ROOTED IN JESUS CHRIST

Rooted in Jesus Christ

Toward a Radical Ecclesiology

Daniel Izuzquiza

WILLIAM B. EERDMANS PUBLISHING COMPANY

GRAND RAPIDS, MICHIGAN / CAMBRIDGE, U.K.

Published 2009 by

Wm. B. Eerdmans Publishing Co.

2140 Oak Industrial Drive N.E., Grand Rapids, Michigan 49505 /

P.O. Box 163, Cambridge CB3 9PU U.K.

Printed in the United States of America

14 13 12 11 10 09   7 6 5 4 3 2 1

Library of Congress Cataloging-in-Publication Data

Izuzquiza, Daniel.

    Rooted in Jesus Christ: toward a radical ecclesiology / Daniel Izuzquiza.

        p.   cm.

    Includes bibliographical references.

    ISBN 978-0-8028-6279-2 (pbk.: alk. paper)

    1. Church.   I. Title.

BV600.3.I98   2009

262 — dc22

                                                    2008048959

www.eerdmans.com

Contents

Prologue

This book proposes a radical ecclesiology in the context of the so-called First World countries. The first part clarifies the relationship between church and society by analyzing four subtopics — the languages of theology, the role of social sciences, the transformation of culture, and a spiritual approach to politics. To this end, I dialogue with some of the main theological proposals of the late twentieth century — Latin American liberation theology, some currents of radical theology in the English-speaking world, and European political theology. The second part of this book offers a more systematic development of this proposal in terms of a radical understanding of the church as the body of Christ. It analyzes the sources of this proposal, the sacraments as alternative Christian practices, the proposal's embodiment in several outstanding witnesses, and its political implications (as a radical counter-politics). Overall, this book elucidates the need, the possibility, and the scope of a radical ecclesiology in the twenty-first century.

What Do We Mean by "Radical" Theology?

First, my proposal is radical in a *political* sense. This book provides a radical alternative to the global capitalist system that is structurally causing so much injustice and death. The dominant order is systematically responsible for the exclusion of millions of persons, of entire populations, and even of continents. Large segments of humanity are left behind, because in fact humanity itself has become superfluous to this liberal-capitalist society. In the face of this situation, the socio-political response of the church must emphasize the creation of a public alternative to this iniquitous system.

Second, my proposal is radical in the *ecclesial* realm as well. The church is currently sharply divided over ideological issues. The church appears to be divided between traditionalists and progressives, conservatives and liberals, those accentuating identity and those stressing dialogue, "Christians of presence" and "Christians of mediation," and so on. I consider these positions to be in fact part of a modern mentality continuum, which is not coherent with the church's self-understanding, and for this reason I propose a radical solution to overcome these divisions. Against conservatives, I argue that the church should voluntarily renounce any form of violence, coercion, power, or imposition on society. Against liberal progressives, I insist that the church ought to humbly but persistently make its voice heard in the public realm by the embodiment of an alternative way of life.

Third, this book is radical in the strictest etymological and *theological* sense. Radical comes from the Latin word *radix*, which means "root." As Christians, we need to go back to the roots of our faith, we need to nourish once again the deep experience of being united to Jesus Christ our Lord. As the letter to the Ephesians puts it, we "are being rooted and grounded in love" (Eph. 3:17). Hence, the title of this book, *Rooted in Jesus Christ*. From this perspective, it can be said that my proposal is profoundly Christological and spiritually grounded.

Fourth, this book is radical in a *personal* sense. It can be read as the theoretical elaboration of a personal and radical journey. A Spaniard born in 1968, I grew up as a Christian in the midst of liberation theology enthusiasm. This starting point will be warmly and critically analyzed in the introductory chapter. The project of this book then developed in the United States; this new context, and the questions aroused by a number of English-speaking theologians and schools of thought, provide the core of the book in its four central chapters. A further step in this journey comes from the fact that the book was finished after my return to Spain. For this reason, the concluding chapter engages in a dialogue with European political theology. I hope that my personal journey, and the lessons I have learned along the way, will be helpful for the reader as well.

Finally, these personal and theological reasons come together in the selection of the conversation partners for this book. In the four central chapters of the first part, I dialogue with four different schools of thought that have claimed the name *radical* for themselves: postliberal theology as radical tradition, John Milbank's radical orthodoxy, the Radical Reformation in the Anabaptist tradition, and the current Catholic radical thought inspired by Dorothy Day. By bringing them together in dialogue, I hope to show how their positive contributions can be strengthened and how their possible dangers can be avoided. The introductory and concluding chapters frame my findings with two other theological positions that can also be considered radical: liberation theology and European political theology. While the first part of the book has an implicit ecumenical thread (I dialogue with Lutheran, Anglican, Mennonite, and Catholic authors), the second part is more catholic in its systematic approach, in its constructive development, and in the authors considered. I am a Roman Catholic theologian, but that does not mean that my proposal is limited to denominational boundaries.

Rhizomes and Roots

The book is divided into two parts, "Rhizomes" and "Roots." Both of these terms are related to the notion of a radical theology, and each of them suggests an important aspect. The notion of rhizome has been used by postmodern authors like Gilles Deleuze not only to describe the pluralistic context of contemporary societies, but also to argue the impossibility of an all-encompassing global discourse that they regard as totalitarian by definition. Deleuze believes that any "root" discourse is dangerous, invalid, absolutist, and inappropriate. Instead, he proposes "rhizome" discourses, that is, fragmentary and reticular diffuse small narratives. There is something correct in this insight, because our world is too complex to be grasped by a single idea, concept, or system. Plurality within society and within the church is a positive reality that we ought to take into consideration. For this reason, the first part of this book deals with diverse proposals ("rhizomes").

At the same time, I disagree with Deleuze's strong thesis. I do not think we can or need to renounce our roots. In order for my proposal to be radical, I need roots. If I keep my discourse at the rhizome level, I cannot avoid superficiality, confusion, and disintegration. To be fully developed, both persons and societies must overcome an insubstantial level of reality by deepening their roots. In the particular case of Christian life and theology, those roots are actually a Root, Jesus Christ. I offer my proposal, with humbleness and conviction, in the midst of a plural and fragmented world. The body of Christ is the real foundation of the world, which I offer in this book at least as another voice in the pluralistic conversation.

Let me add one more thing, from the methodological point of view. My approach in this book is "rhizomatically radical." On the one hand, I attempt to combine not only different authors, traditions, and theological currents, but also diverse disciplines (such as philosophy, politics, economy, and sociology): in this sense, it is a "rhizomatic" method. On the other hand, I articulate and ground those proposals within a spiritual Christology, which is a "radical" attitude, rooted in Jesus Christ.

Synopsis of the First Part (Rhizomes)

One of the most dynamic and influential theological developments of the twentieth century was the irruption of Latin American liberation theology. The introductory chapter of the first part of this book offers a brief presentation of its proposals regarding the relationship between church and society, as well as a critical overview of its current situation. I ask the question, "What is left from liberation theology?" In response, I note that we are left with the method, with God, with the martyrs, and with the poor. I then revisit liberation theology precisely from this fourfold perspective, as a way to invigorate it by going back to its own roots. These four issues provide a guiding trail for the central chapters of the first part of this book.

Chapter 1 focuses on methodological aspects of the general topic. More specifically, I address the question of language in Christian life and theological reflection. The main interlocutor in this chapter is George Lindbeck, considered as a representative of postliberal theology, here understood as a radical tradition. Drawing on Lindbeck's position, but moving beyond it, I propose a dynamic Christian grammar based on the polarity incarnation-eschatology. This provides the basic scheme for an appropriate articulation of three levels of Christian discourse and theological language.

The second chapter introduces the work of the British theologian John Milbank, leader of the so-called radical orthodoxy movement. This chapter also deals with methodological issues, although it concentrates on the use of mediations in theological reflection. In particular, I clarify the relation between theology and social sciences. Following Milbank, I critique the naïve modern assumption of the neutrality of secular sciences — although I also nuance some of Milbank's positions. The primacy of God over all human realities and mediations links this chapter with the second issue in my introductory remarks, and offers an opportunity to articulate a "supernatural sociology" as an alternative to the dominant discourses.

Chapter 3 discusses more systematic issues, namely, the notion of culture and the cultural approach to social transformation. Mennonite theologian John H. Yoder, usually considered to be the finest proponent of Radical Reformation thought in the late twentieth century, is the focus of my analysis. This chapter shows the need for a positive and constructive understanding of the contrast between Christ and modern culture. This radical and countercultural approach is the most appropriate way to promote an authentic transformation of society. Specifically, this chapter deals with the creation of a lived culture of peace and a consistent ethic of life — through personal and communal witnessing to the gospel in a radical and humble way.

Dorothy Day and the Catholic Worker movement offers the basis for the reflections on politics covered in chapter 4. Since Dorothy's death in 1980, there has been a development of a radical Catholic theological tradition that complements or contrasts the mainline discourse within the Catholic Church. Following those insights, this chapter shows how a lived option for the poor is, at the same time, a source for deep spirituality and an impulse for radical politics. I explain how Dorothy Day embodies a new approach to contemplation in action, one that is right and proper for the life in contemporary urban settings, and describe the kind of politics that springs from her spirituality and from the church's theology.

The concluding chapter focuses on European political theology. After the examination of different North American authors in the previous chapters, I am now in a position to consider with new perspectives the four topics outlined in the introductory chapter. Basically formulated in Metz's terms, this chapter revisits the topic of narrative theology, the notion of eschatological reserve, the category of dangerous memory, and the urge for solidarity. A better understanding of those four issues will provide an appropriate basis for the development of a radical ecclesiology for the twenty-first century in the so-called First World countries.

The table below offers a graphical summary of the general architecture of the first part of this book, and provides a clearer appreciation of the way it covers its two main objectives: the elucidation of church-society relations, and the proposal of a radical ecclesiology. This is done through an intermingled argument that combines four topics (language, social science, culture, and politics) with four radical schools of thought. The introductory and concluding chapters provide an overarching frame that brings in two currents that can be also considered as radical theologies.

Liberation Theology	Anglo-American Theology	European Political Theology
Method	Lindbeck and radical tradition: language	Narrative
God	Milbank and radical orthodoxy: theology as social science	Eschatological reserve
The martyrs	Yoder and Radical Reformation: culture of peace	Dangerous memory
The poor	Dorothy Day and radical Catholic politics	Solidarity

Synopsis of the Second Part (Root)

The notion of the body of Christ offers an appropriate tool to develop a radical theology in the twenty-first century. It is rooted in tradition, Scripture, spiritual authors, and the church's practices, and has deep public implications. It provides a catholic response to the results already achieved in the first part and, as such, will be the guiding image in the rest of the book.

Chapter 5 uses a very classical Catholic understanding of the sources of theological reflection. It starts with a consideration of Scripture, focusing on how the New Testament uses the image of the body as a way to refer to the church as a community. I study in particular 1 Corinthians, looking at the socio-political implications of the doctrine of the Eucharist and the church. I recognize that historically in the theology of the church, the notion of the body of Christ has been widely used, and, accordingly, I provide an overview of the evolution of the use, finding nuances of importance for our own contemporary practice. In the twentieth century, the Catholic magisterium used the body of Christ as a powerful image. A closer look at it shows its theological bases and its socio-political implications.

Chapter 6 assumes that every theology shows its fruitfulness as it develops and nourishes a particular set of practices. This is especially true of an ecclesiology. This chapter describes those practices in relation with the understanding of the church as the body of Christ, providing a reading of the seven sacraments recognized by the Catholic Church. While stressing the number seven might seem to present difficulties for the ongoing ecumenical conversation, the approach and the content of this chapter can have cross-denominational validity.

Contemporary theology has learned to integrate its mystical and political aspects in what can be regarded as one of the most important recent renewals. For this reason, chapter 7 relates the systematic approach already found (the church as body of Christ) with the life and the writings of some spiritual authors, especially of the twentieth century. This will allow us to deepen our understanding of some dimensions of reality, such as the broken, silent, cosmic, and transfigured body.

The final chapter offers an overview of some of the public consequences of an ecclesiology of the body of Christ, from political, social, cultural, and economic points of view. This will help us to unfold some of the radical implications of this seemingly neutral notion. Issues like alternatives to the state, nonviolence, plurality, and participatory socialism arise from the core of the theological notion of the body of Christ.

PART ONE

Irruption: Theology as Radical Liberation

Liberation theology irrupted during the second half of the twentieth century as a current of fresh air from impoverished and excluded peoples. If there is a contemporary theology that can be properly characterized as radical in the socio-political sense of the term, it is liberation theology. This Latin American movement provided, starting in the 1960s, a reflective discourse that linked the Christian tradition with revolutionary commitment. For a few decades, liberation theology was at the center of the discussion, not only within ecclesial circles, but also in the public realm. That interest now seems to have faded away, but its social impact is recognizable, for instance, in the Zapatista uprising in Chiapas (Mexico), which has been called "the first postmodern revolution," or in the role of the Brazilian church in opposition to global capitalism through the World Social Forum.

This chapter presents and analyzes some of the major contributions of liberation theology to the universal church and to theological reflection itself. My underlying conviction is that the insights of liberation theology have helped Christians to appreciate substantial issues, including the mission of the church, its relationship to society, and the role of theology in a different way — insights that I consider fruitful and permanent because they recover basic truths of the gospel.

"What Is Left from Liberation Theology?"

In 1995, the Spanish journal *Sal Terrae* devoted an issue to the present relevance of liberation theology in the new post-socialist context. Four theolo-

3

gians — writing from Guatemala, Peru, Brazil, and El Salvador — responded to the question, "What is left from liberation theology?"[1] Their answer clearly indicated that liberation theology has not died: as long as there is oppression in this world and as long as there is a God committed to people's liberation, there will be a liberation theology. More specifically, these authors pointed to four central topics that can be regarded as permanent contributions from liberation theology to theological reflection in general: the method, the Liberating God, the martyrs, and the option for the poor.

The *method* of liberation theology highlights the primacy of praxis and the perspective of the poor. In practical terms, this approach provides a way of looking at reality following the process of "see-judge-act," articulated as a threefold process of socio-analytic, hermeneutic, and practical mediations. More important than the specific procedures, the basic truth of the method is its perspective. Theology is always in danger of becoming a merely theoretical exercise in the academic setting. Liberation theology reminds us that only a theology that starts with and goes back to the ordinary praxis of the people, only a theology that reflects on the life and experiences of the poor, can truly be called Christian theology.

A second reminder may sound obvious: we are left with God, with the *Liberating God.* However, this is not an evident statement. Sometimes theology has dealt with abstract disquisitions more related to human rationality than to God's plan of salvation for humanity; but even more often, theology has become trapped in practical forms of idolatry. Theology has too often been an instrument for the king or the powers that be, in ancient and modern times. Some theologians are providing intellectual support for global capitalism, the new empire, or simply the current unjust status quo. In that task they come close to certain currents of secular thought that take God (and God's poor) out of the public discourse. Idolatry and atheism are, of course, directly related to the exploitation of the poor. Liberation theology reminds us of God's passion for the poor and God's liberating project.

We are also left with the *martyrs.* In recent decades, liberation theology has become a theology of martyrdom. A number of bishops (the best

1. See the articles by Antonio González, Gustavo Gutiérrez, Pedro Casaldáliga, and Jon Sobrino in "Pasión de Dios por la realidad. La teología de la liberación hoy," *Sal Terrae* 83, no. 9 (October 1995): 667-715.

known being Archbishop Óscar Romero in El Salvador, Bishop Enrique Angelelli in Argentina, and Bishop Juan Gerardi in Guatemala), various priests and nuns (including the six Jesuits of the Universidad Centroamericana José Simeón Cañas in San Salvador), and thousands of catechists and members of base communities have been killed for their commitment to the gospel of liberation. These martyrs offer a witness to the meaning and the implications of following Christ in a violent world. Their testimony is much needed to overcome the effects of a cultural context that emphasizes comfort and tends to forget the anonymous victims of injustice.

Finally, liberation theology reminds us of the poor and of the Christian *option for the poor*. When we realize that, according to official data, 825 million people worldwide are severely undernourished, and that 1.4 billion workers (half of the world's workers) earn less than two U.S. dollars per day,[2] it is evident that the specter of poverty has not faded away. Liberation theology attests that a proper Christian approach to this issue cannot be abstract, neutral, or secondary. It must be concrete, committed, and central to our faith and praxis. The preferential option for the poor is, then, a basic truth of the Christian worldview, one that needs to be continually actualized and re-created. The option for the poor becomes, as well, a privileged theological locus. In fact, we talk about our option for the poor because there is a previous and more radical option of God for the poor.

The Method

Liberation theology has developed a method that gives priority to the praxis of Christian communities. As a matter of fact, this opened a new way of doing theology and a new understanding of what theology is about, in the sense that theology is now considered a second step that follows life and practice; theology is critical reflection on praxis.[3] This critical insight has proven to be a fruitful correction to other ways of understanding the theological task. For this same reason I consider it necessary to reflect on

2. Data for 2006, according to two United Nations agencies, the Food and Agriculture Organization and the International Labor Organization. See their web sites at www.fao.org and www.ilo.org.

3. See Gustavo Gutiérrez, *A Theology of Liberation: History, Politics, and Salvation* (Maryknoll, N.Y.: Orbis, 1988), pp. 5-12.

this notion of praxis, the way it is used, and its implications for theology today.

Clodovis Boff, an eminent liberation theologian and author of one of the finest studies on method from this perspective, defines praxis as "the *complexus of practices* orientated to the transformation of society, the making of history,"[4] which, then, has a fundamentally political connotation. This definition of praxis has proven to be fruitful, especially in overcoming the spiritualization of Christian life, most specifically in a Latin American context marked by structural injustice. In fact, the choice of the term *praxis* instead of other possibilities — such as practices, action, or even life — was not a neutral one.

While this choice of terminology makes sense and is coherent, the use of praxis in liberation theology was frequently marked by the dual and conflictual socio-political context in which it was developed. This polarized milieu divided every possible interpretation between capitalist and socialist, conservative and revolutionary, functionalist and dialectical. In so doing, the use of *praxis* became too narrow and eventually was unable to respond to the real practices and lives of the people themselves. In fact, the term *praxis* is not univocal: it could refer to the pastoral praxis of the church, the praxis of the peoples, historical praxis, or the praxis of revolutionary groups — in each case generating a different type of liberation theology. The most common use of praxis favored the political overtones of the term.

From the theoretical point of view, the notion of praxis on which liberation theology depends needs to be and can be expanded and enriched in dialogue with other philosophical discourses.[5] While liberation theology has not misconstrued the notion of praxis, it has used the term in too

---

4. Clodovis Boff, OSM, *Theology and Praxis: Epistemological Foundations* (Maryknoll, N.Y.: Orbis, 1987), p. 6.

5. First, I refer to Maurice Blondel's all-encompassing understanding of action, with its dynamic character that eventually opens itself to the transcendent realm. Second, I consider Hannah Arendt's distinction between three fundamental human activities (labor, work, and action) and her emphasis on action as the human interaction among a plurality of equals, which constitutes the central category of political thought. Third, I mention Alfred Schutz's phenomenology of social interaction in ordinary life as another helpful perspective for a deeper and more fruitful understanding of praxis. Finally, I refer to Jürgen Habermas's analysis of the social setting and the orientation of human action, which provides a threefold division of instrumental, strategic, and communicative action.

narrow a way. While this point lies beyond the limits of this study, I will say a few words about it, drawing on the philosophical categories of Antonio González. This Spanish philosopher and theologian has launched a "friendly" critique of liberation theology, and has developed an original and powerful alternative to its notion of praxis.[6] González distinguishes three kinds of human acts: action, actuation, and activity. Although I cannot fully summarize his position here, two aspects ought to be considered. First, the primacy of praxis, for González, does not place certain acts in opposition to others, but rather integrates all of them. Second, human praxis is not a disaggregated sum of acts, but there is a precise structure that unites them. In this sense, the notion of praxis is not a vague concept opposed to theory or ethically qualified, but includes the whole of human action structurally considered.

These admittedly abstract considerations have a direct effect on the practical level. Using a narrow notion of praxis, priority is not given to people's life and ordinary praxis, but to a preconceived notion of "adequate" praxis. If that were the case (and we must recognize that it has been at least in some situations within liberation theology) we then face the risk of ideological manipulation of the people themselves. A narrow notion of praxis would become associated with, and dominated by, the modern project of liberation. In Hannah Arendt's terms, praxis would be identified with labor (or, in the terminology of Jürgen Habermas, instrumental action): in that case, the real goal would be to achieve success according to an instrumental logic of means and ends. This perspective not only leads to a dangerous and non-Christian hubris, but eventually produces a sense of failure and disappointment when the proposed objectives are not achieved. The result is a new victimization of the poor themselves, because it seems that their revolutionary praxis has led to the triumph of global capitalism, or at least it has proven incapable of stopping its victory.

The alternative I propose is simply to return to the basic insight of liberation theology's method: the primacy of praxis in the life of the poor. But we need a notion of praxis that embraces the whole reality as it really is, not as we would like it to be — recognizing that, occasionally, the enthusiasm or ideological focus of liberation theology may have led to that

---

6. Antonio González, *Teología de la praxis evangélica. Ensayo de una teología fundamental* (Santander: Sal Terrae, 1999), pp. 71-111. For a more detailed philosophical exposition, see his *Estructuras de la praxis. Ensayo de una filosofía primera* (Madrid: Trotta, 1997).

mistake. The focus must be, then, on ordinary or daily life *(vida cotidi-ana)*.[7] I am not proposing a retreat into individualism or an exclusive fo-cus on interpersonal relationships, but I am saying that unless the trans-formation of social structures is rooted in daily life, the poor can be ma-nipulated by certain elites. The notion of praxis ought to be wide enough to include human interaction in its ordinary basis, knowing that only a grassroots revolution will really be effective, only a bottom-up movement finally will be liberating. With such a notion of praxis, we will be able to consider the central role of the poor themselves, integrating daily life with social transformation. This is the source of liberation theology, in accord with its own method, and it also provides the basis for an alternative social resistance to the dominant forces of global capitalism.

God

The contribution of liberation theology to the discovery of a renewed ex-perience and discourse about God cannot be overemphasized. From the earliest writings of this current of thought, there was a significant presence of spirituality. Writers such as Gustavo Gutiérrez, Jon Sobrino, Pedro Casaldáliga, Segundo Galilea, and Leonardo Boff, among others, have helped to articulate the understanding of God's presence in the midst of conflict, injustice, poverty, and social struggles. In a similar vein, more the-oretical authors, such as Ignacio Ellacuría and Juan Luis Segundo, have also dealt with spirituality issues. Other theologians (Franz Hinkel-hammert, Hugo Assman, and Jung Mo Sung) have emphasized the need to clarify the image of the true God, surrounded as we are by idols of death — and by theological legitimations of those idols. Carlos Mesters is the best known among a group of pastoral theologians who have effectively brought the Bible to the people in poor base communities in what may be considered one of the most impressive applications of the Second Vatican Council's recommendations. By and large, then, we see that liberation the-ology has helped to overcome the split between theology and spirituality, and by doing so, to purify the image of God.

---

7. This is one of the contributions of feminist liberation theology. See María Pilar Aquino, *Our Cry for Life: Feminist Theology from Latin America* (Maryknoll, N.Y.: Orbis, 1993).

Nevertheless, there are some aspects in the practice and discourse of liberation theology that appear to be problematic. The legitimate emphasis on social struggle to overcome poverty and to create more just structures led to a much needed engagement at the political and social levels. This took place mainly through secular organizations, such as trade unions, civic associations, political parties, and revolutionary groups. The reason for this strategy seems clear: since the church in Latin America has been a traditional ally of the wealthy and powerful classes of society, it has seemed removed from any felt sense of urgency for structural transformation. However, this option also entailed some unexpected and not-so-positive effects on the praxis of Christians.

From a sheer empirical point of view, a significant number of Christian militants who engaged in revolutionary struggle lost their faith and, in some cases, their social commitment as well. At the same time, large portions of the Latin American poor embraced Pentecostal movements — a complex social reality I cannot analyze here.[8] The necessary distinction between the absolute and the relative sometimes was blurred. A particular

8. Especially at the beginning, liberation theologians looked with suspicion at Pentecostals, arguing that they were financed by foreign interest groups and that they provided an evasive and spiritualist religion, with conservative political consequences. And this critique was probably right. However, while the Catholic Church was making their option for the poor, the poor themselves seemed to opt for the Pentecostals. This situation points to a certain crisis of the practice of the liberation model, and the analysis cannot be superficial. Several authors have argued, from a sociological perspective, that the Pentecostal churches have addressed the challenges of urban poverty in a more effective way than liberation theology's base communities — and this is finally the reason for the rise of Pentecostals in poor neighborhoods. See, for instance, Manuel A. Vásquez, *The Brazilian Popular Church and the Crisis of Modernity* (Cambridge: Cambridge University Press, 1998), and John Burdick, *Looking for God in Brazil: The Progressive Catholic Church in Urban Brazil's Religious Arena* (Berkeley: University of California Press, 1993). My own theological view suggests that this situation can be explained precisely because of the misapprehension of crucial truths of liberation theology. I do not contend that liberation theology was wrong, but just the opposite: the solution for this pastoral and social crisis will only be found by going deeper into and following its basic thrust. It could be said that Pentecostal churches have, paradoxically, embodied some of liberation theology's insights in a more effective way than base communities did. For this reason, I suggest that a theological method that takes into consideration the real praxis of the poor; the absolute priority of God recognized in the community of believers; a way of life that bears witnesses to the gospel in daily situations, even in an aggressive environment; and an honest option for the poor that empowers them — these are essential aspects of a proposal that wants to revitalize a Christian response to oppression among the poor.

commitment to social justice, to revolution, or even to a specific political party seemed to be an absolute demand for everyone, forgetting that God is the only Absolute. Some of the expressions in the context of the Sandinista revolution in Nicaragua seemed to fall under these excesses. But, beyond those situations, perfectly understood given the context in which they took place, I also find disturbing some of the theoretical reflections associated with them, in particular those that leave out the priority of God in liberation.

A significant example can be found in Giulio Girardi, an Italian liberation theologian who has clearly stated his Christian-Marxist integration. His book on Christian identity[9] appeared partly in response to *Libertatis Nuntius,* the first Vatican instruction on liberation theology, and in the context of the increasing influence of the neo-conservative Italian movement Communione e Liberazione. Girardi offers an analysis of Christian identity from the perspective of a sharp dichotomy, that is, either liberation or restoration. For Girardi, favoring liberation means an option for strengthening popular and revolutionary organizations, while any proposal that focuses on the church is dismissed as involutionist. He seems to be trapped in the dichotomy — either you are with the poor or with the church — and surprisingly seems unable to consider the church as the social space of the poor. In doing so, Girardi so stresses the effectiveness of a particular mediation that he almost forgets the absolute priority of God. Positions like Girardi's carry the danger of a unilateral emphasis on the secular realm, forgetting the integral unity with the supernatural order.[10] Their tendency to prioritize secular organizations gives rise to a practical ecclesiology of the "disappearing church,"[11] a position linked to the neglect of God's absolute foundation of any Christian liberation movement.

Of course, I am not implying a direct identification of the church with God's kingdom, but there is a significant ecclesial role in the cause of the people's liberation. Furthermore, we need to strengthen Christian identity — including spirituality, liturgical life, and a factual sense of belonging to the church — as a way to consolidate and intensify our commitment to the

9. Giulio Girardi, *La tunica lacerata: l'identità cristiana oggi fra liberazione e restaurazione* (Roma: Borla, 1986).

10. For a similar and recent "secularist" view, see Juan José Tamayo, *Adiós a la cristiandad. La Iglesia católica española en la democracia* (Barcelona: Ediciones B, 2003).

11. See the interesting analysis of William T. Cavanaugh, *Torture and Eucharist: Theology, Politics and the Body of Christ* (Oxford: Blackwell, 1998), pp. 123-50.

poor. In fact, the church as such may provide an alternative to the unjust system of global capitalism, and should be regarded as a major social subject. The church is a social actor guided by an attitude of service and humility, not by coercion or power, and is a social subject that is the main reference for the commitment of Christians.

Some liberation theologians are already developing the type of reflection that I am proposing. For instance, Benjamín González Buelta reflects on the sense of failure in liberation theology circles following the collapse of political socialism in 1989, and effectively argues for a deeper grounding in God's absolute mystery without withdrawing from social engagement. Echoing Saint Teresa of Ávila, he claims that "God alone suffices"; but he also reminds us that an isolated God who did not care about human beings would not be the Christian God. González Buelta does not renounce the utopian project of a just society, but insists that that utopia is actually embodied in the new life that can already be traced among the poor.[12] Although he does not explicitly develop the ecclesiological implications of this proposal, it follows that the church is the social space in which people are introduced to and nourished in their common search for the transcendence of God in the midst of their historical engagement. The church might not be the only social agent to provide such a possibility, but it is a necessary one and obviously indispensable for Christians. This may sound like an evident conclusion, but it has been overlooked, taken for granted, or regarded with suspicion in recent years.

The Martyrs

"The blood of the martyrs is seed of new Christians." This dictum, common in the church of the first centuries, has resounded anew in the contemporary Latin American church. Bishops, priests, nuns, lay ministers, and numerous unnamed Christians have been killed in recent decades as a consequence of their faith and commitment to reality. While this situation is not new in the church, part of the novelty can be seen in the development of an explicit discourse about martyrdom, including pastoral mate-

---

12. Benjamín González Buelta, SJ, *La utopía ya está en lo germinal. Sólo Dios basta, pero no basta un Dios solo* (Santander: Sal Terrae, 1998). See also his *Orar en un mundo roto. Tiempo de transfiguración* (Santander: Sal Terrae, 2002).

rials and systematic reflection. In fact, these years have seen the development of a theology of martyrdom with consequences for the universal church.[13]

Jon Sobrino is probably the author who has most thoroughly elaborated on these issues, drawing from the general situation in his country, El Salvador, and his own personal and direct experience with well-known martyrs, such as Monseñor Romero and his Jesuit companions at the Central American University.[14] Sobrino has argued that there has been a shift from a theology of liberation alone to a theology of martyrdom, a move that parallels Christological reflection — from an initial focus on just the kingdom to a more mature emphasis on the cross. Sobrino has also defined the martyrs of El Salvador as "Jesuanic martyrs,"[15] since they follow Jesus, dedicate their lives to the cause of Jesus, and die for the same reasons that Jesus died. This very suitable description does not necessarily include, though, thousands of anonymous martyrs killed for the sheer fact that they are poor. Sobrino then establishes a distinction between "active" and "passive" martyrs, and applies to this second group another powerful theological category, taken from Ellacuría, that of the crucified people of God or the suffering servants of Yahweh. All of these considerations have helped to develop a theological reflection that takes seriously the reality of injustice, suffering, and violence in our world today.

Following these insights even further, in the first place, it is important not to forget one of the main contributions of contemporary Christology (including, of course, liberation theology in general and Jon Sobrino in particular): the necessary link between Jesus' death and his life. The cross of Jesus cannot be understood as an isolated sacrificial act, but receives its full meaning as a consequence of his options, way of life, conflicts, and faithfulness to the people and God's project of liberation. A one-sided emphasis on the violence and cruelty of martyrdom would be inconsistent

13. See, for example, the two monograph issues devoted to martyrdom by the international journal *Concilium* in 1983 and 2003. See also "El martirio en América Latina," *Revista Latinoamericana de Teología* 48 (1999): 215-330, and Martin Maier, SJ, "Teología del martirio en Latinoamérica," *Sal Terrae* 92 (2004): 753-64.

14. See a collection of his essays in Jon Sobrino, SJ, *Witnesses to the Kingdom: The Martyrs of El Salvador and the Crucified Peoples* (Maryknoll, N.Y.: Orbis, 2003).

15. See Jon Sobrino, SJ, "The Kingdom of God and the Theological Dimension of the Poor: The Jesuanic Principle," in *Who Do You Say I Am? Confessing the Mystery of Christ*, ed. John C. Cavadini and Laura Holt (Notre Dame, Ind.: Notre Dame University Press, 2004).

with this position. It changes the focus from God to the evil forces that create all of this destruction. A theology of martyrdom should carefully avoid an exaltation of violence, as if being killed were a positive thing.

A second and related consideration can be found in Saint Thomas Aquinas. He states, in an article quoted by Sobrino, that martyrdom is a supreme act of virtue, which may be caused not only by faith but also by some other virtues, including justice (*STh*. II-II, q. 124). In a different part of the *Summa,* Aquinas says that there are three types of baptism (water, blood, spirit) and affirms that, if we consider the sacramental effect, baptism of blood is the most perfect one. One can see the relevance of this point for a theology of martyrdom. But it is also important to remember the reason that he gives for that priority: this baptism of blood includes charity in itself (*STh*. III, q. 66, a. 12, ad. 3). The point I want to stress is that love is central to the notion of martyrdom, not only for the "Jesuanic martyrs," but for the suffering servants of God too. These are not simply theoretical considerations, but they also have important implications for a lived theology of martyrdom.

If our discourse about martyrdom focuses on the violence, suffering, and death operating against the poor people — instead of highlighting their fortitude and endurance — the unwanted effect might be a victimization of the people themselves. In this scheme, the poor would be mere passive recipients of the violence exerted on them, while the real protagonist would be the executioners. The paradoxical outcome of such a theology of martyrdom would be a factual dis-empowerment of the victims, who are left with no other option than silent suffering of their unjust fate. Considered from another perspective, this approach seems to mimic the dominant discourse, with its emphasis on dramatic excesses that may get attention from the mass media. In a sense, the recent film *The Passion of the Christ* might be an example of what a distorted theology of the cross and martyrdom may look like: a bloody and dreadful affair with little connection to human praxis in daily life.

On the other hand, as Sobrino astutely observes, the martyrs can be seen as an event of God's grace, because they challenge and encourage us to love freely and radically, detaching us from a possible hubris that is too confident in our own human initiative. The martyrs witness to the fragility and brutality of human life, and make plain that God can bring salvation through mysterious ways. Instead of efficacy or success, we are invited to discover with confidence the mystery of evangelical fruitfulness. Instead of placing our trust in the modern project of social transformation, we are called to live the reality of the seed that must die and be buried in order to bear some fruit (see John 12:24). A reading of martyrdom that does not focus on suffering (although, obviously, does not neglect it!) enables the victims to overcome their role of victims, that is, empowers them by not victimizing their situation. A Christian theology of martyrdom, then, does not focus on death itself, but on the daily life of the poor. In the midst of unjust poverty, the poor can live Christian life to the fullest and, in so doing, they become witnesses of God's liberating love: they become active martyrs.

Love of one's enemy, for instance, is not just a beautiful phrase to be preached about, but a hard reality to be lived in history and society. From this perspective, forgiveness becomes a powerful instrument in the hands of the victims to bring about reconciliation and social transformation.[16] Although it may seem that forgiveness would be a defeat for the poor, in fact it is a real power (a crucified power, it is true, but a real power nonetheless). Nobody but the victims themselves can forgive the assassins. Forgiveness is not a surrender that leaves unaccountable the persons and the institutions responsible for so many massacres. Rather, it is actually a way to overcome injustice from the perspective of the gospel — it offers the basis for a revolutionary nonviolence. Only great persons and communities are able to forgive. This is just an example of how the crucified people or the suffering servants may also become Jesuanic martyrs. Bearing witness (*martyria*) to the gospel implies taking the cross every day, and following Jesus in his life of service to the kingdom. This approach does not deny Sobrino's interpretation, but intends to take it further and deeper. I do not mean to oppose active and passive martyrdom, nor to imply that the passive one is of lesser quality. John of the Cross makes a distinction between active and passive purification, and this is not only true of individual spiritual life, but also of social movements. We do need to avoid concluding that crucified people are unable to live an active witness of the gospel, and are "only" left with the passive side of it. A responsible understanding of contemporary martyrdom is more coherent with the Christology of liberation, empowers poor people without victimizing them, and provides a fruitful and effective source for conflict transformation.

16. An original interpretation of the relationship between justice and forgiveness is one of the main contributions of Daniel M. Bell Jr., *Liberation Theology after the End of History: The Refusal to Cease Suffering* (London: Routledge, 2001), especially pp. 144-203.

The Poor

Without a doubt, bringing the poor to the center of theological discourse has been one of the main contributions of liberation theology to the universal church, which now includes the option for the poor among its defining features. Formally and explicitly, at least, there is no way to avoid the irruption of the poor in ecclesial life, identity, and reflection. The reality is more complex and less optimistic when we consider the real and concrete relationship of the church, the poor, and the cause of the poor. In fact, there seems to be a tendency among Christians to widen and spiritualize the notion of the "poor." This leads us to forget the real socio-economic process of impoverishment, as well as an interpretation of the preferential option for the poor as if it were something "optional" for the church. The result is a type of ecclesial action that does not challenge the unjust structures that cause poverty. Instead, such action focuses only on a superficial attention to the symptoms of that same poverty.

It is evident that liberation theology does not agree with nor can accept this "soft" version of the poor and the option for the poor. Liberation theology has consistently emphasized an integral view, which includes structural, social, economic, political, cultural, and spiritual aspects. It claims to be a voice of the voiceless, articulating a discourse that springs from the life and struggles of the poor themselves. However, there are some indications that reality might be more complex and that we need to nuance our analysis. For instance, if we consider the emergence of liberation theology, we do not find a simple and naïve bottom-up process through which the poor people themselves became organized and changed the church's perspective.[17] As Christian Smith has shown, following the political process model of social movements, there is a need to evaluate political opportunities, insurgent consciousness, and organizational strength, in order to understand the emergence and development of liberation theology as a social movement. In fact, his analysis focuses on the role of bishops, theologians, groups of priests, publications, and meetings as a key to understanding why and how the option for the poor came about. I am not arguing that liberation theology was an elite ecclesial movement, but Smith's research challenges a simplistic view that merely identifies liberation theology with the poor themselves.

17. Christian Smith, *The Emergence of Liberation Theology: Radical Religion and Social Movement Theory* (Chicago: University of Chicago Press, 1991).

This issue has been effectively addressed by Pedro Trigo. Writing from his daily experience with poor base communities in urban Venezuela, Trigo is one of the most creative and self-critical liberation theologians today, and he has raised serious questions about the coherence of ecclesial practice and reflection, even in liberation theology circles.[18] He believes that the church is reticent to follow a real path of kenotic incarnation in the world of the poor, preferring instead to maintain institutional stands that try to serve the poor while creating distance from them. Trigo's argument goes further, because he reflects on the real praxis in ecclesial base communities, finding a prevalence of top-down communication and a type of relationship that shows an implicit ethnocentrism. He even argues that pastoral agents and leaders of the community themselves have followed an almost Leninist paradigm, in the sense that priority has been given to the role of active minorities ("vanguards") and not to the base. This implicit dualism is just an echo of the Enlightenment approach to the poor characterized by a certain paternalism; we should not forget that contemporary socialism considers itself an heir of the Second Enlightenment. Trigo's analysis shows, then, that not everything within liberation theology was fully respectful of the poor people of Latin America.

Similar concerns were raised early on, among other voices from the Argentinean current of liberation theology. Led by Lucio Gera and Juan Carlos Scannone, this group of authors highlighted the importance of historical-cultural analysis (shared historical memory, culture, popular religion, people's daily praxis) without denying the value of structural socio-economic and political approaches.[19] For this reason, they were more open to the value, significance, and possibilities of liturgy, ritual, symbols, people's culture, and spirituality. They were more attentive to poor social sectors that did not seem to have revolutionary potential. They emphasized the cultural root causes of oppression beyond economic or political struggles. While this current of thought was in a minority position, and some-

18. Among his publications, I specifically refer to Pedro Trigo, SJ, "La base en las comunidades eclesiales de base," *Revista Latinoamericana de Teología* 53 (2001): 153-79. See also his more recent book, ¿*Ha muerto la teología de la liberación?* (Bilbao: Mensajero 2006).

19. For instance, Juan Carlos Scannone, SJ, "'Axial Shift' instead of 'Paradigm Shift,'" in *Liberation Theologies on Shifting Grounds: A Clash of Socio-Economic Paradigms*, ed. Georges de Schrijver, SJ (Leuven: Leuven University Press, 1998), pp. 87-103. See also Juan Carlos Scannone, SJ, *Teología de la liberación y praxis popular. Aportes críticos para una teología de la liberación* (Salamanca: Sígueme, 1976).

times was even suspiciously dismissed by other liberation theologians, the new context has helped to change the perspective. Many analysts recognize that from the 1970s to the 1990s there was an axial shift in liberation theology, moving from the socio-economic to the socio-cultural perspective, without, however, neglecting the former. This move has helped us to focus again on the reality of the poor as they themselves experience it, not as the vanguard leaders or ideological analysis declare it to be.

This renewed emphasis on the role of the poor offers new possibilities for the praxis of liberation. Injustice has shifted from exploitation to exclusion, and at present there seems to be no economic or political alternative to global capitalism. In this new social context, it makes sense to emphasize resistance to this oppressive system. Base communities among the poor provide a social space in which a collective, alternative worldview *(imaginario alternativo)* unfolds and is nourished. The emergence of civil society and new communitarianism among the poor, as well as the "popular economy of solidarity," which stresses the centrality of community, are among the initiatives that sustain hope among the poor, creating new forms of effective solidarity and restoring their basic leadership. It may not seem as successful as other approaches, but it really empowers the poor themselves, focusing on their needs and capacities. Any liberation theology that wants to coherently respond to our current reality would do well to strengthen this perspective, by focusing on the poor.

Conclusion

This introductory chapter has presented a brief summary of the understanding of church and society according to liberation theology, as well as an analysis of the main contributions of Latin American theology to the universal church. Focusing on four major topics (the method, God, the martyrs, and the poor) I have showed the deep and permanent import of liberation theology insights, while also stressing some of the shortcomings found in its positions. My argument suggests that these criticisms are not only fully coherent with the basic thread of liberation theology, but moreover radicalize it in an authentic way that is appropriate for our current historical situation.

The following four chapters, which constitute the core of the first part of this book, can be seen as a reformulation of the four topics I have dealt with in these pages. In chapter 1, the issue of method is developed from the perspective of theological language, drawing on George Lindbeck and following his emphasis on shared Christian practices. Chapter 2 deals with the role of mediations, particularly the social sciences, in theology. I examine John Milbank's helpful attempt to articulate an alternative interpretation that gives priority to God's view. Chapter 3 provides an opportunity to reflect on martyrdom from the perspective of the Mennonite theologian John H. Yoder. This chapter stresses the importance of creating a communitarian alternative to the dominant system, an alternative that bears witness to the gospel by fostering a culture of peace. Finally, chapter 4 analyzes Dorothy Day and the Catholic Worker movement. Here I revisit the political implications of a real option for the poor that assumes the radical consequences of kenotic solidarity embodied in nonviolence.

1. Lost in Translation? The Languages of Theology: Lindbeck and Beyond

This chapter offers the first step toward the clarification of the relationship between church and society in our contemporary world. Its focus is on the type of language that is most suitable for the church's theology in order to fulfill its mission. Paying particular attention to this specific and rather theoretical aspect will clarify some basic problems underlying the more practical topics — those of political philosophy, social ethics and church policy. Subsequent chapters will deal with the use of mediations in theology, with the understanding and transformation of culture, and with the political implications raised by these questions.

For the past twenty-five years, the issue of how to relate particularity and universality has been the core of philosophical, theological, and ethical discussions, as well as of the church's ministerial proposals and policies. Is there a common language that provides the basis for universal ethics in our pluralistic society? Is there a particular Christian voice in the discussion? If so, which one, and how is it articulated? To clarify the theological discussion, there is a need for methodological and epistemological reflection, and George Lindbeck's cultural-linguistic model offers a good starting point from which to re-conceive this issue. Starting from his proposal, I argue that there is a need for a more complex and dynamic analysis of how theological language deals with particularity and universality, since the dominant discourses leave aside important elements of Christian faith and practice.

What Language for the Church?

The *National Catholic Reporter,* in a recent article entitled "Language Becomes Catholic Battleground," argued that language has become one of the mega-debates in the Catholic Church worldwide.[1] In the context of cultural pluralism and fragile identities, the question not only affects the Catholic Church but also all Christian denominations. Given that the era of a unified Christian worldview is gone, Christian communities have to ask themselves about the kind of language they should use. How much can be accepted from the secular culture? How different must Christians be? The question is neither a superficial nor a new one.

In the late nineteenth and early twentieth centuries, for instance, Christian theologians tried to face this new situation through the liberal theology movement. Their attempt to make Christian faith both understandable and relevant for their times meant a translation of New Testament issues into ethical and cultural categories. However, in the final decades of the twentieth century some voices began asking themselves whether this approach was the only possible one, or the most appropriate one. There seems to be a new and growing theological sensibility that wants to overcome the dominant and unchallenged liberal approach without falling back into fundamentalism. At the same time, and not merely by chance, postmodern thinkers have brought a new understanding to the limits of modernity and the liberal project. With this background in mind, what kind of language should Christianity, theology, and the church primarily use?

A Universalistic Approach

The dominant discourse argues this way: "It is a fact that we live in a pluralistic society. At the same time, the Christian message is a universal one, intended to bring salvation to all humankind. It is clear that we cannot remain enclosed within our own circles. So we need to find ways to dialogue with others, to understand them, and to make our message meaningful. We need to learn their language, and try to translate our Christian pro-

---

1. John L. Allen Jr., "Language Becomes Catholic Battleground," *National Catholic Reporter* 40, no. 9 (December 26, 2003): 5-6. See also Benedict XVI, *Deus Caritas Est,* no. 2.

posal into that common language. Only by doing that will Christian salvation have universal relevance in our modern, plural world." Generally speaking, this argument is valid in mainstream Western theological discourse. North Americans tend to emphasize pluralism, while Europeans highlight secularization.

From a philosophical, non-Christian perspective, Jürgen Habermas may be considered the main representative of this universalistic approach. According to Habermas, in modern pluralistic societies there is no shared idea of what "good" is, but there are many different worldviews claiming universal validity to their respective proposals. In this situation, liberal democracies offer the only framework in which agreement can be possibly reached: an emphasis on right procedures, communicative rationality, and discourse ethics is the only way to organize a peaceful society. All particular traditions — Christianity included — should translate their proposals into a shared common language, if they want to be part of public life.[2]

Habermas's proposal has received a great deal of attention from Christian theologians who have pointed out a number of its limitations, but have agreed with his general approach. For instance, Paul Lakeland has used his philosophical system to explain the structure, the mission, and the nature of the church.[3] He actually proposes a "Habermasian ecclesiology" based on the German philosopher's categories, structural principles, analysis, and language. The outcome is a theory of the church as a community of communicative action. This modern approach seems to offer a good framework for the particular Christian contribution to public life in modern pluralistic societies.

However, if we go back to Habermas himself, we find a key concept — what he calls "linguistification of the sacred" — that will be useful in understanding the limits of Lakeland's proposal. Habermas interprets the process of modernity as a fragmentation of classical unified metaphysics into different spheres. Within the Christian worldview, God as the Absolute Being expresses himself as Good, Truth, and Beauty; according to Habermas, God disappears, diluted in ethics, science, and art. The sacred/God becomes translated, and then disappears. The problem is that with

---

2. See Jürgen Habermas, *The Theory of Communicative Action*, 2 vols. (Boston: Beacon, 1984 and 1987).

3. Paul Lakeland, *Theology and Critical Theory: The Discourse of the Church* (Nashville: Abingdon, 1990).

this universalistic approach Christians lose their specific contribution to society. In one of the few positive quotations from Habermas on religion he writes,

> Philosophy, even in its postmetaphysical form, will be able neither to replace nor to repress religion *as long as religious language* is a bearer of a semantic content that is inspiring and even indispensable, for this content eludes (for the time being?) the explanatory force of philosophical language and *continues to resist translation* into reasoning discourses.[4]

In this text, the German philosopher recognizes that religions have a pool of experiences and meanings that cannot be adequately grasped by secular thought. This content cannot be translated, and will continue to offer an alternative worldview only if and as long as religious language continues to resist being translated. By translating their message into secular categories, the churches may end up emptying it.[5] This is the main critique of the next group of authors.

A Particularistic Approach

One of the main philosophical critiques of the modern, liberal project is that of Alasdair MacIntyre. Even before his influential book *After Virtue* (1981), he wrote,

> The most perceptive theologians wish to translate what they have to say to an atheistic world. But they are doomed to one of two failures. Either they succeed in their translation: in which case what they find themselves saying has been transformed into the atheism of their hearers. Or they fail in their translation: in which case no one hears what they have to say but themselves.[6]

---

4. Jürgen Habermas, "Themes in Postmetaphysical Thinking," in *Postmetaphysical Thinking: Philosophical Essays* (Cambridge: Polity, 1992), p. 51. Emphasis added.

5. Following Habermas's own analysis, we could say that by doing this we emphasize the colonization of lifeworld by the system, dangerously losing then the critical input of Christian life.

6. Alasdair MacIntyre, "God and the Theologians," in *Against the Self-Images of the Age: Essays on Ideology and Philosophy* (London: Duckworth, 1971), pp. 19-20.

The alternative to this conundrum seems to be, then, what MacIntyre calls a "closed-circle discourse" in which believer speaks only (or mainly) to believer. This is precisely what some Christian social ethicists — especially Stanley Hauerwas and John Howard Yoder — have been arguing for in recent decades. They both repeatedly state that ethics cannot be done outside a particular community — one of specific practices, values, language, and beliefs embodying God's grace. For this reason, "unless the church and Christians are trained to understand their community's language,"[7] they will fail to serve the world as they are called to. The main contribution that Christian communities can make to social transformation is, precisely, being the church.

A good example of this approach can be found in William Cavanaugh's recent book *Theopolitical Imagination*. After unmasking three modern myths — the state as savior, civil society as free space, and globalization as catholicity — he proposes a Eucharistic counter-politics, directly based on the body of Christ. For Cavanaugh, "the most fruitful way to dialogue with those outside of the Church is through concrete practices that do not need translation into some putatively 'neutral' language to be understood."[8] The works of mercy, when they are lived in a public way and are not limited to an individualistic and superficial approach, provide such practices. It is important to note that Cavanaugh is not forgetting or underestimating dialogue within the pluralistic society, but he wants to emphasize that the most fruitful way for that dialogue to take place is not through "translating" but by embodying and witnessing the Christian worldview.

However, the question from the universalistic side is quite obvious. Isn't this position dangerously pre-modern, sectarian, or fundamentalist? Doesn't it make it impossible for any kind of public agreement in pluralistic societies? To clarify these questions, we need to step back and look at the issue from a different, more theoretical perspective.

---

7. Stanley Hauerwas, "Why the 'Sectarian Temptation' Is a Misrepresentation. A Response to James Gustafson," in *The Hauerwas Reader,* ed. John Berkman and Michael Cartwright (Durham and London: Duke University Press, 2001), p. 102.

8. William T. Cavanaugh, *Theopolitical Imagination: Discovering the Liturgy as a Political Act in an Age of Global Consumerism* (London: T&T Clark, 2002), p. 94.

George Lindbeck's Cultural-Linguistic Model

In 1984, Yale University professor of theology George Lindbeck published *The Nature of Doctrine,* an influential book considered by many a groundbreaking piece of postliberal theology.[9] He tries to overcome the unsatisfactory situation of modern theological studies, dominated by either a cognitive-propositionalist model or an experiential-expressionist view. Lindbeck proposes instead a cultural-linguistic model that provides the basis for what he calls a postliberal theology. We first briefly look at his concept of religion and theology, leaving for the following section a more careful discussion and analysis of his model.

Religion and Doctrines

Lindbeck considers that religion can be viewed as a kind of cultural and/or linguistic framework that shapes the whole life of believers. In doing so, he is applying some sociological, anthropological, philosophical, and linguistic insights to the theological field. According to Lindbeck, religions are "comprehensive interpretative schemes, usually embodied in myths or narratives and heavily ritualized, which structure human experience and understanding of self and world."[10] From this perspective, Lindbeck offers an alternative model that understands religions as idioms, languages, or cultural systems that deal with ultimate questions and with the transcendent.

Doctrines, then, are not to be considered as propositions or symbols, but rather as rules or regulative principles of that religious framework.[11] Given the linguistic analogy, we could distinguish vocabulary and grammar: vocabulary refers to symbols, concepts, rites, and stories, while doctrines are understood as the grammar of a given language. We could say that while vocabulary alludes to single elements in themselves, doctrines explain and regulate the way those elements function and are articulated within the religious-cultural-linguistic system. Some doctrines determine

9. George A. Lindbeck, *The Nature of Doctrine: Religion and Theology in a Postliberal Age* (Philadelphia: Westminster, 1984).

10. Lindbeck, *The Nature of Doctrine,* p. 32.

11. Lindbeck, *The Nature of Doctrine,* pp. 73-90.

the vocabulary, some formulate syntactical rules to use that material in construing the world, and others provide semantic reference. But in general, doctrines are understood in relation to the grammar of a religion, that is, to the way a particular religion structures its constitutive elements. In this sense, doctrines are regulative principles or rules (in accordance, also, to the traditional notion of *regula fidei*).

Theology

Lindbeck then applies his theory to the three major divisions of theology. First, he considers that the task of any systematic or dogmatic theology is to give an articulated, comprehensive, and normative explication of the meaning a religion has for its believers. In the cultural-linguistic approach, this is done intra-textually so that the believer can interpret his or her life and reality within the scriptural narrative.[12]

Second, practical theology addresses the issue of applicability, but Lindbeck emphasizes that this needs to be done using each religion's own internal criteria. Theology should judge religion by its own standards, not by external ones. Paradoxically, religious communities will be practically relevant by concentrating on their own forms of life, instead of trying to be relevant — as the liberal model does.[13]

Third, foundational or apologetic theology deals with intelligibility.[14] Following his linguistic comparison, Lindbeck points out that the grammar of religion, like that of any language, can only be learned and explained by practice, not by theoretical or general analysis of experience. "In short, religions, like languages, can be understood only in their own terms, not by transposing them into an alien speech."[15] His suggestion for the church in contemporary societies is not translation, but catechesis: instead of trying to express the faith in new concepts, postliberal theology would like to teach the language and practices of the religion to anyone interested in listening.

12. Lindbeck, *The Nature of Doctrine*, pp. 113-24.
13. Lindbeck, *The Nature of Doctrine*, pp. 124-28.
14. Lindbeck, *The Nature of Doctrine*, pp. 128-34.
15. Lindbeck, *The Nature of Doctrine*, p. 129.

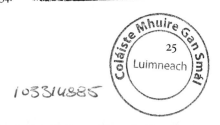

Analysis of Lindbeck's Model

What kind of language is more appropriate for the church in our world? We first investigate two issues that deal with formal aspects — the role of non-theological disciplines and some methodological questions — and then consider two involving theological content, more specifically, the possibility of translation for Christian language and the relation between particularity and pluralism.

The Role of Non-Theological Disciplines

It seems quite obvious that the cultural-linguistic model leans on the analysis and discourse of non-theological disciplines, such as sociology (Peter Berger and Thomas Luckmann), anthropology (Clifford Geertz), or linguistics (Ludwig Wittgenstein, Peter Austin). Lindbeck himself recognizes this fact, and states that the novelty of his proposal is not in the theory itself, but in the theological use he is suggesting.[16] Some may find this approach surprising, dangerous, or at least uncomfortable. But the fact is that Christian theology has done the same through the centuries, sometimes called fundamental or foundational theology (especially on the Catholic side), and sometimes called theological prolegomena (especially on the Protestant side).

The issue, then, is not whether to use non-theological disciplines, but which ones to use — and how. What has happened in recent decades is the so-called linguistic turn in philosophical reflection, which has actually followed the Enlightenment anthropological turn, and has had important effects on the theological realm. The dominant theological reflection is somewhat dependent on post-Kantian philosophical idealism or realism, as in the experiential-expressive or cognitive-propositional models. Instead of doing so, authors like Hans Georg Gadamer, Paul Ricoeur, or some of the proponents of analytical Anglo-American philosophy — including the Oxford school of ordinary language — are explaining reality with socio-phenomenological and cultural-linguistic approaches. Some

16. "What is new about the present work is not, in short, its theory of religion, but the use of this theory in the conceptualization of doctrine, and the contention that this conceptualization is fruitful for theology and ecumenism" (Lindbeck, *The Nature of Doctrine*, p. 8).

talk about a post-metaphysical era as a consequence of this linguistic turn. Any contemporary theology ought to take this context into consideration, while not necessarily assuming an anti-metaphysical or merely nominalist stand. It is in this situation that we need to locate Lindbeck's proposal, and to consider it as a much needed attempt.

At any rate, a number of questions remain unanswered: Is this shift appropriate? Should theology accept it? Will it be fruitful for theological concerns? Are we not losing firm ground on which to construct theology? Doesn't this approach push theology toward non-foundationalism? If so, what are the advantages and risks of such a theological reflection? Lindbeck's response to these questions is twofold. On the one hand, he implies that at least Christians should try it. If contemporary thought is understanding our world with these categories and this theoretical framework, at least theology should try to see if they are helpful for its particular task — provided that theology is not prevented from fulfilling its task. On the other hand, he argues that this approach explains better than the dominant ones — cognitive and emotivist — the problems and issues of the current theological reflection.[17] So the only way to prove the truth or falsity of this attempt is to look at the theological results obtained with this cultural-linguistic model.

A Question of Methodology: Top-Down or Bottom-Up?

Lindbeck is correct in suggesting that theology should not try to look for an outside Archimedean point on which to rest or ground itself. All the previous attempts to do so have led to a situation in which religion and theology are finally dependent on foreign philosophical or ideological systems — transcendental, existential, liberal, capitalist, and dialectic. The cultural-linguistic model emphasizes the fact that the Christian religion is a particular way of life, shared by those who follow Jesus of Nazareth. Its foundations are there.[18]

---

17. The outline of *The Nature of Doctrine* shows that this is Lindbeck's line of argument: while chapter 2 adopts a non-theological perspective, chapter 3 deals with inter-religious issues, leaving the intra-Christian theological discussion for chapters 5 and 6. He begins by saying that this is a possible and relevant approach, before arguing it is a more fruitful one.

18. This last sentence may support some Wittgensteinian critiques of Lindbeck that say he is falling into a new kind of foundationalism, but I cannot see how any Christian theol-

The question is primarily a methodological one, and can be illuminated by a similar debate in contemporary Christology. Actually, the discussion is not between high or low Christologies, but on how to construct a high Christology. While traditional theology has dealt with the person of Jesus Christ from above, with a descending methodology, contemporary authors tend to construct their Christology from below, using an ascending methodology. In both cases, the final outcome is (or should be, or at least can be) a similar one: an affirmation of Jesus Christ as true human and true God in one person. What varies is the method used in each case.

This example may help to clarify our discussion as well, because in a similar vein Lindbeck tries to maintain the basic contents of theology while modifying its method. He argues that the whole modern theological project after the Enlightenment has been a defensive attempt to ground theology not in itself, but somewhere else: a particular philosophical or ideological vision. Lindbeck is not attempting to *empty* our Christian faith by renouncing a metaphysical foundation. He is trying to *fulfill* Christian thinking with Christian life, not with abstract philosophical concepts that finally empty life. In so doing, he is locating his proposal in the new non-foundationalist paradigm that might not be easy to understand — or, when understood, may create uneasiness because of its novelty and apparent lack of solid ground to stand on.[19]

At this point, it is necessary to clarify that Lindbeck is, on the one hand, leaning on non-theological disciplines and, on the other hand, arguing for a self-referential Christian language, centered on Jesus Christ. He consciously borrows from the social sciences a general theory of religion, from which he construes a model; but his interest is strictly theological: he wants to explain the nature of theological doctrines. He thinks we live in a foundationless era — similar to the early centuries of Christianity — and for that reason, his cultural-linguistic model provides an adequate interpretation for theological reflection. He never equates doctrines with mere "language games" or theology with cultural analysis. He moves from those

---

ogy can escape from having Jesus Christ as its foundation, unless it devolves into a form of fideism that gives primacy to human faith, instead of God's salvific events. See, for example, D. Z. Phillips, *Faith after Foundationalism* (London and New York: Routledge, 1988).

19. A general introduction to this topic can be found in John E. Thiel, *Nonfoundationalism* (Minneapolis: Fortress, 1994). For a broader perspective, see William C. Placher, *Unapologetic Theology: A Christian Voice in a Pluralistic Conversation* (Louisville: Westminster/ John Knox, 1989).

disciplines to a coherent theological system. In other words, he is applying an ascending methodology.

Language and Translation

Now that we have clarified these preliminary questions, we can move to the central issue of this chapter, namely, language. Lindbeck argues that the Bible offers a "totally comprehensive framework,"[20] and, for this same reason, is untranslatable. Two conditions are included in this global perspective that make it literally untranslatable: (1) every human experience can be expressed as or translated into biblical terms, and (2) if someone intends to communicate the biblical view in other terms, then something will be missing or will be expressed in an incoherent or partial way. That is to say, the biblical worldview is all-embracing: everything is included within it, and nothing is properly understood outside it.

This may sound like a very strong claim to contemporary ears, probably too strong. But it is the core of Christian faith. The question is not how wide biblical experience is, but how deep. It can probably be best explained with the image of a lens: all reality is seen through the lens of the biblical worldview.[21] For instance, according to this vision all suffering is cruciform and all hopes are messianic. As Lindbeck says, "It is the text, so to speak, which absorbs the world, rather than the world the text."[22] It is important to realize that this is a theological issue, not a technical one. It is not that we have not yet developed the ability to translate correctly without losing meaning; rather, it is not possible. The Bible offers, from the believer's perspective, a complete hermeneutical clue.

In fact, the question is not about language translations, but about conceptual or categorical ones. Let us consider an example from mathematics: the number six can be translated from Arabic (6) to Roman figures (VI), and vice versa; but the number zero (0) cannot be translated into Latin,

---

20. George A. Lindbeck, "The Gospel's Uniqueness: Election and Untranslatability," in *The Church in a Postliberal Age,* ed. James J. Buckley (Grand Rapids: Eerdmans, 2003), p. 232.

21. Let us listen to liberation theologian Clodovis Boff: "Faith is not a landscape to be seen, but eyes for seeing. It is not a world, but a gaze upon the world. It is not a book to read, but a grammar for reading — for reading all books." Clodovis Boff, OSM, *Theology and Praxis: Epistemological Foundations* (Maryknoll, N.Y.: Orbis, 1987), p. 123.

22. Lindbeck, *The Nature of Doctrine,* p. 118.

because it simply does not exist. In a similar way, how can YHWH or the Trinity be translated into a non-monotheistic or secular language? Any religious tradition offers a context (with concepts, practices, rites, beliefs, and experiences) that allows believers to have a shared, personal religious experience. As Lindbeck puts it, "it is necessary to have the means of expressing an experience in order to have it, and the richer our expressive or linguistic system, the more subtle, varied, and richer can be our experience."[23] In fact, language creates the possibility of religious experience rather than expressing a pre-linguistic experience.[24] If one does not have the concept, he or she cannot have the experience.

The experiential-expressionist model considers that all humans have common experiences, expressed with different names in different cultural contexts. However, only within a community of brothers and sisters can we dare to call God Father (or, for that matter, Mother). It would be an error to emphasize the social consequences of the fraternity derived from God as a Father, translating (equating) them into secular terms like social justice, progressive taxation, welfare state, or public health system. Those are clear consequences of the faith in God as Father, but such terms are finally unable to translate the experience of God as Father. For example, Sweden may be the most egalitarian welfare state in the world, but it does not seem that the Swedes experience God's paternity better than, say, Brazilian peasants. It would be a misunderstanding to identify the kingdom of God with the Swedish social democracy. As a matter of fact, it seems that secular Swedish culture fails to provide the cultural-linguistic tools to live the experience of God's paternity, while the impoverished communal Brazilian communities do allow for such an experience to be lived and nourished. Again, we find that in order to experience a certain reality as such, human beings need the cultural and linguistic tools that make that experience really possible.

Particularity and Pluralism

The main problem with Lindbeck's cultural-linguistic model is the risk of sectarianism. Since he emphasizes the untranslatability of Christian lan-

23. Lindbeck, *The Nature of Doctrine*, p. 37.
24. See Sue Patterson, *Realist Christian Theology in a Postmodern Age* (Cambridge: Cambridge University Press, 1999), p. 35.

guage, the relevance of strong religious communities, and the importance of particular traditions, the question is how this proposal can be appropriate for a pluralistic world. This question is central. It could even be said — and Lindbeck would agree on this point — that if postliberal theology cannot explain cultural pluralism and the Christian role within it, then it makes no sense to change the theological model we are using. My argument covers this issue from three different perspectives: socio-political, philosophical, and theological.

The *socio-political* point of view underscores the limits of the liberal approach to pluralism. Since we live in a complex world with different visions of society, the dominant position argues, we need to develop clear procedures that assure certain agreements on a number of practical topics. This process of overlapping consensus (John Rawls) may reach some common ground, but it does so by blocking the riches of every person and tradition. The rule of the majority overcomes minorities, diversity is lost, and plurality is not considered as something to be valued and defended. Some authors, inside this liberal tradition but criticizing it from the feminist and multicultural perspective, have pointed out that the process of building consensus cannot be done by cutting down particularities and their riches.[25]

Hannah Arendt indicates that modernity has created a growing dichotomy between the public and the private realms. Public dialogue refers only to technical issues, while the more personal ones are left for the private space — where intimacy can be shared with relatives or friends. Her analysis shows how this social mechanism has impoverished our public life. In modern public dialogue only certain topics are politically correct, leaving the rest of them to the private realm. Arendt suggests going back to conversation, in its etymological sense of *con-vertere* (to "pour-in-common") as a way of regaining a public space in which different voices can and must be heard. Only through conversation can we create a truly common world in which all pluralistic voices can contribute their own particular tongue. But they should not be concerned about translating their language into a common Esperanto, but rather about speaking as clearly as possible in their own language. We should never forget, says

---

25. See, for instance, Iris M. Young, *Inclusion and Democracy* (Oxford: Oxford University Press, 2000), for a good proposal that comes from the liberal side but moves beyond deliberative democracy.

Arendt, that "human plurality, the basic condition of both action and speech, has the twofold character of equality and distinction."[26] By unilaterally emphasizing equality, the dominant liberal tradition tends to downplay diversity and distinction.

This has been one of the main critiques from the *philosophical* perspective, especially among postmodern authors. This school of thought follows the principle of differentiation, established by Ferdinand de Saussure and now peacefully assumed by contemporary linguistics. According to this principle, linguistic value is determined only by relations and differences with other signs in the language.[27] This is true at the basic phonetic level (for example, if a non-native speaker cannot recognize the difference between two sounds, she or he will be incapable of understanding or pronouncing those different meanings) and also at the more general ones. Difference creates meaning and, for that reason, if differences are blurred, those signs (sounds, words, sentences, languages, cultures, religions) become meaningless. If we combine this principle with Wittgenstein's famous claim that "the meaning of a word is its use in the language,"[28] we can see the practical importance of this question. Any group that wishes to make a significant contribution in a pluralistic world will need to articulate its difference in ordinary practices; if not, it will become meaningless.

If this is the case, then, the emphasis of postmodern authors on difference is not surprising. They claim that modern reason, in its attempt to attain universality, denies particularities; its abstract thread shadows the concrete experience of people; legitimate differences that enrich our life are actually blurred under cultural and political uniformity. The philosophical case for distinction has public relevance, especially from the perspective of minority and excluded groups. This postmodern defense of difference and plurality, with its implied critique of the modern rationale, is a necessary reminder and a positive contribution. While this position is helpful for Christian reflection, it must be nuanced in two ways. On the one hand, we must realize that the emphasis is not placed on the minority

26. Hannah Arendt, *The Human Condition* (Chicago: University of Chicago Press, 1958), p. 175.

27. See Ferdinand de Saussure, *Course in General Linguistics,* trans. Roy Harris (La Salle, Ill.: Open Court, 1986), pp. 112-20.

28. In his *Philosophical Investigations,* § 43. See Garth Hallett, SJ, *Wittgenstein's Definition of Meaning as Use* (New York: Fordham University Press, 1967).

status as such (this might lead to sectarian views) but on difference, that is, providing the basis for an alternative worldview. On the other hand, as Anselm Min has rightly pointed out, difference cannot be absolutized but we must sublate it in solidarity.[29]

With these remarks we can now move to consider the *theological* view of the question of particularity, which is best understood with the image of the city on the mountain: "In days to come the mountain of the LORD's house shall be set over all other mountains, lifted high above the hills. All the nations shall come streaming to it" (Isa. 2:2). God elected Israel as a peculiar people to shine in contrast with its neighbors, to show them a different way of living.[30] This is God's historical plan of salvation in the Hebrew Scriptures. Christian communities must form a society of contrast to serve the world. The church should not dilute its peculiarity, because if it does so, it cannot fulfill its mission.[31] As we have seen, the significance of any public proposal is related to its distinction from other voices, just as its meaning is based on use. A Christian alternative to the dominant system and discourse ought to be based on daily practices that embody a different worldview.

In terms of the New Testament, we can refer to the church as salt and leaven in the world.[32] As Jesus said, if the salt becomes tasteless, it is good for nothing (Matt. 5:13). The church has to maintain its specific taste, flavor, color, and language (!) to be faithful to its mission. Like the salt in the soup, Christians are called to be significant minorities in the midst of this pluralistic world. "Minority" means that the Constantinian worldview is definitively over. It means that Christians should not be worried about in-

29. See Anselm Kyongsuk Min, *The Solidarity of Others in a Divided World: A Postmodern Theology after Postmodernism* (New York and London: T&T Clark, 2004). This book offers, in the first part, a balanced critique of the postmodern notion of difference and, in the second part, a constructive theological assessment of the problem.

30. "Israel was from the very beginning a contrast-society founded in the Exodus of the poor," says Norbert F. Lohfink, SJ, in *Option for the Poor: The Basic Principle of Liberation Theology in the Light of the Bible* (Richland Hills, Tex.: BIBAL, 1987), p. 41.

31. Lindbeck refers to this truth when he suggests an Israel-like ecclesiology in George A. Lindbeck, "Confession and Community: An Israel-like View of the Church," in *The Church in a Postliberal Age*, pp. 1-9. See also his "Scripture, Consensus, and Community," in *The Church in a Postliberal Age*, pp. 201-22.

32. See Marianne Sawicki, "Salt and Leaven: Resistances to Empire in the Street-Smart Paleochurch," in *The Church as Counterculture*, ed. Michael L. Budde and Robert W. Brimlow (New York: State University of New York Press, 2000), pp. 59-87.

fluencing the whole society they live in. "Significant" means that Christian communities must offer a specific contribution of their own to the public space. Instead of following the dominant liberal approach by trying to build majority-overlapping consensus, they should place their emphasis on assuring that their particular voice is heard as it is, and understood. A humble but different voice.

By doing this, the church is following Jesus' path, and his own personal approach to this question of particularity and universality. As Paul Tillich wisely said, "If Jesus is called the Christ, he must represent everything particular and must be the point of identity between the absolute concrete and the absolute universal."[33] In Jesus Christ there is no room for the merely abstract, nor for the merely particular. The problem of the universalistic liberal approach is that it may become too abstract. The problem with Lindbeck's cultural-linguistic emphasis is that he may get trapped in the sheer particular. To overcome these difficulties, the mystery of the incarnation offers an appropriate solution from the Christian perspective. Only through particularity did Jesus achieve universality.

A Radical Proposal: Theological Narrative

So far I have presented Lindbeck's model, highlighting some of its strengths and contributions. I have also suggested some of its limitations: Is it leaning toward cultural relativism? According to this model, is Christian faith just one proposal among others? What kind of truth claims are linked to Christian doctrines understood in this cultural-linguistic paradigm? Does it offer a firm enough foundation? How real is the risk of sectarianism in this proposal? To clarify and eventually solve these questions, a dynamic approach is needed that uses Lindbeck's insights and moves beyond them, offering a radical proposal for Christian communities in pluralistic societies.

Lindbeck's emphasis on the recovery and importance of the particular tradition is a necessary one, for it allows the embodiment of Christian life in specific social practices. But we need to take another step forward to overcome some shortcomings in Lindbeck's argument and to be more

33. Paul Tillich, *Systematic Theology,* vol. I (Chicago: University of Chicago Press, 1951), p. 16.

compatible with the Christian faith. My proposal includes a dynamic Christian narrative — from incarnation to eschatology — which overcomes a static approach and allows the integration of the poles included in the discussion. It is radical in two senses: first, it is rooted in Jesus Christ, and second, it surpasses the current ecclesial "language divide" by going deeper into the issues. On the basis of this theological discourse, I address the open discussion regarding particularity and universality, epistemology and ontology, coherence and correspondence, language and reality.

The Logic of the Incarnation

The logic of incarnation[34] is one of the central features of the Christian faith, with normative value for our understanding of the world and with significant implications for the matters we are dealing with. Regarding the issues I have sought to clarify in this chapter, four aspects need to be considered.

Incarnation shows that the Christian story is, first of all, a *particular* one. From Bethlehem to Golgotha, Jesus is absolutely particular. He spoke Aramaic and lived in Galilee and Judea. Only through this particular incarnation did God's universal salvific plan take place. Jesus is the Christ and Savior for all humankind, but only through his concrete and limited experience. Particularity, then, is a necessary pole or moment of the dialogue and, although it is not the only one, we must start with it.

God's plan, as revealed in Jesus Christ, adopts a particular approach to universal knowledge. His *epistemology* strongly leans on a specific perspective that sometimes may even seem a relative one. Jesus rarely speaks about how things are, but mainly deals with interpretative questions about the Law, social structure, or reality. In this particular moment, then, emphasis is placed on epistemology as such. Jesus starts from a humble position, making claims about what is experienced and known, not about reality as such. Again, this will not be the whole picture, but it is the starting point.

34. See James K. A. Smith, *Speech and Theology: Language and the Logic of Incarnation* (London: Routledge, 2002). In fact, Smith is dealing with a different problem, the paradox of speaking about a transcendent and infinite God with finite and immanent language. But he rightly points to the logic of incarnation as the appropriate Christian solution to this paradox. I draw in part from his insight.

Accordingly, the focus goes to *coherence*. Jesus strongly advocates for coherence in the discourse, but even more important, and more often, he seeks coherence in personal ethical behavior and in lived social settings. "Not everyone who calls me 'Lord, Lord' will enter the kingdom of Heaven, but only those who do the will of my heavenly Father" (Matt. 7:21). There is a need for internal coherence of the discourse, and also for practical coherence in daily life. Lindbeck himself says: "The crusader's battle cry *'Christus est Dominus,'* for example, is false when used to authorize cleaving the skull of the infidel."[35] We must remember that the meaning of a word is given by its use: orthodoxy is linked to orthopraxis, but it is also true that a wrong and continued practice (such as religious intolerance) has effects on the credibility and coherence of a certain doctrine.

At this point, it is also clear that there is a need to emphasize *language*. Jesus speaks as the Jew he is to the Jews in their own terms. And, especially in the final period of his public life, he pays growing attention to his disciples' formation. They must learn the meaning of words such as *Abba, love, service, cross, self-denial, kenosis.* For instance, after Jesus' teaching in the synagogue of Capernaum, some people exclaimed, "This is more than we can stomach! Why listen to such talk?" (John 6:60), while Peter acknowledged, "Your words are words of eternal life" (John 6:68). Deeds and words are integral parts of the message, and both are needed to understand it. With Jesus and in the Christian community, alternative practices embody and nourish alternative language uses.

So far we have considered some consequences of the doctrine of incarnation in the area of foundational theology. We have seen the practice of Jesus as one stressing particularity, epistemology, internal coherence, and language. Is this all? No. Incarnation is a nuclear doctrine of Christian faith, but it is not the only one. It must necessarily be considered in a dynamic equilibrium with eschatology. Lindbeck himself is closer to the incarnationalist-particularist position, but he widens his own perspective when he talks about applicability as futurology, meaning that the purpose of practical theology is "to shape present action to fit the anticipated and hoped-for future."[36] If incarnation emphasizes particularity, eschatology will provide the basis for a Christian approach to universality.

---

35. Lindbeck, *The Nature of Doctrine*, p. 64. This observation offers a very necessary correction to President Bush's "theology of empire" and war in Iraq.

36. Lindbeck, *The Nature of Doctrine*, p. 125.

An Eschatological View

Eschatology refers to the ultimate realities and as such offers a complement to the incarnational view, which focuses on the (limited) achievements in a particular human setting. In fact, this eschatological reading deepens the reality already implied in the incarnation and introduces a dynamic element.

Jesus of Nazareth is the cosmic Christ. The particular moment of Jesus, the Galilean peasant, achieves a full sense only when completed with the *universal* moment of Christ, as ruler over the universe. God's plan is "that the universe, all in heaven and on earth, might be brought into a unity in Christ" (Eph. 1:10). Then, in the new creation, Christ will be all in everyone and everything. As Christians, we can achieve universality only through a particular and specific way, the way of Jesus. But we do recognize that the way of Jesus leads to universal salvation.

For this reason, Christian philosophy cannot stop at the epistemological level. It does make stronger claims about how things actually are (ontology), not only about what we know of them (epistemology). However, those claims are linked to a Messianic future, which can find an adequate conceptualization in Ernst Bloch's anticipatory consciousness of the real Being as Not-Yet-Conscious.[37] According to this vision — which in this regard is very close to Christianity's — reality is truly found in the future: what we already know is real, but it needs to be fulfilled in the kingdom of God. Christian doctrine claims to be not a mere opinion but a real truth; at the same time, it knows that real and definitive truth will only take place in the kingdom of God, in a future that is already anticipated with the incarnation of Jesus Christ but is not fully accomplished yet.

In relation to this Messianic ontology, there is a need for a theory that considers truth not only as coherence but also as *correspondence*. Such a theory, one that suits the Christian perspective, can be constructed in dialogue with the philosophy of ordinary language and its concept of performative utterances. There are some situations in which to say something is actually to do something. Even more, according to J. L. Austin, in perlocutionary acts the speaker performs *by* saying something.[38] This is

---

37. Ernst Bloch, *The Principle of Hope*, vol. 1 (Cambridge, Mass.: MIT, 1986), pp. 114-78.

38. See J. L. Austin, *How to Do Things with Words* (Oxford: Oxford University Press, 1965).

not simply a philosophical novelty, but also a biblical truth: the Hebrew notion of *dabar,* for instance, refers at the same time to "word" and "thing." The Judeo-Christian understanding of the Word of God, then, implies a consideration of performative speech. I want to stress the fact that Christian communities create a new reality as they worship, pray, serve, and live. But they can do so only if they keep faithful to their own shared and inherited expression, if there is correspondence between what they say and what they do. If this is so, for example, when Christians *say* "Jesus is Lord" they are actually *creating* a new reality, an alternative to every empire.[39]

In fact, the Christian conviction is that "these [worldly] things are a shadow of the things that were to come; the reality, however, is found in Christ" (Col. 2:17). It is not only that Christians interpret things in a different way, or that they formulate them in a particular fashion; it is really a different reality. Christians claim that their language is the most appropriate one to understand the core of *reality,* as will be shown in the eschatological times.[40] Of course, one can only anticipate that reality in a partial fashion, but to do so, one needs to have the tools (language, rituals, practices, mystagogical processes, communal relationships, and so on) that made it possible. Without the proper "grammar" one cannot read that pretasted eschatological reality.

Languages of Theology

We come now to the central question of this chapter. What kind of language should the church use, and what type of theological discourse is most appropriate for contemporary pluralistic societies? The best response partly leans on Lindbeck's model but also introduces several modifications as it tries to move beyond it to provide a better solution. It involves three

---

39. See note 35 above for a correction of an obvious paradoxical misuse of Christianity in contemporary politics.

40. This eschatological view offers a solution to the dilemma pointed out by Scott Smith, "Hauerwas and Kallenberg and the Issue of Epistemic Access to An Extra-Linguistic Realm," *The Heythrop Journal* 45 (2004): 305-26. Christianity makes universal claims from its particular forms of life, and at the same time presupposes an access to a real world apart from language. But this second aspect is based on the eschatological anticipation and, as such, can be "proved" only at the end of times.

steps — practical, systematic, and apologetic — and the order is not without significance.

The first step is to recognize that there is a clear need for a context that allows for religious experience. Only strong Christian communities can offer plausibility structures in which to recognize and experience Jesus Christ's acting power in our midst. Contemporary citizens of our secularized world need to have available a pool of Christian language, experience, practices, and habits. Only that will make it possible for them to live and experience God. This is particularly important in our context, because now the general environment does not provide it. This *language of living* is the first and indispensable step for the church's practice and for theological reflection. It is the language of worship, prayer, Christian commitment to the poor, active community life, mystagogical processes for children and adults, and alternative ways of living.

If the first step is that of practical theology, the second one should focus on systematic theology, that is, a *rational discourse* for the community of believers. Although the language of living is necessary, not everything can be evaluated on the level of everyday life practices. As Lindbeck says, "the logic of coming to believe, because it is like learning a language, has little room for argument, but once one has learned to speak the language of faith, argument becomes possible."[41] Christian faith and the Christian understanding of reality are not merely the sum of fragmented non-rational experiences. Christians — as persons and in communities — need internal coherence among the different aspects of reality that only an articulated discourse can offer. This has been traditionally the task of dogmatic or systematic theology (which, by the way, not all religious systems have developed). At the same time, it is important to emphasize that this Christian discourse is formulated within its own language, tradition, and way of expression.

Only then, as a third step, can Christian theology accomplish its necessary role of *dialogue with others,* be they non-believers or believers of different religions. Apologetics, foundational theology, or theological prolegomena is not, in this vision, a preliminary stage, but a subsequent one.[42]

---

41. Lindbeck, *The Nature of Doctrine,* p. 132.

42. Says Lindbeck: "A postliberal approach does not exclude an ad hoc apologetics, but only one that is systematically prior and controlling in a fashion of post-Cartesian natural theology" (Lindbeck, *The Nature of Doctrine,* p. 131). In fact, he adds this nuance:

Of course, it is absolutely necessary to understand other positions and to make oneself understood. It is important to try to build a consensus that is as wide as possible. But this is not the first step. It is a secondary practice and it comes only after the other two steps have been accomplished. Of course, in this process there will be a need for some translation, using what have been called "middle axioms" (J. H. Oldham, Reinhold Niebuhr) or some form of analogy (Karl Barth) to relate Christian positions to those of secular culture.

Let me explain this threefold proposal with an example, regarding the identity of the church. "What is the church and how is it to be explained?" It is necessary, first, to create and to strengthen a real community in which alternative relationships take place; it is necessary to nurture the social embodiment of Christian practices. It is important to provide a communal experience in which everyone is welcomed and no one is excluded. Finally, it is indispensable to build up a community in which God's presence shines. This practical approach is a requisite for any other step, and it will demand a particular language and way of expression (liturgy, sacraments, catechesis, social involvement, prayer, community organization, and relationships). Second, there is a need for a theological discourse that organizes, explains, and helps Christians to live better that shared experience. For instance, the development of a theology of the body of Christ would be of great importance (including scriptural, historical, spiritual, dogmatic, and social arguments, all included in a systematic rational reflection). Third, it could be interesting to find appropriate analogies for a secular vision of that practice and doctrine of the church as the body of Christ — such as participatory democracy, respect for minority cultural groups, nonviolent socialism, or asymmetric solidarity for the poor.

Conclusion

This chapter has focused on issues concerning the language that Christian churches should use in contemporary cultural settings. I have argued that Lindbeck's cultural-linguistic model offers a good starting point, and I have modified it to offer a proposal that considers incarnation and escha-

---

"apologetics becomes primarily a matter of appropriate communal praxis" (Lindbeck, *The Nature of Doctrine*, p. 12).

tology in dynamic terms. As a consequence, I have suggested a Christian movement from particularity to universality, and a three-step proposal for the languages of theology. Some important fields may be analyzed from these results, both in the theoretical-theological area and in the ministerial praxis of the church. Among other things, this model allows one to argue for the need for a specific Christian approach to social issues. Similarly, it highlights the importance of overcoming sectarianism without losing communal identity, the exigency of deep spiritual formation at all levels, and the recovery of creativity in local communities. These aspects, related to the Christian view of culture and politics, will be analyzed in the following chapters. We begin with a closer look at the role of mediations, particularly social sciences, in theological reflection.

2. Can a Gift Be Wrapped?
John Milbank and Supernatural Sociology

"Can a gift be given?" asked John Milbank, ten years ago, when he tried to ground a Trinitarian metaphysic of the gift, in contrast with other phenomenological, anthropological, and ontological approaches to donation.[1] Milbank wanted to emphasize the absolute gratuity of God's revelation; it does not need to be mediated through a particular philosophical system that would represent a human construction, but is offered to humanity as a real free gift. His point was clear and important: God's self-communication is a gift that human beings can only receive as such, and never fully comprehend or apprehend. However, and going beyond the particular interest of that essay, we must also ask some crucial questions: Does this truth nullify the role of mediations in articulating that same revelation? Is there a place for not strictly theological human discourses in that process? Do we need to dismiss all social sciences in theological thought as if they were a human construction in opposition to God's gift? In other words, can a gift be wrapped? Can a gift continue to be a free gift, even if it is surrounded by wrapping paper? Is God's self-revelation less gratuitous if we use the mediation of social sciences in our theological reflection? Or even more, can we even think of a pure gift that does not come somehow wrapped?

A number of current discussions can be formulated within this framework. In the field of economics, is it enough to say that usury is a sin or to proclaim the tradition of a Jubilee year? Do we not need the mediation of

---

1. John Milbank, "Can a Gift Be Given? Prolegomena to a Future Trinitarian Metaphysic," *Modern Theology* 11 (1995): 119-61.

social sciences to articulate a proposal that applies the doctrine on usury to the current situation or makes a contribution to effectively reduce international debt? A second example may be taken from the biological domain, with the evolution-creationism debate. Is there an opposition between the theory of evolution and the biblical doctrine of creation? How are they integrated? In the area of public health, and more specifically in AIDS prevention, we could ask the question about the role of condoms from a Christian perspective. Is the so-called Ugandan model, with its three-fold ABC strategy (Abstinence, Be faithful, Condoms) a suitable one? How are technical issues combined with moral and religious views?

In all these cases, the question is about the role of scientific mediation in articulating Christian thought. If we discard fideism, literalism, and religious fundamentalism (as I do), are we necessarily led to naturalism or "rational fundamentalism"? Of course, I do not think so. Then, we must ask ourselves, what is the proper relationship between science and theology? What does the autonomy of the secular sciences mean, and what is the role of religious beliefs for a global understanding of reality? If faith provides a particular worldview, one that theology articulates in a rational way, what is the role of modern sciences in that process? Given our specific interest in socio-political issues, we must particularly elucidate the interplay between social theory and theology. In 1980 Father Arrupe, general superior of the Jesuits, wrote a famous letter on Marxist analysis, where he mentioned that conflict appears only when the "absolute character" of that mediation contradicts Christian worldview. But he also acknowledged that these problems are not limited to Marxist analysis: "In particular, the type of social analysis used in the liberal world today implies an individualistic and materialistic vision of life that is destructive of Christian values and attitudes."[2] Is there an absolute character in secular social sciences that challenges and opposes Christian theology? Again, can a gift be wrapped or, because it is given, must it remain unwrapped?

This chapter addresses these issues in order to move a step forward in the process of clarifying the relationship between church and society. The previous chapter argued for the need for a specific Christian voice in the

---

2. Father Pedro Arrupe, SJ, "Marxist Analysis by Christians" (December 8, 1980), in *Liberation Theology: A Documentary History*, ed. Alfred T. Hennelly (Maryknoll, N.Y.: Orbis, 1990), pp. 307-13. Original text in "Sobre el análisis marxista," *Acta Romana Societatis Iesu* 18 (1980): 331-38.

public arena, while recognizing the necessity of articulating several levels of language in Christian theology. How can that be unfolded in the area of social sciences? Do secular sciences provide theology with a neutral description of reality, like raw material on which theology can reflect? Or, on the opposite side, can theology be considered a full-blown social theory? What would a "supernatural sociology" imply and look like?

Presentation of Milbank's Position

In 1990, John Milbank published his influential and polemical book *Theology and Social Theory*.[3] Significantly subtitled *Beyond Secular Reason,* this work critically interprets the evolution of modernity as a form of (anti)-theology that leads to nihilism, and proposes Christianity as the only viable alternative. In the process Milbank dismisses as "dead-ends" political economy, sociology, liberalism, modern philosophy, any form of autonomous reason, and all types of theology influenced by them. In the opening lines of the book, Milbank says that "the secular as a domain had to be instituted or *imagined,* both in theory and in practice."[4] The process of secularization consists precisely in this: not in the separation of two spheres (sacred-secular) but in the creation of the secular domain as the space of power. The process actually "invented" the political, the state, the secular, and — as a subproduct — private religion. The secular, as an autonomous object, is at the same time natural and artificial (*factum,* made).

Milbank's critical project seeks to dismantle all modern social theory as a corruption of the previous theological synthesis. Hence, when discussing liberalism in part I, Milbank interprets the new science of politics as concerned with the creation of a new space for the secular, which led not only to the invention of the state and politics, but also to the need to invent private religion. There are two lines of thought in this whole process: first, the natural rights legacy of liberalism and absolutism that Milbank considers Christian deviance or heresy; second, the historicist and humanist perspective of Niccolo Macchiavelli, which argues that political practice must be adapted to customs, manners, religions, and times. Because of its

---

3. John Milbank, *Theology and Social Theory: Beyond Secular Reason* (Oxford and Malden: Blackwell, 1990).

4. Milbank, *Theology and Social Theory,* p. 9.

conception of cyclical time, Milbank considers this approach as a half-return to paganism and falsehood. In other words, modern liberalism is either heretical or pagan. In chapter 2, Milbank considers the new political economy based on contractualism, especially analyzing the work of the Scot economists. While political science dealt with *creation* (institution of a new space), political economy was interested in *providence* (prudent conservation, regulation of desire, regularity of power, the market). For Milbank, "*only* the theological model permits one to construct the *mythos* of the sovereign power."[5] For this reason "the institution of the 'secular' is paradoxically related to a shift *within* theology and not an emancipation *from* theology."[6] We here find the same claim that was made in the previous chapter, one that has importance for theological discourse.

The three chapters in part II are devoted successively to French, German, and American sociology. Milbank himself summarizes the results of chapters 3 and 4: "Instead of a partial admission of 'suspicion,' one should develop a 'meta-suspicion' which casts doubt on the possibility of suspicion itself."[7] Milbank argues that Max Weber is trapped in a very questionable liberal Protestant meta-narrative. If religion is private, and the public is dominated by rationality, there is no space for Christianity as a sphere of charity. Then, he applies this result to twentieth-century sociology of religion, and challenges the fact that we have come to assume that while "religions" are problematic, the "social" is obvious. In fact, sociology (as well as liberal theology and phenomenology of religion) tries to identify and protect a real essence of religion. Thus, religion is regarded as belonging to the Kantian "sublime": the sublime is to be protected and treasured, but it causes no effects on the objective factual world. That is to say, the sublime is "policed," kept behind the possibilities of empirical understanding. Milbank argues that twentieth-century sociology of religion can be seen as a secular policing of the sublime. For this reason, "the sociology of religion ought to come to an end."[8] While it is clear that Milbank is arguing against sociology offering a meta-discourse that theology must accept, this is obviously a strong claim that we need to ponder with some thoughtfulness.

The argument of the rest of the book goes as follows: part III discusses

---

5. Milbank, *Theology and Social Theory*, p. 28.
6. Milbank, *Theology and Social Theory*, p. 29.
7. Milbank, *Theology and Social Theory*, p. 102.
8. Milbank, *Theology and Social Theory*, p. 139.

theology and dialectics in three chapters (G. W. F. Hegel, Marx, and twentieth-century Catholic theology of the supernatural). Part IV starts clarifying Milbank's view on science and hermeneutics, positions he also dismisses. In this context, he says that "theology need only to embrace as absolute its own narrative."[9] Of course, every Christian would agree with this, since any other position would mean capitulation to some other discourses. But the real question is whether theology should embrace, relatively and under Christian narrative, other narratives. That is the key issue we need to clarify in this chapter. The final part of Milbank's book focuses on the postmodern debate: the criticism of ontological violence and the road to nihilism (chapter 10); an analysis of pluralism and virtue in which he follows Alasdair MacIntyre, while criticizing his "general virtue proposal" (chapter 11); and finally, chapter 12 goes back to Saint Augustine's *City of God* and establishes theology as an alternative social theory. The general line of thought of Milbank's work is then clear: modernity necessarily leads to postmodern nihilism; for this reason, Christianity must go beyond secular thought; the only alternative, then, is a Christian narrative that engages and overcomes the postmodern challenge.

Analysis of Milbank's Position

First of all, Milbank's *way of arguing* is not without difficulties. He practices a "hermeneutics of suspicion" that gives the impression of interpreting the authors out of their actual intentions and forcing them into his own framework. This negative and dangerous approach leads him to extrapolate the position of the authors studied and sometimes to misinterpret them (as I show in the following section). While it is important to clarify the possible dangers or hypothetical consequences of a given thinker, overall this does not seem to be a very rigorous method. At the same time, Milbank construes his argument in dialogue or confrontation with a number of key authors, but surprisingly avoids others. For instance, he tends to forget the self-critical tradition within modernity, as developed by Hannah Arendt, Max Horkheimer and Theodor Adorno, and Gadamer, among others. These authors provide a deep criticism of secular reason, while maintaining the noblest insights of the Enlighten-

---

9. Milbank, *Theology and Social Theory*, p. 268.

ment project. It is hard to defend positions as strong as Milbank's without considering the contributions of these thinkers, who have dealt with similar concerns and have offered possible solutions. His method does not seem entirely honest, intellectually speaking. Milbank's way of arguing also sometimes shuts down the dialogue by his use of adverbs; such as *only* (pp. 28, 33, 173, 434). This may seem to be a minor detail, but we ought to remember that prepositions and adverbs are key elements in human dialogue and particularly in doing theology. (For instance, remember the difference between an "either-or" and a "both-and" perspective in Catholic-Lutheran dialogue.) Milbank's unilateral way of arguing has the effect of blocking the conversation.

A second issue refers to Milbank's interpretation of *secularization*. He seems to be right when he defines and critiques the modern sociological task as "policing the sublime," a topic related to the more practical political issue of privatizing religion.[10] It is clear that Milbank's emphasis on a theological root for the secularization process is important for his argument. What remains unclear, though, is the extent to which this analysis is very different from the conventional interpretation of secularization. Again, the reader would look in vain for a discussion with Talcott Parsons, Marcel Gauchet, or Habermas in this respect. Milbank argues that secularization is not an emancipation from theology or the Christian worldview, but simply a movement within theology toward "heretical" or pagan views. One would expect that, before making such strong claims, Milbank would engage in a discussion with those authors who have defended a different position.

A third theme we ought to consider is the critique of *positivism*, the status of sciences, and the implicit "conflict of interpretations" among different disciplines. Milbank is correct when he says: "Sociology of religion cannot claim to be a true metadiscourse about religion, in contrast to theologies which merely represent world views."[11] But he goes too far and misses the point when he concludes that sociology of religion must end. Milbank's argument can be restated in terms of an epistemological critique of positivism, especially since he considers that all social sciences are

---

10. Although this issue is much clearer in Europe than in the United States, see Jim Wallis, *God's Politics: Why the Right Gets It Wrong and the Left Does Not Get It* (San Francisco: HarperSanFrancisco, 2005).

11. Milbank, *Theology and Social Theory*, p. 110.

positivistic. In that case, the point is that, if a philosophical (or theological) argument against scientific positivism does not annul science as such, why should a theological critique of sociology of religion nullify it? There is not a convincing answer in Milbank's work. Again, this is partly because he does not enter into a conversation with authors, such as those espousing the Frankfurt School of Critical Theory,[12] who have argued against positivism and instrumental reason while defending the need for a strong rational discourse.

The *political implications* of Milbank's theory is the fourth focus of analysis. He is usually considered as a conservative theologian because, as Paul Lakeland says, Milbank defends "a shameless reassertion of the premodern superiority of Christendom."[13] However, Milbank clearly (and explicitly) sets the basis for a political platform articulated around socialism, nonviolence, and "inclusive plurality."[14] It is true that Milbank is going against the stream of liberal secularism, but he does so to propose an innovative Christian socialism. As long as the emphasis is placed on the development of this alternative, this theology hardly seems "conservative." Still, one question remains unanswered, because Milbank shuts any possible door to or bridge toward "secular reason" and because he does not correctly acknowledge the fact of secularism and pluralism. He would probably say that it is not a fact, but an imaginary self-interested interpretation produced by the modern mindset. But in fact, we do have to face the fact that there *is* a polytheism of values. The question remains of how to deal with it. Although Milbank argues for a postmodern Christian narrative as a solution in the pluralistic context, he sometimes seems to lean toward a more authoritarian vision that is at odds with the modern perspective.[15]

This introduces the topic of *ecclesiology,* our fifth and final issue in this

12. See, for instance, Max Horkheimer and Theodor Adorno, *Dialectic of the Enlightenment: Philosophical Fragments* (Stanford, Calif.: Stanford University Press, 2002).

13. Paul Lakeland, *Postmodernity: Christian Identity in a Fragmented Age* (Minneapolis: Fortress, 1997), p. 68.

14. Although Milbank has elsewhere developed his thought on this regard, the following three quotes from *Theology and Social Theory* will suffice: "Socialism is grounded in Christianity" (p. 208); "Jesus's commitment to non-violent persuasion as a precondition for the perfect society surpass[es] the conceptions of later 'proletarian' revolutions" (p. 237); "reconciliation of virtue with difference" is the distinctive element of the church (p. 417).

15. For instance, see Milbank, *Theology and Social Theory,* p. 402: "True society implies absolute consensus, agreement in desire, and entire harmony amongst its members, and this is exactly (as Augustine reiterates again and again) what the Church provides."

section. The role and understanding of the church in Milbank's work have received a great deal of attention. Two of the most thoughtful commentaries on Milbank have dealt with this matter, providing what appear to be opposite interpretations. Canadian theologian Gregory Baum finds that Milbank proposes an Anabaptist ecclesiology "as an heir to the radical wing of the Reformation" and "distances himself from any high church tradition."[16] On the other hand, the Jesuit from Leuven Georges de Schrijver notes that Milbank defends a high-church ecclesiology, as opposed to a low-profile one.[17] Schrijver refers to Milbank's emphasis on the church as the visible embodiment of a theological alternative to the modern worldview, a position opposed to the more quiet and low-profile post–Second Vatican Council ecclesial presence in society. Can we integrate both views? Can Anabaptism maintain a high-church ecclesiology? What is Milbank's notion of the church? Is he espousing a pretentious church, as Schrijver suggests, or an irrelevant one, as Baum implies?[18] The key to solving this issue is to maintain the two poles in tension: the church must be visible and present in the public arena, while at the same time being humble. Only then will the church be relevant and not pretentious, meek and not diluted.

A Theological Critique of Milbank

Milbank finds in Christian practices the alternative to the modern organization of life, and in theology an alternative to dominant secular social theories. If we accept for the moment his point of view it will become evident that the only discussion that may challenge Milbank's position will be a

16. Gregory Baum, "For and Against John Milbank," in *Essays in Critical Theology* (Kansas City: Sheed & Ward, 1994), pp. 53-54.

17. Georges De Schrijver, SJ, "The Use of Mediations in Theology: Or, the Expansion and Self-Confinement of a Theology of the Trinity," in *Mediations in Theology: Georges De Schrijver's Wager and Liberation Theologies,* ed. Jacques Haers, SJ, Edmundo Guzmán, Lope Florente Lesigues, and Daniel Franklin Pilario, CM (Leuven: Peeters, 2003), p. 48.

18. I take these two adjectives from two articles that are not referred to Milbank, but throw some light on this topic. Eugene B. McCarraher, "The Church Irrelevant: Paul Hanly Furfey and the Fortunes of American Catholic Radicalism," *Religion and American Culture* 7 (1997): 163-94; Miroslav Volf, "Against a Pretentious Church: A Rejoinder to Bell's Response," *Modern Theology* 19 (2003): 281-85.

theological one. Since he assumes that Christian theology out-narrates secular reason, we need to engage in a theological discussion to clarify the validity of Milbank's proposal. This section presents three theological views (Karl Barth, Henri de Lubac, liberation theology) and analyzes Milbank's reading of them. It then provides a theological framework for a sound understanding of the relationship between theology and social sciences.

The Analogy of Being and Social Sciences

It is clear that Milbank comes close to Barth's position in his desire to go "beyond secular reason." As Gregory Baum has pointed out, Milbank "claims with Barthian vehemence that there is no good society, no valid ethics and no true wisdom apart from the life and message of Jesus Christ."[19] Baum then denies that Milbank is a Karl Barth *redivivus,* saying instead that he is an Anabaptist or Mennonite Barth. In fact, in the more than four hundred pages of *Theology and Social Theory,* Milbank only mentions Barth once — in a tangential reference.[20] There is another implicit — but more central and critical — allusion to Barth:

> Certain styles of neo-orthodoxy that insist on the absolute contrast between the revealed word of God and human "religion," which as a mere historical product can safely be handed over to any reductive analyses whatsoever. However, this sort of neo-orthodoxy is itself but a variant of liberal Protestantism.[21]

Milbank conceives of Barth's position as one of absolute contrast (between faith and religion, Word and culture, and so on), which he interprets as an influence of Immanuel Kant's modern division between *noumenon* and *phenomenon.* The consequence of this view, according to Milbank, is that Barth's project is trapped inside modern philosophy and eventually falls back into liberal theology.

---

19. Baum, "For and Against Milbank," p. 52. See also Neil Ormerod, "Milbank and Barth: A Catholic Perspective," in *Karl Barth: A Future for Postmodern Theology?* ed. Geoff Thompson and Christiaan Mostert (Hindmarsh: Australian Theological Forum, 2000), pp. 276-89.

20. Milbank, *Theology and Social Theory,* p. 328.

21. Milbank, *Theology and Social Theory,* p. 101.

In order to do justice to Barth's position, however, we need to clarify his understanding of the analogy of being. Although this issue has stirred a lively debate among both Protestant and Catholic theologians, I simply follow Hans Urs von Balthasar's analysis, because it provides a solid interpretation by an author close to Milbank's views. In summary, von Balthasar considers that *analogia fidei* can assume *analogia entis* in itself, purifying and modifying it. He concludes his detailed analysis by saying that these formulas are not battling one another (*analogia fidei* against *analogia entis*) but are two ways of understanding the one revelation of God. "Barth's way of understanding God's revelation in Christ includes the analogy of being within the analogy of faith," while the Catholic doctrine "allows the analogy of being to gain its density and concreteness only within the wider analogy of faith."[22] It is important to realize that von Balthasar gives priority to *analogia fidei,* which assumes the analogy of being *within* itself. The analogy of faith, then, is the context that allows the possibility for *analogia entis.* In other words, the priority is given to God's initiative.

Karl Barth's understanding of analogy, at least according to von Balthasar, can be summarized in three points. First, Barth gives absolute priority to *analogia fidei.* Second, this presupposes and implies God's initiative that, in a movement of descent, freely decides to reach humans. Third, this analogy of faith assumes within itself the analogy of being. These three dynamically intertwined results form a methodological tool that helps to analyze and comprehend several theological issues, such as the relationship between faith and reason, faith and justice, love and justice (Reinhold Niebuhr), and grace and nature. Since *analogia fidei* assumes within itself *analogia entis,* the Word of God is able to assume human words, cultures, and even religions. In other words, the priority of a Christian theological discourse *(analogia fidei)* does not impede, but actually demands, a secondary role of secular sciences *(analogia entis)* within itself. In conclusion, Milbank's vehement claim that theology out-narrates and excludes social sciences ought to be nuanced precisely for theological reasons given by authors not likely to be considered "liberal" or "modern," such as Barth and von Balthasar.

22. Hans Urs von Balthasar, *The Theology of Karl Barth: Exposition and Interpretation* (San Francisco: Ignatius, 1992), p. 382.

The Supernatural and Social Sciences

In chapter 8 of *Theology and Social Theory,* Milbank offers an original and polemical analysis of the twentieth-century nature-grace debate among Catholic theologians. It is provocative in that he establishes a sharp distinction (even opposition) between Henri de Lubac and Karl Rahner. According to Milbank, while the French "supernaturalizes the natural," the German "naturalizes the supernatural."[23] Drawing on Maurice Blondel and retrieving the patristic synthesis, de Lubac avoids an extrinsicist understanding of grace while retaining its gratuity. Nature, history, and human existence become "supernaturalized" by grace. Milbank's presentation of Rahner, though, finds that his notion of "supernatural existential" leads to universal humanism and an autonomous secular order. Milbank then argues that Rahner's view has been the dominant influence in European political theology and Latin American liberation theology, both of which are subject to the same criticisms: they maintain an implicit dualism, underestimate the public role of the church, and miss the opportunity for a real Christian alternative to the dominant system. In short, they adopt a "natural" view that makes them finally dependent on secular political groups. Although Milbank's position has the ability to point out some problems apparently unnoticed by other views, his whole argument seems problematic.

Milbank acutely formulates two possible approaches to the nature-grace discussion. However, the opposition he draws between de Lubac and Rahner seems overstated. As a matter of fact, both authors refer to the other in a generally positive manner. They see themselves in broad agreement with each other.[24] Rahner explicitly accepts de Lubac's contribution as the general frame for his own reflection, hoping to guarantee the "unexactedness" of God's grace. De Lubac even says that "it is not the ancient concept of *natura pura,* but the system which has grown around it in modern theology and profoundly changed its meaning, which seems to me could be set aside without any loss."[25] This is close to Rahner's understanding of pure nature as a residual or remainder concept *(Restbegriff).*[26]

23. Milbank, *Theology and Social Theory,* p. 207.

24. See, for example, de Lubac's positive allusions to Rahner in Henri de Lubac, SJ, *The Mystery of the Supernatural* (New York: Herder and Herder, 1967), pp. 72 and 132.

25. De Lubac, *The Mystery of the Supernatural,* p. 42.

26. Karl Rahner, SJ, "Concerning the Relationship between Nature and Grace," in *Theological Investigations,* vol. 1 (New York: Crossroad, 1982), pp. 297-317; here, p. 313.

It is not clear that assuming this position necessarily leads to a political dualism or implicit endorsement of secularism, as Milbank claims. It seems that Milbank reads too much (of his own views and of the current ecclesial situation) into these foundational texts and, in doing so, actually misses the point.

While Milbank might be correct in emphasizing de Lubac's version, he errs when he radically opposes de Lubac and Rahner. In doing so, Milbank not only misconstrues Rahner's position, but also the whole nature-grace debate. Because of his interest in highlighting the differences between the two currents, Milbank develops a flawed argument with important consequences. In fact, one of the main arguments of de Lubac is the integration of nature under grace — which of course leaves the door open for an integration of the secular realm within a supernatural worldview. That is to say, social sciences must be integrated within a Christian theological worldview. If there is no nature-grace dualism, there is no possible "secular social science" that cannot be assumed by theology. In other words, although Milbank claims that sociology must come to an end, de Lubac's interpretation of the supernatural demands that it be integrated within Christian reflection.

Liberation Theology and the Role of Mediations

The next step in Milbank's argument is the application of this debate to post–Second Vatican Council political and liberation theologies, specifically focusing on the mediating role of social sciences for theology. He considers that these theological proposals have mostly built on Rahner's notion of the supernatural, leading to an erroneous acceptance and "baptism" of secular society, a paradoxical understanding of salvation as private transcendence, and a dependence on social sciences. Milbank's discussion with Clodovis Boff is very significant: "Theology, then, does not *require* the mediation of social science, in Boff's sense that social science presents theology with the social object perfectly described and perfectly explained."[27] If that were Boff's account of the relation between theology and social science, Milbank would be right because Boff would be forgetting that only *analogia fidei* is able to found any other possible analogy, or

27. Milbank, *Theology and Social Theory*, p. 248.

that there is no real "pure nature." For this reason we need to pause for a moment and analyze Boff's position and Milbank's reading of it.

Boff proposes an instrumental use of analytical mediations in dialectical reference to praxis, and always subordinated to the hermeneutical principle of faith.[28] It is not accurate to say, as Milbank does, that Boff's method assumes a social object defined by secular sciences. It is true, though, that Boff affirms that "the theology of the political begins where the discourse of the sciences of the social ends"[29] and that could seem to indicate a division of tasks in which social sciences provide theology with "raw material." But Boff's point is simply to recognize the complexity of reality: "A theology of the political has no more access to society apart from the sciences of the social than it does to revelation apart from an adequate interpretation and understanding of scripture."[30] Boff is not advocating a "neutral" definition of reality by autonomous secular sciences, he is just acknowledging that theology can only comprehend its object (God's active revelation in history) through the use of socio-analytic mediations. In this sense, Milbank's attempt is a positive and necessary reminder that theology should not give priority to social sciences as if they were in charge of defining reality. But he misreads Boff,[31] and eventually misses the point by entirely rejecting the mediating role of social sciences.

A second aspect we need to clarify is Milbank's case for a stronger emphasis on the role of the church as the social embodiment of a just society. In fact, he thinks that the main mediation for social transformation is actually an ecclesial mediation. However, Milbank contends that liberation theology "presents a very minimal ecclesiology,"[32] an argument that we already encountered in the previous section. The underlying discussion, though, is about the specific character of Christian praxis and the related

28. This is the basic argument of Clodovis Boff, OSM, *Theology and Praxis: Epistemological Foundations* (Maryknoll, N.Y.: Orbis, 1987).

29. Boff, *Theology and Praxis*, p. 82.

30. Boff, *Theology and Praxis*, p. 82.

31. I am not the only one who reaches such a conclusion. Thus, Baum, "For and Against John Milbank," says that Milbank "misreads the starting point of liberation theology, which is practice" (p. 67) and "wrongly accuses liberation theology of embracing a 'liberal' notion of freedom" (p. 68). In a similar way, Schrijver, "The Use of Mediations in Theology," contends that "Milbank theorize[s] in a way that is academically unacceptable" (p. 52) and "ultimately, Milbank makes a caricature of liberation theology" (p. 53).

32. Milbank, *Theology and Social Theory*, p. 246.

issue of ecclesial distinctiveness from modern society. Boff clearly states his position: "There is no such thing as a *Christian* practice as such. . . . What really exists is practice *inspired* by faith and *interpreted* as being 'Christian,' or 'supernatural,' or 'salvific.'"[33] Milbank defends an opposite view, and precisely grounds his understanding of theology as social theory on this claim, when he says that "there can only be a distinguishable Christian social theory because there is also a distinguishable Christian mode of action, a definite practice."[34] Does a specific Christian practice exist? Is Christian sociology possible?

Toward a "Supernatural Sociology"?

The previous section launched a theological critique of Milbank's proposal. Its results demonstrate the need for an integrated understanding of theology and social sciences that gives priority to the perspective of faith (*analogia fidei,* the supernatural, or Christian vision of reality) while assuming within itself, in a derivative way, the other pole (*analogia entis,* a graced nature, or the mediation of social sciences). This section explores the implications of such findings for the development of a Christian social theory, or "supernatural sociology,"[35] and outlines some of its possible features. The first part is more theoretically oriented, while the second part focuses on practical examples.

The Project of a Supernatural Sociology

John Milbank is not alone in proposing a Christian social theory. This is true, although this term does not refer to an area of sociology of religion that studies the Christian church, nor to the Catholic magisterial social

33. Boff, *Theology and Praxis,* pp. 102-3.

34. Milbank, *Theology and Social Theory,* p. 380.

35. I am well aware that *supernatural sociology* is an odd term for contemporary ears, but this section shows the reason we need to explore its possible fruitfulness. See Gregory Baum, "Do We Need a Catholic Sociology?" in *Essays in Critical Theology,* pp. 139-70. He asks whether it makes sense to "reintroduce the notion of a Catholic sociology" from the perspective of the option for the poor, and concludes: "I do not think it would be a useful strategy" (p. 164). I want to explore this same issue.

teaching. Rather, *Christian* or *supernatural sociology* alludes to a full-blown social theory that is grounded on the Christian worldview, practices, and theology. On the one hand, it is not limited to what is usually called "sociology," since it includes political theory, social psychology, economics, anthropology, and social work as well. On the other hand, it can provide a complete meta-narrative that springs from the gospel and Christian practice and shed light on the whole of reality. Such a contention is at odds with the general discourse in contemporary societies. For this reason we now explore a significant precedent along the same lines.

In 1936 Paul Hanly Furfey, a priest associated with the Catholic Worker movement and professor of sociology at the Catholic University of America, published the book *Fire on the Earth*, which includes a first chapter titled "Supernatural Sociology."[36] He acknowledges two sources for a strictly Catholic social thought: revelation and the lives of the saints. In doing so, Furfey emphasizes the importance of lived practices as the basis for social theory. In particular, he underscores the need of Christian practices for a supernatural sociology. Not only does he affirm that every important problem must take into account supernatural reality, but he also recognizes the contrast between two logics. On the one hand, "worldly prudence tells us that our reliance should be upon the best modern, tested, scientific methods."[37] On the other hand, to understand the real social doctrine of the church we ought to accept the folly of the cross as lived by the saints. "A thoroughgoing social Christianity must be an opposition movement. It must expect the antagonism of the most respected classes."[38] Instead of looking for prudent and "reasonable" compromises with the dominant order, Furfey stresses the need for Christian contrast and alternative, as manifested in the cross of Jesus Christ.

For this reason, Furfey proposes a personalist understanding of politics (we must remember, though, that personalism is radically opposed to individualism). This vision does not place emphasis on social, technical, institutional, and legal reform, but on the "personal practice of social virtues,"[39] which leads to a deeper and nonviolent revolution. He develops three aspects of this practice in the final chapters of his book: the duty of

36. Paul Hanly Furfey, *Fire on the Earth* (New York: Macmillan, 1936), pp. 1-21.
37. Furfey, *Fire on the Earth*, p. 19.
38. Furfey, *Fire on the Earth*, p. 76.
39. Furfey, *Fire on the Earth*, p. 94.

bearing witness as a clear, persuasive presentation that leaves space for divine grace; the technique of nonparticipation as an "action de rupture" that combines non-cooperation with civil disobedience in certain cases; and, finally, the pragmatic test that does not consider efficiency as the most important criterion, but does embody its principles in specific social practices that respond to concrete needs.

Now, given this framework, we can go back to the central point of our discussion: the use of mediations in theology, in particular, the role of social sciences. Furfey explicitly accepts "the importance of such purely scientific investigations, even in supernatural sociology."[40] The task of developing a Christian social theory "involves the use of the most modern scientific methods. Sociology, economics, and the cognate sciences must be called into service."[41] This is something that Milbank tends to forget in his attempt to go beyond secular reason. Furfey insists: "Supernatural sociology, of course, does not despise these [scientific] methods, but it attaches more importance to the supernatural."[42] And this basic reminder is too often overlooked in contemporary social thought.

In summary, we see that Furfey's proposal anticipates Milbank's critique, but does so in a more balanced way. Furfey's supernatural sociology is in agreement with the general theological framework I developed in the previous section: while *analogia fidei* and the supernatural have an absolute priority for theological reflection, they do so in a way that integrates within themselves *analogia entis* and the natural realm. In other words, theology can function as a full-blown social theory, but it must include within itself, in a derivative way, the mediating role of social sciences. In the following paragraphs I provide three contemporary examples of what such a program would look like.

Three Examples

There are three authors who are close to the theological framework I have sketched (especially the overcoming of dualism through the integration of *analogia entis* within *analogia fidei,* an intrinsic understanding of super-

---

40. Furfey, *Fire on the Earth,* p. 9.
41. Furfey, *Fire on the Earth,* p. 106.
42. Furfey, *Fire on the Earth,* p. 138.

natural grace, and a derivative role of social sciences in Christian discourse). We will briefly look at each of these thinkers to clarify the analysis and proposals in the areas of politics, economy, and social action.[43]

William Cavanaugh has challenged, in a polemical but rigorous way, the view of the *modern state* as a savior that provides peace among religions.[44] According to the dominant opinion, religions are fanatical and dangerous realities that must be controlled and kept out of the public arena: this is the "great achievement" of the peaceful modern state. Cavanaugh, however, considers this vision of the state as a myth that actually "created religion" in the modern sense (as a separate realm) and led to the privatization of the church. It is interesting to note that Cavanaugh's historical analysis focuses on the sixteenth- and seventeenth-century "wars of religion," precisely the same period of the Baroque Scholastic development of the concept of "pure nature." The nature-supernature split runs parallel to the division state-church, as if the state were a neutral, uncontaminated sphere of reality. It is no wonder, then, that Cavanaugh's solution focuses on the church as the body of Christ, that "transgresses both the lines which separate public from private and the borders of nation-states, thus creating spaces for a different kind of political practice."[45] One can see here the influence of Henri de Lubac's integrated nature-grace anthropology, as well as his emphasis on the church.

The practical dimension of this new style of politics rediscovers the role of direct action and participatory democracy, in the tradition of anarchism[46] and nonviolent resistance, in opposition to the formalities of representative liberal democracy. More recently, Cavanaugh has treated this topic again, insisting on the same ecclesiological conclusions: "The urgent task of the Church, then, is to demystify the nation-state and to treat it like the telephone company. At its best, the nation-state may provide goods and

43. A fourth example could be an analysis of cultural action and practices, which I provide in the following chapter. See Tracey Rowland, *Culture and the Thomist Tradition: After Vatican II* (London: Routledge, 2003).

44. William T. Cavanaugh, *Theopolitical Imagination: Discovering the Liturgy as a Political Act in an Age of Global Consumerism* (London: T&T Clark, 2002), especially pp. 9-52.

45. Cavanaugh, *Theopolitical Imagination*, p. 90.

46. Cavanaugh himself proposed a move "toward eucharistic anarchism," but has later shied away from that suggestive position. See William T. Cavanaugh, "The City: Beyond Secular Parodies," in *Radical Orthodoxy: A New Theology*, ed. John Milbank, Catherine Pickstock, and Graham Ward (London: Routledge, 1999), pp. 182-200.

services that contribute to a certain limited order."[47] As we can see, Cavanaugh does not completely discard the role of the nation-state, but emphasizes that the church should not subordinate its public action to the state. We Christians are not to "kill or die" for the telephone company but we can make telephone calls; likewise, we should not regard the state as savior, but we could still use it as an instrument to foster some advances toward a more just society. Again, we find that *analogia fidei* must incorporate *analogia entis* within itself, that the nature-grace split is an error, that there is a place for technical social sciences within supernatural sociology.[48]

The second area that shows the practical implications of my proposed theological framework refers to *economy and the market*. Steve Long has shown how the "dominant tradition" in moral ethics gives economics its independence through the Weberian fact-value distinction.[49] Within this framework, the role of religion is limited to the area of values, and it may take either the form of legitimating capitalism by providing the adequate core of values (the classical Weberian thesis of Calvinism, or the contemporary Catholic one of Michael Novak), or the more critical stand of some Christian ethicists such as J. Philip Wogaman. The problem with these two positions is that they share a common view that incapacitates them so they cannot provide an alternative. We can again recognize the effects of a nature-grace dualism, which now provides a "neutral" space for capitalist economy and the market, while leaving for the church or religious traditions the role of merely "preaching" spiritual values. De Lubac's integrated vision provides a stronger critique (not only a critique, but an alternative) since it pushes to embody Christian virtue in practices that overcome the material-spiritual division, thus creating a new reality. Let me briefly present a good and significant example.

47. William T. Cavanaugh, "Killing for the Telephone Company: Why the Nation-State Is Not the Keeper of the Common Good," *Modern Theology* 20 (2004): 243-74; here, p. 266.

48. It is only in this sense that I agree with the following critique directed against Milbank: "while political liberalism is not sufficient for supplying our theological commitments and religious needs — and in that sense we must go beyond it — it can be seen to be necessary for certain forms of religious and theological creativity, such as, for instance, Radical Orthodoxy. It is one of the oldest textbook errors to mistake non-sufficiency for non-necessity." Christopher J. Insolde, "Against Radical Orthodoxy: The Dangers of Overcoming Political Liberalism," *Modern Theology* 20 (2004): 213-41; here, p. 238.

49. D. Stephen Long, *Divine Economy: Theology and the Market* (London: Routledge, 2000), pp. 9-80.

The so-called communion economy was successfully launched by the Focolare ecclesial movement in 1991, and now comprises some eight hundred businesses that link efficiency and solidarity in a new style of economic action. The project emanates from a spirituality of communion lived in everyday life, and relies on the strength of the culture of giving to change economic behavior.[50] Two aspects need to be mentioned here. First is the primacy of practice, as Milbank puts it: "there can only be a distinguishable Christian social theory because there is also a distinguishable Christian mode of action, a definite practice."[51] Communion economy is, first of all, a practical initiative of small enterprises in which new economic realities, new social relationships, and new spiritual insights take place. Second, this reality becomes a new "object" for scientific study. In fact, since 1995, more than 120 theses and dissertations on communion economy have already been defended in various universities all over the world. Social sciences and techniques play a role within supernatural sociology, in a derivative way. They are like tools that may be used, but they cannot create or dominate reality, as if they could say what is possible and what is not. The reality of a communion economy based on giving not only changes reality as such, but also the scientific method used to analyze it. As Milbank has effectively argued, social sciences and methodological strategies are not neutral. If we can still use those sciences, we cannot do so in a naïve way. Supernatural sociology will tend to privilege some methods over others (for example, qualitative methods will usually be more fruitful than quantitative ones). Likewise, it will privilege some approaches that the dominant discourse tends to discard (for example, participatory action-research). Finally, it may eventually need to develop new tools that adequately respond to the new practices and realities.[52]

50. See Luigino Bruni (coord.), *Economía de comunión, Por una cultura económica centrada en la persona* (Madrid: Ciudad Nueva, 2001), as well as their web site at www.edc-online.org.

51. Milbank, *Theology and Social Theory*, p. 380.

52. Other examples are the experience of the participatory budget started in Porto Alegre, Brazil, and now effectively working in various other cities in America and Europe; the theoretical constructions of Michel Albert (*parecon*, or participatory economy) and Luis Razeto (popular economy of solidarity); and the different proposals for a universal basic income. Although they are very different in their theoretical background and practicalities, it is possible to see a convergence in what Milbank has called "socialism of the gift in a complex space." See John Milbank, "Politics: Socialism by Grace," in *Being Reconciled: Ontology and Pardon* (London: Routledge, 1999), pp. 162-86.

A third example can be found in the area of *social services,* and most specifically in the practice and understanding of hospitality. Harry Murray has contrasted the rehabilitation model to the hospitality perspective in dealing with the homeless.[53] While the former locates the problems in the individual, the latter adopts a more structural vision that locates the problem in society and finally intends to "rehabilitate society" away from its own illnesses of exclusion, inequality, dehumanization, and insolidarity. This perspective can still be found in the example of the Catholic Worker movement, although Murray rightly notices that the rehabilitation model dominates the contemporary landscape, as a consequence of Weber's rationalization. This evolution has led in modern times to a shift from personalist hospitality to a professional services approach, which seems to be more efficient, but may eventually contribute to the dehumanization of urban life. The Christian viewpoint should carefully distinguish fruitfulness from efficacy, not allowing the economic rationale to dominate its practices. If we look carefully, we find that the underlying principle of the bureaucratic professional model is a dualistic distinction between life and work that mirrors the nature-grace split. Just as some positions defend the supernatural order by positing a realm of pure nature that is independent of grace, modern social service providers isolate a pure professional and technical space dominated by the rehabilitation logic, leaving aside the social interaction of personalist hospitality. The clarification that my theological framework provides should warn Christians against an aseptic approach to social intervention, while encouraging practices that embody a much more integrated anthropology. That is to say, within the Christian worldview any attempt to sharply distinguish between daily life, rehabilitation processes, faith, and technical resources should give rise to a unified vision based on communities of solidarity. Within that context, but not outside of it, professional rehabilitation techniques have their own space. Just as *analogia entis* finds its place within *analogia fidei,* social sciences may be incorporated into a supernatural sociology.

53. Harry Murray, *Do Not Neglect Hospitality: The Catholic Worker and the Homeless* (Philadelphia: Temple University Press, 1990).

Conclusion: Can a Gift Be Wrapped?

We are now in a position to go back to our initial question: Can a gift be wrapped? Taking into account our previous considerations, first of all, a gift is given; that is, a theological priority must be present in our understanding of reality. In this I agree with Milbank's position, including his claim that secular sciences are never neutral but imply a certain worldview that we must always consider. Although this point may seem clear, there is a tendency to forget it or take it for granted. In this sense, Milbank's reminder is a necessary one and provides the possibility for the development of a "supernatural sociology."

However, the question remains open (and it is the second element of my conclusion). Can a gift be wrapped? Can we use the mediation of social sciences in our theological reflection? Can the gift of God's active revelation be wrapped in paper, in non-theological language? I think it can be. The gift is always the gift, while the paper is just secondary. But the fact that there is a wrapping paper does not affect the reality of the gift. From this perspective, Milbank's contention that theology is a full-blown social theory that must lead to the suppression of any other social science is a misleading overstatement. Within the general framework of a supernatural sociology, there is plenty of room for secular social analysis and techniques, as long as they do not intend to supplant the Christian worldview, as long as the wrapping paper does not take over the gift itself.

Furthermore, my third point affirms that gifts are better when wrapped in paper. I deny the possibility of a purely naked gift, just as I think that any supernatural sociology ought to include within itself a moment of secular discourse that, on the one hand, will improve its analytic capacity and, on the other hand, will help to develop a necessary self-critique. We can never forget that theology itself is a human construction that needs to be criticized. Non-theological disciplines are very useful in that regard, just as extra-ecclesial criticisms may also be a means of purification toward internal coherence in the church's practices.

As long as this Christian way of life remains faithful to the gospel, rooted in Jesus Christ, it will become an alternative to the dominant system. In fact, it will provide a radical and authentic transformation of culture, from its very roots. This is the topic of the following chapter.

3. Athens and Jerusalem, or Bethlehem and Rome? John H. Yoder and Nonviolent Transformation of Culture

The two previous chapters have argued for a position that stresses Christian identity, language, practices, and worldview as distinct from the general culture in contemporary societies. Although I have already tried to balance this emphasis with a genuine concern for the wider reality, we need to address the issue of how this approach can effectively promote social transformation. By emphasizing the identity of the Christian community and its difference from secular society, it would seem that I am favoring a disengagement from socio-political matters. On the contrary, this particular focus provides a real alternative for the radical transformation of society toward a more just and peaceful reality in which the poor of the earth are no longer excluded. This is the purpose of this chapter.

The underlying rationale of this chapter is simple. First, I assume that matters of culture are crucial for understanding and transforming social reality. While not denying the role of politics or economics, any social transformation will be very limited unless it considers issues of worldviews, styles, ways of life, social imagination, and interactions — that is, culture. Economic structures and political processes are all rooted in the daily culture of societies. Unless we deal with culture, all our attempts will be too narrow or superficial. Second, I contend that Christian communities are constituted by a set of practices that embody an alternative social configuration. As long as Christian communities, faithful to their vision, nourish these practices and habits, they will provide a different social setting and imagination. This is true not only for individuals in small groups, but also has clear implications in the public realm of politics and economics, fostering a real cultural transformation.

The primary interlocutor in this chapter is John H. Yoder, a contemporary representative of the Anabaptist Radical Reformation. In a paper initially prepared in 1955 for a conference of the Mennonite Church, Yoder argued "that is possible for the Christian or the Christian church to address to the social order at large or the state criticisms and suggestions."[1] This is an obvious position for mainline Catholic and Protestant ethicists, but not for those of his Anabaptist tradition, which maintains "that Christian ethics is for Christians"[2] and not for the general society. It is clear that his approach tries to balance the distinctiveness of Christian community and its responsibility to the wider society. Yoder's approach will allow for a fruitful understanding of the way Christians engage in cultural transformation.

Yoder's Theological Views

John H. Yoder (1927-97) was probably the finest and most influential Anabaptist theologian of the twentieth century. This Mennonite professor taught at the University of Notre Dame for thirty years. This significant fact helps to explain his extensive influence beyond the boundaries of his own church, somewhat surprising if we consider not only the Mennonite Church's minority position, but also its traditional isolationist tendency. In fact, Yoder is a great example of how to remain faithful to one's own tradition while at the same time creatively expanding its views. His teaching position in a prominent Catholic university provided a more pluralistic setting and a more acute concern for the wider society. Yoder's main book, *The Politics of Jesus*,[3] makes the case for interpreting the gospel as social ethics. He defends his strong nonviolent position, claiming its validity for the whole church, as well as its political relevance.

I will now analyze Yoder's main theological positions because this is a necessary step for clarifying his ethical, social, and political views. Although Yoder deals mainly with issues of social ethics, he cannot be correctly understood if we forget the underlying theological system.

1. John H. Yoder, *The Christian Witness to the State* (Newton, Kans.: Faith and Life 1964), p. 5.
2. Yoder, *The Christian Witness to the State*, p. 28.
3. John H. Yoder, *The Politics of Jesus. Behold the Man. Our Victorious Lamb* (Grand Rapids: Eerdmans, 1994 [orig. ed., 1972]).

Foundational Theology

What is the relationship between Athens and Jerusalem, between reason and faith? This question has been present in philosophical and theological reflection from Tertullian to Jürgen Habermas. In the contemporary theological discussion, the mainline position has always tried to achieve an agreement or at least a common understanding between the Christian proposal (Jerusalem) and the nonreligious discourse (Athens). Yoder adopts a different perspective: the key relation to be analyzed is not Athens and Jerusalem, but Bethlehem and Rome. He is convinced that what happened in Bethlehem, Galilee, and on the cross has a clear relevance for Rome — that is, for every empire. That does not mean that Christians should forget the task of announcing the Word to everyone, making themselves and their ethical proposal heard. On the contrary, he thinks that "we [Christians] report an event that occurred in our listeners' own world and ask them to respond to it. What could be more universal than that?"[4] It is the particularity of Bethlehem that universally challenges the supposed universality of the empire.

This specific position regarding the role of reason and revelation has a parallel in the use of the Bible in ethical studies. Richard Hays has studied the hermeneutical strategies of several contemporary theologians as they use the New Testament for their respective Christian ethics programs. Two of them are Reinhold Niebuhr and Yoder, representatives of realist and radical positions, respectively. Hays finds that in Niebuhr's writings "Scripture stands in the background as the ultimate source of the ideals that inform moral judgment, but its relation to specific political choices is distant and indirect." In that sense, Niebuhr is a significant representative of the mainline way of reasoning that Yoder challenges by insisting that the New Testament's portrayal of Jesus remains fundamentally normative for Christian ethics. Hays's summary of his own fundamental guidelines includes this: "Extrabiblical sources stand in hermeneutical relation to the New Testament; they are not independent, counterbalancing sources of authority."[5] As we will see, this principle will

---

4. John H. Yoder, "'But We Do See Jesus': The Particularity of Incarnation and the Universality of Truth," in *The Priestly Kingdom: Social Ethics as Gospel* (Notre Dame: University of Notre Dame Press, 1984), p. 59.

5. Richard B. Hays, *The Moral Vision of the New Testament: Community, Cross, New Cre-*

play a significant role in clarifying the relationship between Christ and culture.

Christ and Trinity

In line with this fundamental theology, Yoder affirms that the norm for Christian ethics is the affirmation that Jesus is the Lord. H. Richard Niebuhr points out that, by saying so, Yoder forgets the Trinity and its ethical consequences — he does not acknowledge the ethical implications derived from the Father and creation (natural law), or from the Spirit who indwells in every human person (moral autonomy). Against this, Yoder argues that Niebuhr's theology is almost tri-theist and modalist. Yoder insists that it is not correct to affirm three sources of Christian morality. "The reference to the Trinity seems therefore rather to be a slogan, symbolizing the author's urban, pluralistic concern for a balance between Christ and other moral authorities."[6] In fact, there is only one norm and authority: Jesus is the Lord — which actually includes a Trinitarian affirmation.

In his very interesting study of Christ and culture, Glenn Stassen explains H. Richard Niebuhr's position using the testimony of his life's evolution. In 1934 Niebuhr received an insight on the sovereignty of God, displayed in three main themes: the universal rule of God, the independence of the living God from subjective values, and the manifestation of God within our history. Stassen interprets them in a Trinitarian way[7] and, in so doing, nuances Yoder's criticisms. Stassen then suggests a particular embodiment of authentic transformation (pp. 225-46) by linking the transformative faith in the Trinitarian God with the church's responsibility as apostle, pioneer, and pastor (which Niebuhr explained in his 1943 article "The Responsibility of the Church for Society"). Stassen proposes certain concrete Christological norms for transformation (pp. 156-70) and con-

---

ation: A Contemporary Introduction to New Testament Ethics (New York: Harper Collins, 1996), pp. 224 and 310.

6. John H. Yoder, "How H. Richard Niebuhr Reasoned: A Critique of 'Christ and Culture,'" in Glen H. Stassen, D. M. Yeager, and John H. Yoder, Authentic Transformation: A New Vision of 'Christ and Culture'. With a Previously Unpublished Essay by H. Richard Niebuhr (Nashville: Abingdon, 1996), p. 63.

7. Glen H. Stassen, "Concrete Christological Norms for Transformation," in Stassen, Yeager, and Yoder, Authentic Transformation, pp. 130-33, and p. 267 n. 13.

nects them with Yoder's. Finally, he repeats a similar approach when he talks about Jesus Christ as normative for Christian discipleship (pp. 206-11). However, it is not clear whether those norms are Niebuhr's or Stassen's, so the question of normativity in Niebuhr remains open. In any case, Christological normativity is beyond doubt for Yoder.

The Church: Radical Catholicity

Yoder is a Mennonite, heir of the Anabaptist radical tradition often considered by mainline theologians as sectarian. Faithful to this tradition, he points out the vital role of Christian communities in social ethics. This helps to shed light on another of Yoder's emphases: he tries to show that he is actually representing a very catholic position — probably because readers will consider him a priori as a sectarian. For this reason, Yoder has devoted time and energy to explaining his vision of the church, one that comes from the Radical Reformation, as a true radical Catholicity.[8] He especially addresses this issue in his books *The Royal Priesthood: Essays Ecclesiological and Ecumenical* (1994) and *For the Nations: Essays Evangelical and Public* (1997). He understands "the radical reformation model as a paradigm of value for all ages and communions, rather than as an apology for a denomination claiming the last — or the best — word."[9] It is important to realize that this is Yoder's own understanding and the goal of his project because it will clarify the relevance of Yoder's proposal for the whole church.

Yoder's Ethical Views

Love and Justice

Mainline theology assumes that Jesus proposed a very high ethical ideal, so high that it is not meant to serve as a principle of social, economic, or po-

8. See Michael W. Cartwright, "Radical Reform, Radical Catholicity: John Howard Yoder's Vision of the Faithful Church," introduction to John H. Yoder, *The Royal Priesthood: Essays Ecclesiological and Ecumenical* (Grand Rapids: Eerdmans, 1994), pp. 1-49.

9. John H. Yoder, *The Priestly Kingdom: Social Ethics as Gospel* (Notre Dame: University of Notre Dame Press, 1984), pp. 4-5.

litical organization. It tends to consider the ethic of Jesus as a personal ethic, since in the gospel "there is no social ethic in the ordinary sense of the word."[10] Of course, Yoder firmly rejects such a sharp division. It could be said that his whole theological project, and clearly his argument in *The Politics of Jesus*, is directed at demonstrating the social ethic of Jesus and its political relevance. From the first page to the last, Yoder claims that "Jesus is, according to the biblical witness, a model of radical political action" and that "the difference it makes for political behavior is more than merely poetic or motivational."[11] He even denies the notion of "the social implications of the Gospel," as if these were merely second-hand derivations. He firmly argues that the new reality brought about by Jesus needs to be socially embodied in Christian community, as a sociological entity in its own right with specific social practices.[12]

The Role of the State and Political Authority

Following the tradition of the radical reformers and free churches, Yoder maintains a strong reserve toward the state. He does not exactly defend an anarchist or anti-state political view, but he does deny the practical alliance of church and state that has dominated Western history. He frequently critiques the Constantinian shift that occurred in the fourth century, because it changed the church's self-understanding: instead of being the social embodiment of a new kind of human relations, the church has considered itself as the soul of the existing society. Its role has been that of the chaplain. But for Yoder it is clear: "God's pattern of Incarnation is that of Abraham and not of Constantine."[13]

---

10. Reinhold Niebuhr, "The Ethic of Jesus and the Social Problem," in *Love and Justice: Selections from the Shorter Writings of Reinhold Niebuhr*, ed. D. B. Robertson (Louisville: Westminster/John Knox, 1992), p. 30.

11. Yoder, *The Politics of Jesus*, pp. 1 and 247.

12. John H. Yoder, "Why Ecclesiology Is Social Ethics: Gospel Ethics Versus the Wider Wisdom," and "Sacrament as Social Process: Christ the Transformer of Culture," in *The Royal Priesthood*, pp. 102-26 and pp. 359-73. See also his "The Kingdom as Social Ethics," in *The Priestly Kingdom*, pp. 80-101.

13. John H. Yoder, "Let the Church Be the Church," in *The Royal Priesthood*, p. 172. See also his "The Constantinian Sources of Western Social Ethics," in *The Priestly Kingdom*, pp. 135-47.

Abraham, like Moses, Jesus, and many others, is a prophet heard only by a minority. Christians in the contemporary world — after all these centuries of Constantinism — are beginning to understand themselves as a voluntary minority. This, in fact, is not a statistical observation, but a theological one, and should lead to clear ethical consequences in understanding the church as the "new rest of Israel" and a "contrast-society" (Gerhard Lohfink). According to Yoder, Christian social ethics has being trying to tell the rulers what they should do, trying to organize this society, to influence politics. But that should not be its role. Christian communities should incarnate an alternative way of living; that does not mean that they retreat from society, but that they embody a radically different approach to political activism.

The Question of Means and Ends

In a statement that clearly represents mainline Christian ethics, Reinhold Niebuhr affirms: "we regard all problems of social morality in pragmatic rather than absolute terms."[14] That implies that any socio-political issue (of an economic, political, or educational nature; related to peace, social justice, or international relations) has to be decided not by general principles, but by a careful rational analysis of pros and cons, especially regarding the consequences of any decision. Niebuhr is very much aware of the unwanted effects of naïve policies, what he calls the "irony of history," which takes a different direction than the one that was supposedly guiding it.

As a matter of fact, Yoder admits the question of means and ends, but sees it in a new way. He is willing to talk about political efficacy, but from a different perspective. For him, "the cross of Christ is the model of Christian social efficacy, the power of God to those who believe."[15] Yoder believes that the equation "to renounce violence is to renounce power" is a mistaken one. The question, then, seems to be: What kind of realism are we talking about? Is it a historical-political realism (Niebuhr), or is it a biblical realism (Yoder)? Who is defining reality? What are the real alternatives? Only within this frame of radical Christian realism will Yoder admit

---

14. Reinhold Niebuhr, "Why I Leave the F.O.R.," in *Love and Justice,* p. 257.
15. Yoder, *The Politics of Jesus,* p. 242.

the use of middle axioms as a mediation to formulated Christian norms in pagan terms.[16]

The Debate about Nonviolence

Pacifism is usually one of the main topics in any discussion involving Yoder. The question of pacifism is just an example — clear and important, but just an example — of the general discussion of social ethics between the mainline and the radical schools of Christian thinkers. Moreover, I think it is important to study the issue in a wider perspective: that of active nonviolence, which necessarily includes social justice. It has to be kept in mind that active nonviolence includes much more than mere passivity or nonresistance; it includes an active engagement for justice in social struggles. This is the view of Yoder, although he sometimes uses the more traditional and ambiguous term *nonresistance*.

To clarify this issue it will be helpful to refer again to the significant position of Reinhold Niebuhr, who was for a time a member of the Quaker-based pacifist group Fellowship of Reconciliation. His classic book *Moral Man and Immoral Society* (1932) remains the most influential critique of nonviolence ever written in the United States. In an article first published in 1939,[17] Niebuhr criticizes modern Christian pacifism as heretical. These followers tend to believe that man is essentially good, forgetting the reality of sin and making God's grace irrelevant. Niebuhr reminds us that any total ethic must include a permanent tension between different poles of reality: Christian ethics does not only refer to the law of love, but also recognizes the fact of sinfulness and the deep need for God's mercy to overcome human tragedy. To forget this is to fall into a senseless and confusing naïve moralism. This is what the modern pacifist heresy is doing.

Yoder directly responded with theological arguments regarding the notion of redemption.[18] The work of the Holy Spirit, or God's active grace, creates a new people who are called to embody a new reality. Niebuhr's ar-

16. Yoder, *The Christian Witness to the State,* pp. 71-73.

17. Reinhold Niebuhr, "Why the Christian Church Is Not Pacifist," in *The Essential Reinhold Niebuhr: Selected Essays and Addresses,* ed. Robert McAfee Brown (New York and London: Yale University Press, 1986), pp. 102-19.

18. John H. Yoder, "Reinhold Niebuhr and Christian Pacifism," *Mennonite Quarterly Review* 29 (1955): 101-17.

guments may be correct generally speaking, but not when they are referred to the church. The body of Christ is a new social reality in which the distinction between moral man and immoral society is simply false. Here is a theological reason why pacifism — or better, Christian nonviolence — is not only not heretical, but radically and deeply orthodox.

Eschatology

One of Yoder's most important essays on peace bears the significant title "Peace without Eschatology?"[19] In fact, as Helmut Thielicke wrote in the conclusion of the pages he devoted to his study of the place of evangelical ethics between the two aeons, "theological ethics is eschatological or it is nothing."[20] Only by taking a closer look at the eschatological principles of Yoder will we be able to understand fully his ethical views.

Yoder on Eschatology

The discussion on where and when to locate the eschaton has been at the center of the theological reflection in the twentieth century, a discussion with clear ethical influences. Albert Schweitzer offers the vision of an apocalyptic Jesus, who merely announces a future kingdom and offers a radical ethics until his second coming (interim ethics). Against him, C. H. Dodd presents a present-time realized eschatology that Jesus announces with his words and actualizes with his deeds. Oscar Cullmann maintains a third position, understanding hope as salvation in history, with a tension between the kingdom already present and the kingdom not yet fully accomplished.

Yoder's position is influenced by Cullmann and his emphasis on the "already–not yet" of the kingdom; that tension, as embodied in Christian communities, is a key aspect of Yoder's social ethics.[21] It allows him to focus on Jesus as the Savior King (Victorious Lamb over all the powers on the cross) to be imitated in obedience to God. The church is the community

---

19. Yoder, "Peace without Eschatology?" in *The Royal Priesthood,* pp. 143-67.

20. Helmut Thielicke, *Theological Ethics,* vol. 1: *Foundations* (Grand Rapids: Eerdmans, 1979), p. 47.

21. Philip LeMasters, *The Import of Eschatology in John Howard Yoder's Critique of Constantinianism* (San Francisco: Mellen Research University Press, 1992), pp. 31-90.

that anticipates the new age inaugurated by Christ, and for this reason it is necessary that it stand in stark contrast to the world. His ethical proposal is primarily centered on radical obedience, and against a consequentialist approach to moral reasoning.

Social Ethics, Eschatology, and Culture

Lynn Mitchell has written an analysis about the implications of eschatology for social ethics that I find helpful in drawing some conclusions.[22] He does not particularly study the authors I have been considering, but he does compare the Augustinian-Lutheran and Anabaptist traditions, with which Niebuhr and Yoder are respectively related. Mitchell argues that an eschatological duality is indispensable for developing an adequate public ethic. That duality implies a two age–two community understanding of reality: fallen creation and redeemed creation, history and eschaton, church and civil society.

Three emphases need to be noticed. First, the temporal and sequential aspect of the two ages offers a dynamic vision that allows a transformational approach to social ethics. Second, the duality of the two communities is rightly understood in the sense that the church is not against the world, but rather for the world. The risk of isolationism is thus avoided. Third, the eschatological community is clearly against the status quo and has to show this in a concrete alternative *modus vivendi*, that is, through a shared way of living, a culture.

Cultural Transformation

Christian eschatology grounds Yoder's approach to social ethics, with its focus on providing an alternative to the system. One can see the contrast with mainline positions that seek political influence as a way to modify the system. Following the reflection on the eschatological reserve, the question we address now is how that radical proposal of an eschatological ethics is effective in social transformation. To do that, the focus of my analysis is on the Christian understanding of the role of culture for social ethics.

22. Lynn E. Mitchell Jr., *The Vision of the New Community: Public Ethics in the Light of Christian Eschatology* (New York: Peter Lang, 1988).

H. Richard Niebuhr's Typology

In his very influential book *Christ and Culture*, H. Richard Niebuhr offered an analysis of the "enduring problem" of the double relation of the church with the Lord and with the cultural society it lives in.[23] He suggested a very clear typology of the possible approaches to that relationship, characterizing each of them, offering some examples (from the Bible era, and from the history of Christianity), critiquing every position, and offering a balance. His great success has gone beyond this particular field, and his influence can still be seen in various theological typologies. The chart below summarizes the basic contents of the whole book, more as a clarifying reminder than as a detailed summary, providing a more general map of Niebuhr's argument.

Christ against Culture	Christ above Culture	Christ Transforming Culture	Christ and Culture in Paradox	Christ of Culture
New law	Architectonic	Conversionist	Oscillatory	Natural law
Radical tension	Synthesis	Synthesis of synthesis	Paradox	Accommodation
1 John	Some motifs in Matthew's Gospel	Fourth Gospel	Pauline writings	James, Gnostic writings
Tertullian, Benedictine monasticism, Quakers	Thomas Aquinas	Augustine, John Calvin, Jonathan Edwards, F. D. Maurice, Karl Barth	Martin Luther, Nikolai Berdyaev, Ernst Troeltsch, Reinhold Niebuhr, Emil Brunner	Clement of Alexandria, Abelard, liberal Christians (Albrecht Ritschl)

Niebuhr and Yoder on Cultural Transformation

Besides the classification itself, there is a second element in the book that sometimes gets overlooked. Niebuhr not only presented five possible ways

---

23. H. Richard Niebuhr, *Christ and Culture* (New York: Harper and Brothers, 1951). Pages from this book will be referenced in the text parenthetically.

of understanding the relation of Christ and culture, but he also opted for one of them, the conversionist or "Christ transforming culture" model. In an already mentioned and very clarifying study, Yoder has shown several shortcomings in Niebuhr's book.[24] There are two main points in Yoder's argument.

The first point is strictly theological. Niebuhr presupposes that virtue lies in the middle of a bipolar dualism in which Jesus is one of the extremes. He recognizes that the radical position (Christ against culture) is the closest of the five to Jesus himself and he assumes that it is a necessary but inadequate position. If the discussion is between Jesus and culture, and if Jesus is placed in one of the extremes, then it will be no wonder that Niebuhr leans toward the middle. But, by doing so, the final criterion for solving the Christ-culture dilemma is the individual Christian (which is a very modern notion, but not quite evangelical) rather than the gospel.

The point that Yoder rightly notices is precisely the fact that Jesus is the real criterion. The discussion should not be between Jesus and culture, but between eschaton and incarnation, with Jesus Christ as the only valid criterion who lies in the middle. With this framework of analysis, it would be clear that the radical position is not only necessary, but the only adequate one from the Christian point of view. In fact, it is the position that offers a real possibility for an authentic transformation of culture — that is, Niebuhr's own view.

The second difficulty in Niebuhr's argument is methodological and betrays a certain lack of internal coherence. Following Bronislaw Malinowski, Niebuhr first defines culture as everything people do: "language, habits, ideas, beliefs, customs, social organization, inherited artifacts, technical processes, and values" (p. 32). But later on, when he is discussing the radical positions of Tolstoy and the Mennonites/Quakers, he says they are anti-cultural because they follow their own "economics and education" (p. 56). So it seems that for Niebuhr culture now means the dominant position of a given society. He denies the possibility of an alternative culture, precisely what radical Christians claim to be — a path to the authentic transformation of culture.

---

24. John H. Yoder, "How H. Richard Niebuhr Reasoned: A Critique of 'Christ and Culture,'" in Stassen, Yeager, and Yoder, *Authentic Transformation*, pp. 31-89.

The Authentic Transformation of Culture

In a second article, "But We Do See Jesus," Yoder affirms that "only this evangelical Christology can found a truly transformationist approach to culture."[25] To do so, Christians often try to find "tactical alliances" with the Enlightenment or with the Gandhian vision, with the socialists or the alter-globalization movement. But that tactical situation is never definitive. Culture is not monolithic, although Niebuhr seems to think it is: it can be accepted or rejected in part, after careful discernment. But in any case, the criterion is Jesus the Lord, not any kind of compromise between Christ and that culture.

A restatement of this position can be found in a somewhat related reflection in Aquinas's *Summa*. Aquinas is considering the norm of virtue, that is, whether acts of virtue should be extremist or observe the mean in their performance. Following Aristotle, Aquinas thinks that moral and intellectual virtues must observe the mean, which is a rational mean controlled by prudence. However, and this is the point I want to highlight, he clearly says that theological virtue does *not* observe the mean. The reason for this is that God is the object of theological virtue, and "there is no sinning by excess against God" (*STh.* I-II, q. 65, a. 4). In other words, we should not try to find a middle ground between Christ and culture, looking for the rational mean, but we should affirm the excess of our love, faith, and hope for Christ in our very culture.

As Charles Scriven rightly points out, "the question of Christ and culture does not concern *whether* the church should participate in cultural life, but *how* it should participate."[26] And he goes on to say that the church performs its transformative task in the world precisely by its radical solidarity with Christ. Niebuhr's own thought, if taken seriously in the transformation direction, is best developed through small, radical communities that reshape the world through their solidarity with and in Christ. Authentic transformation of culture will not come through a compromising synthesis, but through a radical countercultural contrast.[27]

25. Yoder, "But We Do See Jesus," p. 61.

26. Charles Scriven, *The Transformation of Culture: Christian Social Ethics after H. Richard Niebuhr* (Scottdale Pa.: Herald, 1988), p. 192.

27. I am obviously defending a countercultural position of contextual theology, as explained in the last chapter of Stephen B. Bevans, SVD, *Models of Contextual Theology,* revised

There is another question that needs further clarification, the question of dualism. Mainline theologians of the liberal tradition usually accuse radical Christians of being sectarians and dualists, of drawing too sharp a distinction between church and world, a position that does not work in contemporary pluralistic societies. On the other hand, theologians of the radical tradition say liberals are the real dualists, with their strong separation between public and private: since modern political theories only consider individuals, everything that relates to God and religion must be set aside, in the intimate and private realm. Since the real Christian alternative comes with community life, with this dualistic approach, it is impossible to achieve any cultural transformation. So it is necessary to offer radical alternatives that break liberal dualism — although they may be misunderstood as dualistic themselves.

The fact of the matter is that the remnants of the dualistic model are very much present in contemporary thought, in a particular Western-modern way — a dualism coined by René Descartes as *res extensa–res cogitans,* or by Kant as *phenomenon-noumenon.* In the field of socio-political and moral reflection, a similar dualism can be found in the influential distinction of Weber between fact and value. According to this view, religion or theology provides a core of values that may support or critique a particular state of affairs given as an objective reality. Conservative interpretations of religion will try to maintain the status quo (for example, the whole discourse about family values provides the moral basis for capitalism) while progressive interpretations of religion supply a prophetic critical voice. However, it seems that both visions have failed to overcome dualism. As long as we accept this dual distinction between fact and value, there will be no authentic transformation of culture.

An alternative approach to this value discourse occurs in a different category, that of virtue. According to Aquinas, virtue is a good operative habit, which implies relation to an act (*STh.* I-II, q. 55, aa. 1-3, and q. 49, a. 3). In this sense, virtue is intrinsically connected with action and cannot be understood as something extrinsic or superimposed to some neutral facts or actions (as it seems to happen under the fact-value distinction). From this perspective, Christian morality and political engagement are

and expanded ed. (Maryknoll, N.Y.: Orbis, 2002 [orig. ed., 1992]). See also Michael L. Budde and Robert W. Brimlow, eds., *The Church as Counterculture* (New York: State University of New York Press, 2000).

based on virtues, habits, and actions necessarily embodied in shared social practices. This virtue-focused theological reflection has been recently
recovered in moral thought.[28] It is much more coherent with the unified
anthropology and intrinsic understanding of grace in contemporary
Catholic theology, and it provides an adequate framework for an authentic and radical transformation of culture. By focusing on virtue, this approach liberates the forces of Christianity in a creative and transformational way.

Authentic Transformation and Revolutionary Nonviolence

What kind of cultural transformation are we referring to? In short, the
Christian worldview proposes a culture of justice and peace. However,
given the situation of violence and injustice we live in, we must ask how
deep this Christian transformation is. In fact, common wisdom tends to
identify revolution with violence, while identifying nonviolence with either a reformist position or with passivity that maintains the status quo.
Good reasons appear to support this interpretation, because of the extreme caution with which the church has traditionally engaged in social
reform movements, not to mention the spiritualizing tendencies among
some religious groups. The traditional term within the Anabaptist tradition has been *nonresistance,* which only adds more suspicion to the ears of
groups committed to a real struggle against structural injustice. Those justice fighters rightly ask, in the face of suffering and injustice, how can we
fail to resist evil?

However, this identification is a fallacy. Actually, the opposite is true.
History teaches that violent revolutions have been normally incapable of
changing the structures of reality. After a violent overturn, what usually
happens is simply that the oppressed become new oppressors, but the deep
structures remain unchanged. On the other hand, nonviolence is far from
accepting a system of domination and inequality, nor mere superficial
changes that maintain the same oppressive structures. For this reason, I
have consistently used the term *nonviolence* (as opposed to *nonresistance,*

28. See, for instance, James Keenan, *Virtue for Ordinary Christians* (Kansas City, Mo.:
Sheed and Ward, 1996) and Stanley Hauerwas, *A Community of Character: Toward a Constructive Christian Social Ethic* (Notre Dame: University of Notre Dame Press, 1981).

non-violence, or *non violence*)[29] to refer to this reality of active, creative, revolutionary nonviolence.

Revolutionary nonviolence implies, then, not only the abolition of war, armies, and violent "solutions" to human conflicts, not only a transformation of political, economic, and social structures, but also a deeper transformation of mentalities, relationships, worldviews, values, attitudes, behaviors, daily life, that is, an authentic transformation of culture. It has probably been among the Latin American current of nonviolent liberation theology, that — decades ago — the praxis and reflection on nonviolent revolution became more acute and persuasive.[30] More recently, some grassroots groups have explicitly formulated their proposal as nonviolent revolution toward decentralized self-managed socialism.[31] Longtime activist Jean-Marie Muller, one of the most important representatives of the well-developed French nonviolent current, has written that today "revolution is more necessary than ever"[32] and that we need to reinterpret our notion of human beings and society, because up until now, revolution has been identified with violence: the first revolution, then, ought to be a cultural one. We need to develop a culture of peace and nonviolence, realizing that such a culture is more difficult, needs more care, more attention, and more "cultivation" than the prevalent culture of violence and death.

From a strictly Christian perspective, a similar position was argued by Etienne Trocmé in his famous study *Jesus and the Nonviolent Revolution.*[33] Originally published in 1961, it was very influential on Yoder's view, for example. Along these same lines, Bible scholar Walter Wink has made the case for a Christian approach to socio-political conflicts, engaging the

29. The term *nonresistance* gives the impression of being a passive attitude. *Non violence* and *non-violence* seem to imply a mere absence of violence. By using the neologism *nonviolence* I want to highlight the active, creative, and revolutionary character of this position.

30. See Adolfo Pérez Esquivel, *Christ in a Poncho: Testimonials of the Nonviolent Struggles in Latin America,* ed. Charles Antoine (Maryknoll, N.Y.: Orbis, 1983), and Jean Goss and Hildegard Goss-Mayr, eds., *La no-violencia evangélica, fuerza de liberación. Encuentro de obispos de América Latina* (Barcelona: Fontanella, 1978).

31. Colectivo Tortuga, "La revolución noviolenta," in *Socialismo, Autogestión, Noviolencia* (Elx-Alacant: Tortuga, 2003), at www.nodo50.net/tortuga.

32. Jean-Marie Muller, *El coraje de la no violencia. Nuevo itinerario filosófico* (Santander: Sal Terrae, 2004), p. 15.

33. Etienne Trocmé, *Jesus and the Nonviolent Revolution,* edited with an introduction by Charles E. Moore (Maryknoll, N.Y: Orbis, 2004).

powers of oppression through Jesus' nonviolent third way, which provides a solution to the alternative violence-cowardice, fight-flight. Wink's original reading of a key passage of Matthew's Gospel provides three clear examples and a thesis statement absolutely central for a correct understanding of Christian nonviolence.[34] I am convinced that this is a fruitful way of showing the meaning of nonviolent revolution and authentic transformation of culture.

The three examples are located in the context of the Sermon of the Mount, when Jesus says: "if anyone strikes you on the right cheek, turn the other also; and if anyone wants to sue you and take your coat, give your cloak as well; and if anyone forces you to go one mile, go also the second mile" (Matt. 5:39-41). Sometimes, these ordinances have been read as counsels of perfection, directed only to a few people specially called. Other times, they are interpreted as only valid for individual morality in interpersonal relationships, but not for socio-political conflicts. Moreover, the general sense is that Jesus is here advocating a passive and servile attitude. Nothing is further from reality, as Wink shows. To strike the left cheek necessarily means a backhand, which then has the clear meaning of insulting, humiliating, and degrading. By turning the cheek, the "inferior" person is affirming his or her dignity against the aggressor, who now *must* treat him or her as an equal. The second example also shows a way in which the poor can practice assertive nonviolence in a court setting: by giving the undergarments after being stripped of the coat, the poor debtor leaves the court naked — a strategy that makes plain the essential cruelty of an unjust system. The third case, going the second mile, is related to the fact that Roman imperial soldiers could coerce people in such way, but only for a mile. Again, Jesus proposes here a creative strategy in which the oppressed person takes the initiative, surprises the soldier, and shows the political relevance and revolutionary consequences of imagination and humor.

Although this analysis has been extremely brief, I hope it will suffice to show how Jesus' approach offers the basis for an authentic transformation of human relationships at all levels. He offers a creative alternative that empowers the poor in their struggle against oppression. The thesis statement of that same pericope is usually translated as "do not resist evil" (Matt. 5:39) but we have already seen that an attitude of nonresistance to

---

34. Walter Wink, *Engaging the Powers: Discernment and Resistance in a World of Domination* (Minneapolis: Fortress, 1992), pp. 175-93.

evil would be a really odd conclusion, incoherent with Jesus' praxis and teachings. Taking into account that the Greek word *anthistēnai* (literally "stand against": *stēnai-anti*) is, in the Bible, a technical term for "warfare," the expression means in fact "do not resist violently, do not engage in armed insurrection." It seems much more appropriate to render it as "do not mirror evil" or "do not react violently against the one who is evil." Jesus is then proposing to break the spiral of violence: he did not propose a violent revolution, but he did lay the basis for a real nonviolent revolution. This is the way toward an authentic and radical transformation of culture: a movement from culture of death to a culture of life and peace.

Performing Nonviolence as Authentic Transformation

We have already seen that radical transformation of culture, from a Christian perspective, implies a holistic approach that embraces all levels of human reality. On the one hand, it not only refers to social, economic, political, institutional, and technological changes, but also to worldviews, relationships, structures, and spirituality. On the other hand, authentic transformation is not oriented toward attitudes, but focuses on actions and practices; it does not emphasize isolated actions, but stresses the importance of habits; revolutionary nonviolence avoids a merely value-driven perspective, but nourishes the strength of moral virtues. This final section briefly presents three examples that show how the practice of revolutionary nonviolence brings about authentic transformation. While all reality is not going to be changed by these proposals, Christ-centered social action can bring about deep transformation of culture.

Transforming Conflicts

Conflicts are part of human life, society, and history. They are here to stay and they are not necessarily a bad thing. They show that reality is complex, that different persons have different views, social settings, and particular needs. This human reality may provide opportunities for change and progress in our midst. We find conflicts in personal and family relations, in the social realm, in the economic arena, and in the international field. The issue is not whether conflicts exist, but how we deal with them. Traditionally, human societies have relied on a violent strategy for conflict management (authoritarian resolutions, crime punishment, violent revolutions, war). Is this the only possible approach? Is it effective at all?

Let us focus for a while on the level of conflicts that are internal to a given society, not considering the issue of international conflicts. The overwhelmingly dominant model is called "retributive justice," and consists basically of an attempt to control crime and to administer punishment to the perpetrator who violates the law. The focus is actually on the law, and for this reason, the victim is considered to be the state, not the individual who was hurt. This impersonal system maintains and reinforces the conflict between adversaries. The perpetrator is punished, jail being the most clear example. The victim is not restored at all: in fact she or he is doubly victimized — by the crime itself and by the judicial system. Overall, the conflict is not resolved or transformed, it is more acutely invigorated because the focus is on blame, guilt, and punishment, and not on restoration.

An alternative strategy is found in "restorative justice" and conflict transformation.[35] Instead of focusing on the law, this approach concentrates on the harm done to persons or to relationships in community. The aim of justice is, then, to identify the needs and obligations of the parties in conflict, and to promote effective healing. The basic components of a restorative system include meetings of the parties in conflict, communication among them, an agreement by the parties, an apology by the offender, restitution to the victim, a change in the offender's behavior, respect shown to all the parties, assistance provided to any party that needs it, and inclusion of the parties.[36] Even this brief summary is enough to show that this model of restorative justice creates a change in the social system: the final situation is different from the initial one, and it implies that the whole community or society is engaged in the process, not only the offender, some "experts," and possibly the victim. This integrative approach generates a dynamic of social transformation that goes much deeper than merely punishing crime.

It is not surprising that this alternative paradigm is found in societies

35. See Howard Zehr, *Changing Lenses: A New Focus for Crime and Justice* (Scottdale, Pa.: Herald, 1990).

36. Daniel W. van Ness, "The Shape of Things to Come: A Framework for Thinking about a Restorative Justice System" in *Restorative Justice: Theoretical Foundations,* ed. Elmar G. M. Weitekamp and Hans-Jürgen Kerner (Devon, U.K.: Willan, 2002), pp. 1-20.

with a strong communal sense centered on collaborative engagement (for instance, Native Americans or traditional Aboriginal tribes of the Pacific islands). Christian roots are explicitly found, among other places, in chapter 18 of Matthew's Gospel and in traditional practices of community conflict resolution.[37] In fact, it is widely recognized that the retrieval of these alternative experiences and the articulation of a modern restorative justice system is closely linked to the contribution of Christian communities, especially the historical peace churches.

Transforming a Culture of Death

In recent years, it has become relatively common to describe and critique contemporary Western societies as embodying a culture of death. Pope John Paul II, in his 1995 encyclical *Evangelium Vitae*, said that contemporary society "is characterized by the emergence of a culture which denies solidarity and in many cases takes the form of a veritable 'culture of death'" (no. 12). The reasons and cases for such a harsh label are well known: abortion, the death penalty, war, euthanasia, and hunger, among others. Deeper insights will also refer to the production and trade of weapons, to the unjust conditions of international trade, to the scandal of millions of persons without health insurance in the wealthiest countries of the earth, to the destruction of tropical forests and many other attacks on the environment, to violence against women and children, or to accidents that could be easily avoided with better job conditions. All these realities point to a situation in which human life is not considered to be the center of social organization. Other realities, such as profits and comfort, have taken the place of humanity at the core of our societies. The result is a pervasive culture of death.

The late Cardinal Bernardin launched in 1983 an integral proposal known as the "seamless garment," in order to promote a "consistent culture of life"[38] that would not leave aside any of the major issues related to this basic, broad, and interconnected topic. He not only argued the need for such a consistent ethic of life, but also sketched the attitude necessary

37. For a scriptural approach to this topic, see Christopher D. Marshall, *Beyond Retribution: A New Testament Vision for Justice, Crime, and Punishment* (Grand Rapids: Eerdmans, 2001).

38. Joseph Cardinal Bernardin, *A Consistent Ethic of Life: An American-Catholic Dialogue*, http://www.hnp.org/publications/hnpfocus/BConsistentEthic1983.pdf

to sustain it and the principles required to shape it. In other words, he proposed a general worldview and culture that seeks to embody "an heroic social ethic." He wrote:

> If one contends, as we do, that the right of every fetus to be born should be protected by civil law and supported by civil consensus, then our moral, political and economic responsibilities do not stop at the moment of birth. Those who defend the right to life of the weakest among us must be equally visible in support of the quality of life of the powerless among us: the old and the young, the hungry and the homeless, the undocumented immigrant and the unemployed worker. Such a quality of life posture translates into specific political and economic positions on tax policy, employment generation, welfare policy, nutrition and feeding programs, and health care.

The internal coherence of the ethical discourse clearly requires that we consider with equal force the "right to life" and "quality of life" issues. A legal approach to these issues will not solve them, however. While recognizing the importance of judicial matters (legal decisions on abortion, international debt relief, or going to war have real consequences on people's lives), there is another aspect that is often overlooked. This is the practice of a consistent ethic of life in our daily lives. The problem we are facing is not a legal system that does not protect life, but a culture of violence, death, profit, and self-interests that undermines the basis for life and peace. The contribution of Christian communities must include the creation of a shared environment in which opting for the poor, bearing children, welcoming immigrants and refugees, practicing gender equality in day-to-day situations, helping prisoners and persons with addictions, or taking care of the elderly are common practices promoted and nourished by the community as such. Only then will we be able to talk consistently about a culture of life and peace, embodied in people's minds, worldviews, actions, habits, relationships, institutions, and structures.[39] Only then will

---

39. Two recent and complementary contributions, one from the Roman Catholic Church, the other from the historic peace churches, can be found in Luke Gormally, ed., *Culture of Life — Culture of Death: Proceedings of the International Conference on 'The Great Jubilee' and the Culture of Life* (London: The Linacre Centre, 2002) and in Fernando Enns, Scott Holland, and Ann Riggs, eds., *Seeking Cultures of Peace: A Peace Church Conversation* (Telford, Pa., and Geneva: Cascadia-WCC, 2004).

we be able to talk about authentic transformation of culture toward radical nonviolence.

Transforming Consumerism

One of the most obvious features of Western societies is the widespread presence of consumerism, which can be regarded as capitalism embedded in daily life. Its pervasive effects are well known and its influence cannot be exaggerated. Consumerism has managed to structure societies around a particular way of producing, marketing, and consuming material goods that creates victims among the poor and disenfranchised, destroys the environment (thus handicapping future generations' development), and pushes middle classes of wealthy societies to a stressful and meaningless life. John Kavanaugh, bringing together Marx's concept of fetishism of commodities and the Hebrew prophets' critique of idolatry, has explained consumerism using the notion of "commodity form."[40] He considers consumerism as a way of perceiving and valuing reality that affects every level of existence and touches us in a systematic way. In a more complex analysis, Vincent Miller has argued that consumerism does not constitute a particular worldview, a culture as such, but "a set of interpretative habits and dispositions supported by a variety of practices and infrastructures for engaging elements of any culture."[41] For this reason, the solution cannot merely be a value-driven attempt to live more frugal and austere lives, but a deeper change of "power relations, structures, and practices."[42]

Is there an alternative that religions, particularly Christianity, can offer? Although it is clear that the church is also deeply influenced by the reality of consumerism,[43] and this fact limits its real possibilities of being an alternative, the church has more than enough resources to promote an authentic transformation of consumer culture. Kavanaugh opposes to the

40. John Kavanaugh, SJ, *Following Christ in a Consumer Society: The Spirituality of Cultural Resistance,* rev. ed. (Maryknoll, N.Y.: Orbis, 1991).

41. Vincent J. Miller, *Consuming Religion: Christian Faith and Practice in a Consumer Culture* (New York: Continuum, 2004), p. 194.

42. Miller, *Consuming Religion,* p. 31.

43. This point has been analyzed by Michael Budde, *The (Magic) Kingdom of God: Christianity and Global Culture Industries* (Boulder, Colo.: Westview, 1997). See also Miller, *Consuming Religion,* pp. 73-106.

commodity form the "personal form" of a countercultural community life that embodies revolutionary holiness through self-critique, moral consistency, prayer, sacramentality, social justice, and closeness to the dispossessed.[44] Miller offers similar suggestions, but emphasizes a tactical approach against commodification instead of a strategic one that focuses more generally on consumption. Tactics challenge the habit of interpretation, which is the key to the consumer culture. He argues that theology is not enough, because what is needed to overcome consumerism is not just a narrative, but real alternative practices. For example, Miller affirms that "sacramental operation has a subversive tactical value against commodity abstraction,"[45] but his practical suggestions are too abstract and, for this reason, partly disappointing.

It seems clear, in the final analysis, that against a conservative emphasis on values, which actually legitimates capitalism, the Christian alternative to consumerism should focus on virtues, practices, and shared habits of the Christian community in the world. The real tension between commodification and the Christian worldview involves a battle to control human desires.[46] A hundred years ago, Sigmund Freud showed the importance of desire in human behavior: we may forget or overlook the role of desire, but it is deeply rooted in us, as consumer culture clearly knows. A Christian alternative, then, ought to be rooted in Jesus Christ as the real polarization of human desires, embodied in communal practices (sacraments) which are socio-political in scope. Only then can an authentic transformation of culture take place.

Conclusion: Radical Transformation as a Christological Paradox

The objective of this chapter has been to analyze how Christian theology envisions social transformation. John H. Yoder's radical perspective provides the most coherent approach from the Christian perspective and, at the same time, the most efficient one from the social point of view. This position, best termed *radical transformation*, assumes the main insights

44. Kavanaugh, *Following Christ in a Consumer Society*, pp. 131-72.

45. Miller, *Consuming Religion*, p. 190.

46. Although his focus is not directly on consumer culture, this is a basic point in Daniel M. Bell Jr., *Liberation Theology After the End of History: The Refusal to Cease Suffering* (London: Routledge, 2001).

from the *radical* Christian tradition, but agrees with H. Richard Niebuhr on the importance of cultural *transformation.*

Radical transformation is a paradox. While the mainline discourse in social ethics usually considers the alternative between either a radical revolutionary vision or a moderate evolutionary one, radical transformation proposes revolutionary nonviolence (which actually is both radical and evolutionary!). Deeply considered, radical transformation derives from and expresses a Christological oxymoron. In Jesus Christ there is no room for the merely abstract, nor for the merely particular. He completely assumes everything concrete and everything universal. Instead of trying particular or abstract proposals (Jerusalem, Athens), only by being concrete (Bethlehem) Jesus offers a universal alternative to the empire (Rome). In Jesus Christ, God demonstrates a very specific approach to human cultures: he embodies a countercultural inculturation,[47] normative for Christians. This is the way of authentic Christian radical transformation, revolutionary nonviolence. This is the way to create and nourish a true culture of peace.

47. See Daniel Izuzquiza, SJ, "Una inculturación contracultural. Meditación ante el Misterio de la Navidad," *Sal Terrae* 92 (2004): 931-43.

4. Kenotic Revolution:
The Spiritual Politics of Dorothy Day

Politics from a Radicalist Perspective

During the past few decades, the dominant discussion in social ethics has been the debate between communitarians and liberals, and its corresponding liberal-conservative political argument. Both stances can be found within the Catholic community, and no less an authority than David Hollenbach maintains that the U.S. bishops offer a synthesis of liberal and communitarian perspectives, based on their endorsement of institutional pluralism and social differentiation.[1] However, Michael Baxter has rightly argued that both positions are in fact mere variations of a common "Americanist" tradition that supports a fundamental harmony between Catholicism and the U.S. socio-political system.[2] As an alternative to this dominant discourse, Baxter proposes the retrieval of a Catholic "radicalist" tradition that finds inspiration in the life and works of Dorothy Day. This proposal is not a mere theological interpretation, but it is also historically well grounded in the concrete reality of the Catholic Worker.[3]

1. David Hollenbach, SJ, "Liberalism, Communitarianism, and the Bishops' Pastoral Letter on Economy," in *The Annual of the Society of Christian Ethics 1987,* ed. D. M. Yeager (Washington, D.C.: Georgetown University Press, 1987), pp. 19-40.

2. Michael J. Baxter, "Notes on Catholic Americanism and Catholic Radicalism: Toward a Counter-Tradition of Catholic Social Ethics," in *American Catholic Traditions: Resources for Renewal,* the annual publication of the College Theology Society 1996, vol. 42, ed. Sandra Yocum Mize and William Portier (Maryknoll, N.Y.: Orbis, 1997), pp. 53-71.

3. See, for instance, Mel Piehl, *Breaking Bread: The Catholic Worker and the Origin of*

As a matter of fact, Dorothy Day and the Catholic Worker movement are one of the main sources of inspiration for a contemporary theological school that can be labeled as "Catholic radicalism." This current also has connections with postliberal theology, radical orthodoxy, and the Anabaptist tradition, and for this reason, this book could be considered a part of it. Michael Baxter, himself a Worker and national secretary of the Catholic Peace Fellowship, is one of the leading figures of the group, with his emphasis in denouncing "the bourgeois perspective of [mainline] Public Theology and unmasking Public Theology as a discourse which legitimates the nation-state."[4] Along the same lines, but with a more constructive thread, is the contribution of William Cavanaugh. Cavanaugh is engaged in the task of developing a Eucharistic counter-politics that, based on the body of Christ, provides an alternative to the nation-state from the perspective of the poor.[5] A third author to be mentioned in this group is Fritz Bauerschmidt, who has also worked on the political implications of the Catholic spiritual tradition.[6]

It is in this current of theological reflection that I inscribe my own proposal of a radical ecclesiology. Having studied three theologians in the previous chapters (Lindbeck, Milbank, and Yoder), I now turn my attention to Dorothy Day. Given that this woman was not a theologian, but a social activist and a journalist, I use a different approach in organizing this chapter, as compared to the previous ones.

Catholic Radicalism in America (Philadelphia: Temple University Press, 1982), pp. 145-80, and William D. Miller, A Harsh and Dreadful Love: Dorothy Day and the Catholic Worker Movement (London: Darton, Longman & Todd, 1973).

4. Michael Baxter, CSC, "'Blowing the Dynamite of the Church': Catholic Radicalism from a Catholic Radicalist Perspective," in Dorothy Day and the Catholic Worker Movement: Centenary Essays, ed. William Thorn, Philip Runkel, and Susan Mountin (Milwaukee: Marquette University Press, 2001), p. 93. See also his review article "The Non-Catholic Character of the Public Church," Modern Theology 11 (1995): 243-58.

5. Besides the works already cited in previous chapters, see his "Dorothy Day and the Mystical Body of Christ in the Second World War," in Thorn, Runkel, and Mountin, Dorothy Day and the Catholic Worker Movement, pp. 457-64.

6. Frederick C. Bauerschmidt, Julian of Norwich and the Mystical Body Politic of Christ (Notre Dame: University of Notre Dame Press, 1999), especially pp. 191-201. See also his "The Politics of the Little Way: Dorothy Day Reads Thérèse of Lisieux," in Yocum Mize, and Portier, American Catholic Traditions, pp. 77-95.

A Note on Method: Biography and Theology

The first difficulty we face in this endeavor of founding a radical theological politics is the fact that Dorothy Day was not a theologian or a social ethicist. As Robert Ellsberg has said, "it was not what Dorothy Day wrote that was extraordinary, nor even what she believed, but the fact that there was absolutely no distinction between what she believed, what she wrote, and the manner in which she lived."[7] Along the same lines, Markha Valenta has noticed that in her autobiography *The Long Loneliness,* Dorothy Day "does not present her readers with a carefully reasoned, systematized and correspondingly abstract 'theory' or ideology with which to order her account and life, much less the world."[8] It is true that Dorothy was not a theologian, but it is also obvious that she lived a God-saturated life — a "theological life" — on which we can do theological reflection. Her life, an embodied expression of following Christ, provides optimal material for a political theology.

The methodological approach of this chapter requires some adjustments. While Melchor Cano, in the sixteenth century, considered the lives of the saints as a *locus theologicus,* the modern split between spirituality and dogmatic theology left little opportunity for theologians to adequately cultivate that insight. The rediscovery of biography as a theological resource has come with the development of contemporary narrative theology. For example, James McClendon has argued that in the context of an ethics of character-in-community, "theology must be at least biography" and "biography at its best will be theology."[9] According to McClendon, the lives of significant persons "tell us what in doctrine must be stressed and what may for their part be laid aside."[10] His proposed method, then, is to look into the life of concrete Christians to find their central vision, expressed in a central image or cluster of images. Those images function as

---

7. Robert Ellsberg (ed. and introduction), *Dorothy Day: Selected Writings* (Maryknoll, N.Y.: Orbis, 1997), p. xv.

8. Markha Gabrielle Valenta, *The Radical Folly of Love in (Post)modern America: The Autobiographical Narratives of Dorothy Day* (Iowa City, Iowa: Graduate College of the University of Iowa, 1999), p. 279.

9. James Wm. McClendon Jr., *Biography as Theology: How Life Stories Can Remake Today's Theology,* new ed. (Philadelphia: Trinity Press International, 1990 [orig. ed., 1974]), p. 22.

10. McClendon, *Biography as Theology,* p. 80.

lived propositions of the gospel in a particular life and context. It is clear, then, that McClendon's defense of a biographical theology does not renounce a propositional one. A similar point is argued, from a more theoretical perspective, by German theologian Michael Schneider, when he says that "the lived and exemplary theology of those theological existences develop an 'experimental dogmatic' that leads to bear witness to faith, not from concepts, but from life itself."[11] Following these suggestions, this chapter grounds a radical political theology in the life of Dorothy Day.

My own methodological approach combines biographical-narrative aspects with more systematic ones. In this regard I distance myself from McClendon, who argues for a more strict narrative method, but I think that it is important to make explicit the interpreters' theological frame. It would be too naïve to attempt a purely neutral approach to the life of a person like Dorothy Day, hoping to unfold her theological vision as such. In fact, McClendon himself offers a good example of what I am saying. His own reading of Dorothy Day as a biographical-theological source focuses on her contribution to peace.[12] This is a legitimate claim, but it seems that the final reason for that choice (instead of, say, focusing on hospitality or on the option for the poor) is directly related to McClendon's overall theological project. For this reason I prefer to explicitly develop the theological lenses I use to read Dorothy Day's life. And so, the remainder of this chapter consists in a preliminary introduction to the core of her life (taking for granted a general knowledge of her contribution), an explanation of the theological framework I use, a reading of Dorothy's lived politics in the Catholic Worker, and a further development of those insights for our contemporary situation.

From Conflict to Synthesis

Dorothy Day's spiritual journey can be seen as the unfolding of a deep synthesis she discovered and embodied, a synthesis between faith and justice, tradition and revolution, religion and politics. In the early stages of her

11. Michael Schneider, *Teología como Biografía. Una fundamentación dogmática* (Bilbao: Desclée de Brouwer, 2000), p. 28. Original edition: *Theologie als Biographie: Eine dogmatische Grundlegung* (St. Ottilien: EOS-Verl., 1997), p. 19.

12. James Wm. McClendon Jr., *Ethics: Systematic Theology,* vol. 1, rev. ed. (Nashville: Abingdon, 2002), pp. 279-99.

life, those aspects were seen as polarities in conflict, as unavoidable oppositions. In this respect, I disagree with June O'Connor, when she writes: "Day did not belabor any opposition or dichotomy between 'public' and 'private,' 'historical' and 'personal,' nor did she struggle to combine or integrate two aspects of life which were somehow preconceived or experienced as opposed or conflictual. As a communitarian radical by inclination and choice, Day operated out of a fundamental sense of connection between the public and the private."[13] Dorothy Day did achieve such an integrated synthesis, but it was not without struggle to overcome the opposition. For instance, as late as 1936 we find traces of this dichotomy: "*The Catholic Worker* admits the importance of political action, but is much more interested in the importance of private action, in the creation of order out of chaos. *The Catholic Worker* admits the importance of public responsibility for the poor and needy, but is much more interested in the importance of personal responsibility for the hungry, thirsty, naked, homeless, sick, criminal, afflicted, and ignorant."[14] For this reason it is necessary to take a closer look at Dorothy's own biographical account.

Before even going to college, she writes, "I wanted, though I did not know it then, a synthesis."[15] She was only fifteen. Months later, after joining the Socialist Party at the University of Illinois and reading the great Russian novelists, she noticed that "there was a real conflict going on in me" (*LL*, p. 42), a conflict between religion and the new realities she was discovering. "I felt that my faith had nothing to do with that of Christians around me" (*LL*, p. 43). Toward the end of the second part of her autobiography, under the title "A Time of Searching," she observes that "it was the great mass of the poor, the workers, who were the Catholics in this country, and this fact in itself drew me to the Church" (*LL*, p. 107) and helped her to integrate the conflict into a still fragile new synthesis. By 1926, she writes, "I had become convinced that I would become a Catholic; yet I felt that I was betraying the class to which I belonged, the workers, the poor of the world, with whom Christ spent his life" (*LL*, p. 144). Her struggle did

13. June O'Connor, *The Moral Vision of Dorothy Day: A Feminist Perspective* (New York: Crossroad, 1991), p. 31.

14. Dorothy Day, "For the New Reader," *The Catholic Worker* (December 1936), 6. Accessed from Dorothy Day Library on the Web at http://www.catholicworker.org/dorothyday, doc. #310.

15. Dorothy Day, *The Long Loneliness*, introduction by Robert Coles (New York: HarperCollins, 1997), p. 39. Hereafter, I will refer to this book, in the main text, as *LL*.

not end with her formal and full incorporation into the church, of course. She continued to find a tension between her conviction that the church was the church of the poor and the scandals she found in it. "There was plenty of charity, but too little justice" (*LL*, p. 150). And she pours out her deepest feelings: "How I longed to make a synthesis reconciling body and soul, this world and the next. . . . No wonder there was such a strong conflict going on in my mind and heart" (*LL*, p. 151). In the midst of this situation, she went to Washington, D.C., as a reporter to cover the communist-led Hunger March, in what I consider to be the key episode in her struggle to overcome this ongoing conflict and the discovery of a new synthesis.

This passage is located in the final pages of the second part of *The Long Loneliness*, and it records a period of deep personal search, at the age of thirty-five. She talks about mixed feelings of joy, pride, bitterness, self-absorption, sinfulness. She wonders, "where was the Catholic leadership in the gathering of men and women together?" (*LL*, p. 165). And, in that particular situation, she went to the national shrine. She describes what happened: "I offered up a special prayer, a prayer which came with tears and with anguish that some way would open up for me to use what talents I possessed for my fellow workers, for the poor" (*LL*, p. 166). More than forty years later, she recalls: "Today is our anniversary. In 1932 I prayed at the Washington Shrine to the Blessed Mother to open up a way to work for the revolution! When I got back to New York Peter Maurin was waiting for me."[16] Peter himself "wanted to make a new synthesis" (*LL*, p. 170) and that eventually took place in the Catholic Worker. Considering the narrative dynamic of *The Long Loneliness*, the practical consequences that came immediately after this prayer, and the personal testimony of Dorothy Day, it seems clear that this episode is actually the key turning point of her search for a synthesis.

A similar general conclusion can be found in Roger Statnick's dissertation, although surprisingly he does not point to the Washington event as a key turning point in the narrative. This is how he portrays her religious character: "Dorothy Day seeks an internal synthesis of spirit and matter, belief and experience, just as she seeks an external synthesis of religion and world justice. . . . The plot of Dorothy Day's story is the discovery she

---

16. William D. Miller, *All Is Grace: The Spirituality of Dorothy Day* (Garden City, N.Y.: Doubleday, 1987), p. 191. This particular quote comes from a letter to Nina Polcyn, December 8, 1975.

makes of her destiny both in God and in the world."[17] He concludes: "The plot of her life story is the search for a synthesis of matter and spirit."[18]

How did Dorothy Day articulate this new synthesis? It is honest to say that she did it in a theological, albeit implicit, way. For instance, Stephen Krupa[19] has rightly noticed that the key for Dorothy Day's revolutionary nonviolence is her spirituality, her personal relationship with Jesus. She does not obtain active nonviolence from her leftist background nor from the Catholic doctrine itself. It was the discovery of the gospel and her daily personal relation with Jesus Christ that nourished her faithfulness to pacifism throughout her life. Yet there was no sharp separation between spirituality and theology. Dorothy Day used the theological notions that were broadly available in her time, appropriated them in a very personal and creative way, and radically explored and exploited their implications. An accurate formulation is found in Statnick's remarks: "The doctrines of the incarnate presence of Christ in humanity and of the Mystical Body of Christ are the guide wires for her personal vision of faith." In fact, "the story that conveys Dorothy Day's Catholic Christian transformation shows what is entailed when one claims to believe in the incarnate presence of Christ in the world and in the communion of His Mystical Body."[20] The following section offers a theological framework with which to read Dorothy Day's life and spiritually rooted political involvement.

Theological Framework

Dorothy Day's life and spirituality followed "the downward path" of the gospel, a kenotic movement of revolutionary consequences. Dorothy believed in and lived kenosis as the deepest reality from a Christian perspective. Following Jesus in his radical descent (see Phil. 2:5-8), she emptied herself and humbly shared her life with the poor and weak of society. This upside-down evangelical logic has socio-political consequences, ground-

17. Roger A. Statnick, *Dorothy Day's Religious Conversion: A Study in Biographical Theology* (Notre Dame: Graduate School, Department of Theology of the University of Notre Dame, 1983), p. 74.

18. Statnick, *Dorothy Day's Religious Conversion*, p. 317.

19. Stephen T. Krupa, SJ, *Dorothy Day and the Spirituality of Nonviolence* (Berkeley, Calif.: Graduate Theological Union, 1997).

20. Statnick, *Dorothy Day's Religious Conversion*, pp. 310 and 313.

ing a real kenotic revolution. Dorothy's kenotic revolution was not the revolution of efficacious organizing of influential leaders, but the humble and permanent service to and with the poor. It was not a revolution aimed at seizing power, but was powerless. It was the radical upside-down revolution or, even better, the right-side-up revolution of Mary's *Magnificat*. In sum, the spirituality of personal identification with the kenotic Christ has political consequences, generating a bottom-up alternative to the dominant system, an alternative that might not be brilliant or sparkling but is profoundly revolutionary.

The objective of this section is to develop a theological framework for a correct understanding of the Christian revolution embodied by Dorothy Day and the Catholic Worker. This theological framework consists of a threefold articulation of basic Christian doctrines and its implication for socio-political life. These principles of faith are the incarnation, eschatology, and creation, but the main point in this proposal is the order in which they are combined. While the usual organization of theological discourse follows a chronological sequence (creation, incarnation, eschatology) my proposal, albeit probably counterintuitive, has firm theological foundations, as I show in the following paragraphs.

The first step can be called the "politics of the incarnation." We as Christians find our main political source by contemplating Jesus, the incarnate God, as he lives in Bethlehem, Nazareth, and Galilee, and finally dies on Mount Golgotha. We discover a completely new approach to politics embodied in Jesus: one that is humble, opts for the poor, is based on service, and follows a kenotic process of descent. The life of Jesus cries out that the kingdom of God has come, is already here, among the people. He proclaims that the promises for the poor have been finally accomplished "today" with his coming (Luke 4:21). But its presence is so humble that it can even go unnoticed: it is present as a mustard seed. When talking about politics we tend to think about power, budgets, structures, influence, lobbying, and so on. We as Christians should never forget that the politics of Jesus, the politics of the incarnation, has a different approach.

We then experience the tension between the present and the future of the kingdom. We are called to recognize, to embody, and to strengthen the reality of the kingdom of God on this earth, but at the same time we know that we do not belong to this world (John 15:19). "Do not be conformed to this world," Saint Paul reminds the Romans (Rom. 12:2). Besides saying "yes" in the way of incarnating a humble alternative to this unjust system, we are invited to say "no" to the logic of the anti-kingdom. In the third place, then, we can be open to everyone and make proposals for the general organization of society. Universality springs from incarnation. Our concern for the common good is not an abstract one, but is rooted in the particular experience within the faithful community. To sum up, then, we are faced with a threefold strategy: first, the positive alternative of the incarnation; then, a permanent eschatological criticism; and finally, a realist interest in the wider society.

This primacy of the incarnation implies that the church is called to embody the real presence of Christ in the world and, by doing so, the Christian community fleshes out a real alternative to the dominant system. As Christians, our first word is "yes," since we have already experienced the novelty of Christ, and are invited to show its reality in the public realm. As Stanley Hauerwas puts it, "The church does not have a social ethic, but rather is a social ethic. She is a social ethic inasmuch as she functions as a criteriological institution, an institution that has learned to embody the form of truth that is charity as revealed in the person and work of Christ."[21] This "politics of the incarnation" is the first and most important step, but in our current theological situation it is often forgotten or misunderstood.

Before moving to the next steps of my theological framework, I will clarify briefly the relevance of this politics of the incarnation. In our contemporary pluralistic context, the reasonable concern about a shared common view has led some theologians and social ethicists to subordinate the incarnation to the doctrine of creation. Instead of focusing on the incarnation (which would lead to a particularistic ethical view), mainline ethicists prefer to ground their proposal in creation, which offers a wider embrace to all human beings. We saw an example of this debate in the previous chapter, when we compared Niebuhr and Yoder. Michael and Kenneth Himes[22] provide another example of the dangerous oblivion of this primacy of the incarnation: they link the incarnation, not to the church, but to patriotism. Even within the Hebrew Scriptures, the doctrine of creation is subordinated to the doctrine of redemption, as Gerhard von Rad demonstrated in his 1936 classical and influential article. The doctrine of creation is just an expansion of the concrete experience of liberation.[23] More

---

21. Stanley Hauerwas, "The Politics of Charity," *Interpretation* 31 (July 1977): 262.

22. Michael J. Himes and Kenneth R. Himes, OFM, *Fullness of Faith: The Public Significance of Theology* (New York: Paulist, 1993), pp. 125-56.

23. See Gerhard von Rad, "The Theological Problem of the Old Testament Doctrine of

recently, Stephen Long has proven that, in the area of socio-economic ethics, the consequence of such a move (the priority of creation over incarnation) has been the adoption of the liberal-capitalist dominant view.[24] For these reasons, I want to emphasize the priority of the incarnation, as a way to embody a real Christian alternative to the prevailing and oppressive system.

Once the need for a "politics of the incarnation" is established, we are in a position to move forward and articulate a proposal that maintains in creative tension two other aspects: the "politics of eschatology" and the "politics of creation." In political terms, this tension is often referred to as the dialectic between denouncing and announcing. Ignacio Ellacuría formulated the issue with the notions of utopia and prophecy:

> The prophecy of denunciation, on the horizon of the Kingdom of God, marks out the ways that lead to utopia. Prophecy's "No," prophecy's negation pointing beyond in itself generates utopia's "Yes" by virtue of the promise that is the Kingdom of God already present among human beings.[25]

What this text shows is the need for a Christian proposal that combines the prophetic eschatological "not yet" with the more positive vision of the utopia "already" realized, at least in part, and discovered in our created history. The following section illustrates how Dorothy Day and the Catholic Worker lived this threefold theological framework (incarnation, eschatology, creation) in their daily approach to politics.

The Politics of Dorothy Day and of the Catholic Worker

It is not easy to articulate the political stand of the Catholic Worker. Its co-founder Peter Maurin used to summarize his vision with the slogan "cult,

---

Creation," in *The Problem of the Hexateuch and Other Essays* (New York: McGraw Hill, 1966), pp. 131-43.

24. D. Stephen Long, *Divine Economy: Theology and the Market* (London: Routledge, 2000), pp. 44-80.

25. Ignacio Ellacuría, SJ, "Utopia and Prophecy from Latin America: An Essay of Historic Soteriology," in *Towards a Society That Serves Its People: The Intellectual Contribution of El Salvador's Murdered Jesuits*, ed. John Hasset and Hugh Lacey (Washington, D.C.: Georgetown University Press, 1991), p. 58.

culture, cultivation."[26] Other times, he would talk about houses of hospitality, "agronomic universities" or farming communes, and roundtable discussions, as can be seen as early as the second number of *The Catholic Worker* newspaper.[27] In a very interesting study, Frederick Boehrer[28] has focused on the meaning of anarchism within the Catholic Worker and finds four characteristics of its political practice: an alternative to state definitions of social life, the practice of personalist community, the practice of personalist social movement, and, only after 1980 (that is, after Dorothy Day's death), prophetic discipleship as an alternative to church definitions of Christian living. Although this vision is helpful, Boehrer's description may not present an accurate account of the Worker's general position. In fact, Dorothy Day was hesitant about the very notion of anarchism, and even dismissed it when she found that it led to some misunderstandings.[29] The threefold theological view developed in the previous section offers a wider overarching framework for interpreting the politics of Dorothy Day and the *Catholic Worker*.

The Politics of the Incarnation

The first and obvious example of the politics of the incarnation in the Catholic Worker is found in the *houses of hospitality*. In them, a new reality emerges. They embody the vision of an alternative Christian reality and in that sense they focus not on the rehabilitation of the homeless person, but on the rehabilitation and transformation of society. The houses of hospitality offer a social space in which the poor, homeless, unemployed, disenfranchised, and marginalized recover their dignity. The houses represent a

26. For example, see *LL*, pp. 171 and 275. Very often this triad occupied the central pages of *The Catholic Worker*.

27. See his three easy essays that first appeared in *The Catholic Worker* 1 (June-July 1933).

28. Frederick G. Boehrer III, *Catholic Anarchism and the Catholic Worker Movement: Roman Catholic Authority and Identity in the United States* (Syracuse, N.Y.: Graduate School of Syracuse University, 2001).

29. The political vision of Dorothy Day and the Catholic Worker is a complex one, and it cannot be grasped with a single notion, be that anarchism or any other, such as socialism, Christian communism, distributism, economic voluntarism, communitarian personalism, revolutionary nonviolence, decentralization, or political localism.

dual project of providing hospitality and building community. These must exist in creative tension.[30] When this happens, they create an alternative to the professional social work model that dominates the contemporary social scene with its bureaucratic and rehabilitational mindset.

The Catholic Worker houses of hospitality, in contrast with other social service institutions, do not focus on efficacy. In fact, as Mel Piehl puts it, "The rigorous practice of the works of mercy in Worker Houses indicated not only a firm rejection of any conventional form of religiously inspired politics, but a radically antitriumphalist approach to the spread of Catholic values in America as well."[31] This radical understanding of politics seems closer to Jesus' own approach in the incarnation, from his birth in Bethlehem to his death on the cross. And it has been recognized as such, since "the [Catholic Worker] movement's influence lay not in its numbers or even in its visibility to the world, but in its moral and spiritual integrity."[32] There might be other aspects of politics that eventually may be important to consider, but from the Christian perspective it seems clear that the incarnation speaks about silent service, humbleness, and powerlessness. And we must not forget that those attitudes, when lived faithfully in the public sphere, have political meaning.

The second example of the Catholic Worker embodiment of the politics of incarnation can be found in the *farming communes*. If the houses of hospitality are intended to be a direct and immediate response to the injustice of modern society, the farming communes aim at a long-term program of radical alternative to the whole "rotten system" of industrialism, capitalism, and consumerism. Peter Maurin's "green revolution" proposed a decentralized economy, somewhat idealized and based on the medieval ideal of social integration. But, even in the first generation, the failure of the Catholic Worker back to the land movement seems to be clear and acknowledged by almost all observers.

Deeper reflection shows two aspects of this failure. One is the fact that the farms have maintained a power of attraction for younger generations dissatisfied with urban life and the ecological crisis. Furthermore, many of the urban houses of hospitality have developed a "mixed" lifestyle, either

---

30. Harry Murray, *Do Not Neglect Hospitality: The Catholic Worker and the Homeless* (Philadelphia: Temple University Press, 1990), especially pp. 246-59. See also Jean Daniélou, "Toward a Theology of Hospitality," *The Catholic Worker* 12 (December 1945): 2.

31. Piehl, *Breaking Bread*, p. 141.

32. Piehl, *Breaking Bread*, p. 179.

by connecting with an actual farm or by having a small garden that provides the human contact with the land. In the era of "sustainable development" and Green parties, this aspect is obviously political as well.

The farming experience also shows a second feature that is deeper and even more important than the first one: the "politics of failure." Admittedly, the farms have failed. But, from a Christian perspective, I refuse to accept that politics ought to necessarily lead to success or victory. This does not mean, though, that our political action has to be oriented to failure as an objective, but simply that we do not admit that failure is a complete and definite disaster. As Dorothy Day wrote, "the Christian point of view was to keep in mind the failure of the Cross" (*LL,* p. 216). She elsewhere reflected on the effects of the Catholic Worker, with these words:

> How little we have attempted, let alone accomplished. The consolation is this — and this is our faith too: By our sufferings and our failures, by our acceptance of the Cross, by our struggle to grow in faith, hope, and charity, we unleash forces that help to overcome the evil in the world.[33]

Any Christian political project must accept a certain degree of this politics of failure, unless it wants to become an imperial or capitalistic theology of permanent and misleading triumphs.

The Politics of Eschatology

Roger Statnick has shown the central role of eschatology in Dorothy Day's religious conversion: "This eschatological logic is the rule of life for the life style of the Catholic Worker which, in turn, characterizes this way of life as eschatological."[34] And he explains it with this nuance: "The logic governing Dorothy Day's viewpoint is not simply a mechanism of realized eschatology. . . . Instead, the eschatological logic that marks Dorothy Day's converted horizon is a *realizing* eschatology."[35] In other words, eschatology is the moving power that nourishes and strengthens the Worker's alternative lifestyle.[36]

33. Dorothy Day, *Loaves and Fishes* (New York: Harper and Row, 1963), p. 204. Hereafter, I will refer to this book, in the main text, as *LF.*

34. Statnick, *Dorothy Day's Religious Conversion,* p. 255.

35. Statnick, *Dorothy Day's Religious Conversion,* p. 205.

36. See John Stuart Sandberg, *The Eschatological Ethic of the Catholic Worker* (Wash-

Christian eschatology functions as a permanent corrective to all human achievements, since they are always partial and provisional. If the incarnational position tends to say "yes" by providing a concrete alternative, the eschatological view says "no" to the works of the "anti-kingdom of God." Within the Catholic Worker and in the socio-political realm, this eschatological vision is fleshed out as active nonviolence and civil disobedience. More specifically, three strategies are to be mentioned: conscientious objection to war and refusal to register for the draft, nonpayment of taxes, and going to jail. Since the consistent pacifist position of Dorothy Day is well known, I now focus on the other two facets.

Dorothy wrote: "I have been behind bars in police stations, houses of detention, jails, and prison farms (whatsoever they are called) eleven times."[37] From the time when she was just twenty until the age of seventy-six, the *experience of jail* was present in her life. The consensus among the scholars seems to point to seven imprisonments throughout her life: twice before founding the Catholic Worker (in 1917 and 1922), and five times afterward (during the protests against the Civil Defense Act between 1955 and 1959, and finally in 1973, when she joined the United Farm Workers in their struggle). While Dorothy was not obsessed with the idea of civil disobedience as if it were a permanent necessity, she did not fear going to jail when needed in coherence with her nonviolent stands.

Imprisonment had clear effects on Dorothy's life and worldview. Going to jail, of course, is not an end in itself, although it shows that Christians must go beyond utilitarianism and overcome the obsession with efficiency. Statnick offers this insightful reflection:

> What metaphor does for language, imprisonment does for Dorothy Day's life style. As metaphor shocks a person into perceiving a new dimension of reference in the language he or she uses, jail for Dorothy Day disrupts her expectations of the ordinary, assumed practices, so that a new way of life can unfold. It embodies the metaphoric vision of the divine reality bound to and yet active within the human condition

---

ington, D.C.: Catholic University of America, 1978). This dissertation offers a good description and analysis of the main practices and ideas of the Catholic Worker but fails to provide a sound theological discussion of the role of an eschatological ethic in Christian life.

37. Ellsberg, *Dorothy Day: Selected Writings*, p. 352. Taken from "On Pilgrimage," *The Catholic Worker* (May 1974).

of pain and suffering. The Catholic Worker life style is this kind of incarnate metaphor.[38]

Again we find here the creative tension between incarnation and eschatology, between the Christian "yes" and the Christian "no" to the world, which also expresses a particular embodiment of the spiritual and political option for the poor.

The second aspect of active nonviolence as lived by Dorothy Day and the Catholic Worker is *tax resistance.* This is a practice that brings together the anarchist, distributist, and pacifist aspects of the Catholic Worker personalist worldview in a concrete public practice. Knowing that "war is the health of the State" (*LL*, pp. 263-73) and that a significant percentage of those taxes go to the military budget, the Catholic Worker practiced what can be called "fiscal conscientious objection." In fact, it usually only refers to federal taxes, assuming that local and state taxes are oriented to provide social services. In this sense, probably the best homage that Dorothy Day received when she died was the decision of Archbishop Raymond Hunthausen of Seattle to urge citizens to refuse to pay 50 percent of their income taxes in protest of government spending on nuclear weapons in 1981, an action that created a national commotion.

There is another facet of the specific approach of the Catholic Worker to tax resistance that I want to underline, namely, the connection with its daily life of voluntary poverty. Normally, tax resistance is expressed by a public statement of refusal to pay taxes, but the Catholic Worker has been able to do it using a simpler and more radical way: by remaining below the poverty line, Workers do not have to pay taxes. This tactic, less confrontational but as public as the usual one, allows them to establish more clearly the connection between military expenses and social inequality. It also offers a constructive alternative that is not superficial or merely symbolic, one that grounds political protest in their living together with the poor, and verifies the practice of nonviolence on a daily basis.[39] In other words, it creates a nexus between the politics of the

---

38. Statnick, *Dorothy Day's Religious Conversion,* p. 221.

39. "Many Workers find the practice of nonviolence within the house of hospitality even more challenging and personally demanding than its use in the public, political sphere. Still, the movement's commitment to nonviolence means that the Worker houses have themselves been a daily, living laboratory of experiments in nonviolence for 65 years," writes Patrick G. Coy. "Beyond the Ballot Box: the Catholic Worker Movement and Nonviolent Di-

incarnation (voluntary poverty) and the politics of eschatology (tax resistance).

The Politics of Creation

At this point in our discourse, the modern, progressive, and liberal voices in our midst will rise to say that Dorothy Day and the Catholic Worker are forgetting the big picture, that they are withdrawing from the political realm, or that they are not really concerned with the common good. The definition of the political realm or the common good, however, does not need to be done within a Constantinian framework, as if the role of the church were to organize the whole of society.

There is a place for the "politics of creation" that includes all members of society. But this politics of creation, in Christian theology, is subordinated to incarnation and eschatology. Among contemporary theologians, Yoder argues that the only way to general validity is the kenotic way: "The ordinariness of the humanness of Jesus is the warrant for the generalizability of his reconciliation. . . . The particularity of incarnation *is* the universality of good. There is no road but the low road."[40] This low road is what Dorothy Day calls the downward path (*LL,* p. 59) and what I have named the kenotic revolution.

From this particular perspective, we are now in a position to consider how Dorothy Day and the Catholic Worker deal with the larger social picture. Although it would be helpful to study in some detail the concepts of economic decentralization and political localism as important aspects of the Catholic Worker's position, in this section I focus only on two issues: labor and clarification of thought.

It is often said that Peter Maurin and Dorothy Day had a different understanding of *labor,* the latter being much closer to trade unionism than the French peasant was. A glimpse of this difference of opinions can be found in Dorothy's own words: "Despite Peter's oft-repeated dictum, 'Strikes do not strike me,' we did what we could by word and deed to help

---

rect Action," in Thorn, Runkel, and Mountin, *Dorothy Day and the Catholic Worker Movement,* pp. 169-83; quote from p. 183, note 1.

40. John H. Yoder, *The Priestly Kingdom: Social Ethics as Gospel* (Notre Dame: University of Notre Dame Press, 1984), p. 62.

the worker in his fight for better conditions and higher wages" (*LF,* p. 38).[41] Especially during the first years after its foundation, the Catholic Worker was actively involved in labor issues. It gave some support to the New Deal's National Recovery Act of 1933, backed the Children Labor legal reform in 1935, and supported the unions in various conflicts and strikes, the most famous being the seamen strike of 1936-37.

In those days, Dorothy Day wrote an editorial piece explaining their stand on strikes: "Let us be honest and confess that it is the social order which we wish to change. The workers are never going to be satisfied, no matter how much pay they get, no matter what their hours are. And it is to reconstruct the social order that we are throwing ourselves in with the workers, whether in factories or shipyards or on the sea."[42] That is to say, the Catholic Worker understood that fighting for wages is not enough. Dorothy knew that "unions still fight for better wages and hours, though I have come more and more to feel that that in itself is not the answer" (*LF,* p. 83) since that approach maintains the same logic of the capitalist system. As an alternative, Dorothy Day proposes a civilization based on voluntary poverty.

A common criticism is that this position mistakenly forgets or over-looks the structural issues of injustice in modern societies (for instance, how wealth is produced and distributed), and by doing so it actually toler-ates the existence of an unjust system.[43] In fact, this was Dorothy Day's ini-tial critique of the church, where she found "plenty of charity but too little justice" (*LL,* 150). Years later she also wrote: "Breadlines are not enough, hospices are not enough. I know we will always have men on the road. But we need communities of work, land for the landless, true farming com-munes, cooperatives and credit unions."[44] It would be inaccurate to inter-pret the diverse emphases on these texts as showing an evolution in Doro-

---

41. For this topic of labor, see *LL,* pp. 204-22, and Thorn, Runkel, and Mountin, *Dorothy Day and the Catholic Worker Movement,* pp. 257-319.

42. Ellsberg, *Dorothy Day: Selected Writings,* p. 242, from "Our Stand on Strikes," *The Catholic Worker* (July 1936).

43. For a balanced position, see Francis Schüssler Fiorenza, "Justice and Charity in So-cial Welfare," in *Who Will Provide? The Changing Role of Religion in American Social Welfare,* ed. Mary Jo Bane, Brent Coffin, and Ronald Thiemann (Boulder, Colo.: Westview, 2000), pp. 73-96.

44. Ellsberg, *Dorothy Day: Selected Writings,* p. 252, from "Of Justice and Breadlines," *The Catholic Worker* (January 1972).

thy Day's thought.[45] Rather, they display a complex and radical approach to those issues. It is complex, because it considers the different aspects; and it is radical, because it does not stop with a superficial solution.

The second topic that shows how the Catholic Worker lives and understands the "politics of creation," or the *universality of socio-political matters,* is related to the intellectual dimension. Dorothy Day was a journalist herself, and as such she established the Worker first of all as a newspaper. Peter Maurin was a scholar. He established roundtables of discussion for the clarification of thought, which were an essential part of the Worker from the very beginning. It seems clear, then, that the Catholic Worker never subscribed to a sectarian and naïvely charitable approach to social issues, but always searched for the improvement of the whole society.

The Catholic Worker newspaper "stands as a rare example of an ideological publication whose editorial posture and internal structure approach congruence"[46] so that the movement and the paper mutually reinforce each other. The circulation of the paper reached a record high distribution of 190,000 in May 1938, which is astonishing for a radical publication. The roundtables for clarification of thought also show a desire to reach out and spread the constructive vision of a new society.

A related aspect is what Mark and Louise Zwick have called the "training ground": "From the earliest years, being a Catholic Worker was not necessarily a permanent vocation. Many came to join in the work for a few days, a few weeks, a few months, or a few years. The Catholic Worker became a kind of training ground for living the Gospel."[47] Dorothy herself puts it this way: "'What is it all about — the Catholic Worker movement?' It is, in a way, a school, a work camp, to which large-hearted, socially conscious young people come to find their vocations."[48]

In particular, one can recognize the influence of the Catholic Worker

45. Nancy Roberts finds that "the singular editorial consistency" of *The Catholic Worker* newspaper from 1933 to 1982 is a rare phenomenon in American journalism. See Nancy Lee Roberts, *Dorothy Day and 'The Catholic Worker,' 1933-1982* (Minneapolis: Graduate School of the University of Minnesota, 1982), p. 54.

46. Roberts, *Dorothy Day and 'The Catholic Worker,'* p. 216.

47. Mark and Louise Zwick, introduction to Dorothy Day, *On Pilgrimage* (Grand Rapids: Eerdmans, 1999), p. 28.

48. Ellsberg, *Dorothy Day: Selected Writings,* p. 354, from "On Pilgrimage," *The Catholic Worker* (March-April 1975).

in mainline Catholic progressive forces of the social, political, and intellectual American life. I mention only four examples. The Association of Catholic Trade Unionists, small but very significant, was created in 1937 by an ex–Catholic Worker, John Coy. *Commonweal* magazine, one of the most respected voices of liberal lay Catholics in the United States, had former Chicago Workers John Cogley and James O'Gara as its editors from 1949 until 1984. Dorothy herself wrote more than thirty articles for the magazine. In the political arena, Michael Harrington's experience in the Catholic Worker, expressed in his book *The Other America,* was very influential in the War on Poverty federal program of the 1960s. More recently, one should not forget the role of Robert Ellsberg as editor-in-chief of Orbis Books, after living five years at the New York Catholic Worker house.

In summary, Dorothy Day understood the complexity of social reality and the need for an equally complex response. She was convinced that Christians should always keep in mind the call to be with the poor and to create alternatives from that specific social setting. She also knew that the followers of Jesus Christ, crucified because of his faithfulness to the God of the poor, are invited to reproduce his opposition to the forces and powers of evil. And finally, she acknowledged that there is a Christian responsibility for the common good, which springs from the other two steps and which may call for some particular vocations. But it is important to recognize the order of these three aspects, which is not only a chronological order, but a theological and political one as well. This is what I have called the politics of the incarnation, the politics of eschatology, and the politics of creation.

An Integrated Proposal

Some interpretations of the Catholic Worker movement lean toward the sectarian side, failing to weigh the implications of their retrieval from the general political arena. They are right in saying that the mainline Constantinian approach is misguided and dangerous, but sometimes they may forget that a retreat from state politics will only worsen the situation, especially for the poor. I have tried to show that Dorothy Day and the Catholic Worker, although emphasizing a radical perspective, have been able to acknowledge the complexity of reality, considering different aspects at the same time, and knowing that different contexts demand different emphases.

Following their inspiration, I offer a threefold proposal for Christian contribution to social transformation. In my opinion, the first issue is very often forgotten today by Christians. For this reason it becomes the most important and urgent one.

1. *Political imagination.* There is a clear need for real and radical alternatives to this oppressive capitalist system. We Christians must show that it is possible to move from private property and armies to a nonviolent socialism. We have to make visible that another world is possible. Every Christian person and community should get involved in this task. It is a matter of faithfulness to our way of life, and the key contribution that we Christians can make. First, it will create spaces of social resistance against the empire. Second, it may create a global alternative to the system.

2. *Nonviolent direct action.* Sometimes, Christians will have to say a clear and direct "no" to certain decisions that states, governments, or corporations may make. Different actions of non-cooperation and civil disobedience may then be needed. Although only a few Christians will be called to that kind of radical action, they would be supported by everyone in their communities and by the church as a whole.

3. *The common good and the welfare state.* In the meantime, Christian churches should not forget daily political life and policy making, since many important decisions are made in that area, decisions that heavily influence the poor. For instance, it is very important to maintain the social conquests of the welfare state against neo-liberal attacks proposing a minimal state. This is the most common approach for Christians trying to get involved in social issues. In the framework I am proposing, however, this step is not the most important one and should actually be derived from the first two. Some Christians with strong technical formation should be in charge of these proposals, always supported by the alternatives generated by the whole community (as explained in the first step).

If we look closely at this proposal, we find that it is actually an adaptation of the classical *principle of subsidiarity* of Catholic social thought, which was so influential in Dorothy Day's life and vision. Whatever can be done by small communities and local entities should be done at that level. It is an injustice and a disturbance to assign to a greater and higher association what lesser and subordinate organizations can do. This should be the main emphasis, especially in these days when this level is often forgotten. However, at the same time the principle of subsidiarity states that greater socio-political entities (nation-states or international institutions) must powerfully and effectively do all those things that belong to them alone because only they can do them.

Let me explain this proposal with some examples from the political, economic, and cultural realms. Consider, first, the Christian ethical position on violence, war, and peace as a way to deal with the main *political* question, namely, the use and limits of power. Although the twentieth century saw the advance and limited success of political nonviolence, there has been no real advance toward the abolition of armies as a way of solving international conflicts. Christians have contributed to the creation of nonviolent alternatives, but there has not been a significant and communal option in the church for it. What would happen if, for instance, the same number of Christians working as military chaplains were devoted to full-time research, development, training, and planning of nonviolent defense alternatives during the next fifty years? This would be one of the best contributions of the church to world peace. However, in the meantime, should the church be silent regarding war, military research, weapons trade, and so on? No, the church should lift up its voice. Finally, as a third step, those Christians who feel themselves called to direct actions of civil disobedience should continue to do so, but clearly their actions would be much more meaningful and powerful in the context I am proposing.

My second example comes from the *socio-economic* arena, and it deals with the possibility of socialism. The usual approach among socialist Christians consists in trying to influence partisan politics so that social policies might become as progressive as possible regarding welfare, taxes, public services, and so on. I usually agree with those proposals. I have no problem with that agenda — except for the fact that policy-making discussions are so technically sophisticated that Christian inspiration may lose influence in that particular field. Anyway, what I affirm is that the main contribution of socialist Christians should not be in the field of policy making, but in creating real alternatives to capitalism. That is, emphasis should be placed on the lived experiences of shared property, in communal institutions that break the market logic, in imaginative experiments that show how it is possible to live otherwise. Sometimes these persons or groups may need to express their "no" to capitalism with certain public tools of non-cooperation, such as boycotts.

The *socio-cultural* example deals with immigration. The Christian approach to this issue should emphasize the creation of a real community of "nationals" and immigrants with or without legal papers, regardless their origin, language, economic status, or cultural background. Showing the real possibility of an integrated community with no divisions whatsoever would be our main political contribution to the immigration reality. That includes a whole different way of understanding integration, education, health care, work wages, legal status, worship, neighborhood relations — a real alternative. Of course, it would also be good for some Christians to make technical proposals for better legal regulation of immigration policies and international relations, and for other Christians to fight more directly in opposition to current unjust laws. But I want to stress that only a real Christian alternative would provide a context in which our proposals and actions could be realistically considered as coherent.

Conclusion: Body of Christ as Radical Ecclesiology

One final set of questions arises: Is there an overarching concept or image that can unify fragmented communities and provide a real alternative to the capitalist system? Can these radical attempts establish the basis for a new political ecclesiology?

The main ecclesial image in post–Second Vatican Council theology is the people of God, which has proven to be a good and fruitful notion, but has also shown its links with the modern Enlightenment project that seems to be unable to solve our contemporary problems. In the 1960s there was an optimistic way of looking at reality that thought that the people (and especially the people of God) would be able to bring about integral liberation. The people were seen as a collective subject, strong enough to turn back history. However, we do not have that collective subject or people anymore, especially in the Fourth World and in inner-city settings. What we find there is a number of persons who suffer such a degree of dehumanization that they can hardly be considered subjects of any revolution. In this context, I find much more realistic and powerful the notion of the body of Christ.[49]

---

49. Anselm Kyongsuk Min, "Solidarity of Others in the Body of Christ: A New Theological Paradigm," *Toronto Journal of Theology* 14 (1998): 239-54. See also John H. Yoder, *Body Politics: Five Practices of the Christian Community before the Watching World* (Nashville: Dis-

The body of Christ image speaks clearly and directly to issues of human rights violations such as torture, domestic violence against women, death corridors, sexual abuse of children, abortion, anorexia, bulimia, adolescent pregnancy, and rape. The body of Christ embraces junkies with AIDS-filled bodies who crawl through the streets of every big city, children with their inflated bellies because of famine and thirst, bodies crippled by bombings or mines, injured bodies of uninsured workers, homeless bodies lying on street benches, dead bodies of those who tried to cross the Rio Grande border, and bodies of inmates in lonely prison cells. As the 1940 "Aims and Purposes" of the Catholic Worker movement states it:

> This teaching, the doctrine of the Mystical Body of Christ, involves today the issue of unions (where men call each other brothers); it involves the racial question; it involves cooperatives, credit unions, crafts; it involves Houses of Hospitality and farming communes. It is with all these means that we can live as though we believed indeed that we are all members one of another, knowing that when "the health of one member suffers, the health of the whole body is lowered."[50]

The body of Christ speaks about communion, inclusive relations, unconditional welcoming, union-in-difference, incorporation in a common reality. The body of Christ talks about the Eucharist, about our Lord Jesus and his healings, about the cosmic Christ and the final recapitulation of every body, caress, hug, and tear of human history. The body of Christ builds up the church as a real and visible alternative to the system. The body of Christ shows that another world is actually possible.

I finish by quoting the reflections of two anarchist thinkers, Toni Negri and Michael Hardt, who write:

> Globalization must be met with a counter-globalization, Empire with a counter-Empire. In this regard we might take inspiration from Saint Augustine's vision of a project to contest the decadent Roman Empire. No limited community could succeed and provide an alternative to im-

---

ciple Resources, 1992), and William T. Cavanaugh, *Torture and Eucharist: Theology, Politics and the Body of Christ* (Oxford: Blackwell, 1988), especially pp. 205-81.

50. Dorothy Day, "Aims and Purposes of the Catholic Worker Movement," *The Catholic Worker* (February 1940), 7. Accessed from Dorothy Day Library on the Web at http://www.catholicworker.org/dorothyday, doc. #182.

perial rule; only a universal, catholic community bringing together all populations and all languages in a common journey could accomplish this. The divine city is a universal city of aliens, coming together, cooperating, communicating.[51]

They conclude their book with these words: "Militancy today is a positive, constructive, and innovative activity. This is the form in which we and all those who revolt against the rule of capital recognize ourselves as militants today. Militants resist imperial command in a creative way. . . . This militancy makes resistance into counterpower and makes rebellion into a project of love."[52]

Radical Christian communities in solidarity with the poor (as exemplified by the Catholic Worker) are our way of embodying God's project of love in the real counter-empire, the body of Christ. A radical ecclesiology such as the one espoused and lived by Dorothy Day (firmly rooted in Jesus Christ, in the living church, and in the poor peoples of our societies) provides a political alternative to the system that impoverishes the majority of our brothers and sisters.

51. Michael Hardt and Antonio Negri, *Empire* (Cambridge, Mass.: Harvard University Press, 2000), p. 207.

52. Hardt and Negri, *Empire*, p. 413.

Interruption: Toward a New
Radical Political Theology

The shortest definition of religion: interruption.

JOHANN BAPTIST METZ[1]

This book is simultaneously analytic and systematic, author-driven and topic-oriented. I have dealt with different authors (Lindbeck, Milbank, Yoder, and Day) by studying four aspects of the relationship between church and society (language, mediation of social sciences, culture, politics). This chapter, which concludes the first part of the book, maintains the same dual character. As was stated in the prologue, my journey started with Latin American liberation theology and engaged English-speaking authors but now needs to return to Europe. Johann Baptist Metz is my main interlocutor in a very simple way: I use his main theological categories to reformulate the general thread of this book. At the same time (and this is the constructive and systematic side of the chapter) I want to revisit some of the assumptions of European political theology in the face of secularization, in accordance with the conclusions of this book up to this point.

Summary of the Preceding Chapters

As I argued in chapter 1, the main contribution of Lindbeck and post-liberal theology for our constructive proposal is the emphasis on Christian

1. Johann Baptist Metz, *Faith in History and Society: Toward a Practical Fundamental Theology*, trans. David Smith (London: Burns & Oates, 1980), p. 171.

practices in ordinary life. This provides a firm basis for theology in the context of pluralism and fragmentation that we live in. We need to recognize the difference, or distinct contribution of Christian praxis, if we want to make a significant proposal for our world. The problem with this approach, if taken unilaterally, is that it may fall into an uncritical assumption of tradition leading to merely conservative positions. Or, at least, there is the risk of not fully acknowledging the task of a critical reflection that maintains theology's independence from Christian witness and is open to external interdisciplinary critiques.[2] From this perspective, the project of Milbank's radical orthodoxy provides a complement to this deficiency in Lindbeck's proposal.

The contribution of John Milbank engages in a deep critical discussion with secular reason and, more specifically, with postmodern thinkers.[3] As Milbank himself states, in agreement with Lindbeck, Christian theology is rooted in Christian practices. But our English theologian is aware of the need for a critical reflection on the tradition we inherit: if this analytical view were absent, the affirmation of tradition would lead to a mere repetition of ancient practices, or to fundamentalisms of various kinds. In this regard, Milbank's sophisticated analysis provides a good complement to Lindbeck's view. One cannot say that radical orthodoxy offers a naïve or simplistic analysis of the Christian tradition; its engagement with postmodern thought is a serious intellectual undertaking. At the same time, Milbank's own position is not without dangers. His defense of Christianity as a master narrative that actually out-narrates all other narratives, combined with his affirmation of its political implications, makes one wary of the totalitarian or theocratic impulse that is implied in this position. It seems that we need a more humble and evangelical — that is, *Jesuanic* — view.

2. This is one of the points of the insightful analysis of David G. Kamitsuka, *Theology and Contemporary Culture: Liberation, Postliberal and Revisionary Perspectives* (Cambridge: Cambridge University Press, 1999). Kamitsuka finds a balance in David Tracy's revisionary and public theology, while I pursue a similar goal through a critical reading of Milbank's radical orthodoxy.

3. While in my second chapter I referred basically to Milbank's *Theology and Social Theory*, because of my focus on the role of social sciences in theological reflection, it is important to consult some of his more recent works, especially *The Word Made Strange: Theology, Language, Culture* (Blackwell: Oxford, 1997) and *Being Reconciled: Ontology and Pardon* (London: Routledge, 2003), as well as the programmatic volume he edited together with Catherine Pickstock and Graham Ward, *Radical Orthodoxy: A New Theology* (London: Routledge, 1999).

John H. Yoder and the Anabaptist tradition provide an excellent complement to these possible excesses. If Milbank's stance may be seen as aggressive or even violent, as leaning toward a totalitarian imposition of Christian views on the wider society, or as an attempt to take over the whole world in a presumptuous expression of superiority, Yoder's view offers a sound and fruitful contrast. In his proposal we find peace and nonviolence, dialogue and consensus, a patient offer and a meek witness to the world, an attitude of true humility. At the same time, Yoder's position also contains shortcomings and potential dangers. Emphasis on consensus and peace may lead us to overlook the reality of conflicts caused by structural situations of injustice. Stressing the role of communities, vital as it is, may also cause us to neglect the social setting of these communities, with the unwitting effect of maintaining or strengthening a bourgeois religion that turns its back on the impoverished victims of our world.

A fourth step is needed, then, and Dorothy Day has been our guide for it. Her life of radical solidarity with the poor, as embodied in the Catholic Worker houses of hospitality and witnessed in her writings, offers an alternative to a comfortable Christianity that may be co-opted by the dominant system. Here we find a creative combination of Lindbeck's practices, Milbank's critical stance, and Yoder's nonviolence. However, there are still some remaining ambiguities in this view. In particular, there is the danger of a merely symbolic or ornamental critique of the capitalist system. While the prophetic stance of an eschatological ethics is crucial, the concern for the wider society also plays a role in the Christian worldview.

We can also offer a summary of our findings from an ecumenical point of view, implicitly present in this book. From this perspective, one could say the Lutheran Lindbeck provides a basic stress on *sola fidei*, which at the same time may be dangerous if it overlooks the use of reason. Milbank, an Anglican, is more used to and aware of the need for a rational engagement with the world, but he does not always avoid the risks of a state-church that may eventually lean toward theocracy. Our Mennonite author, Yoder, moves away from any Constantinian understanding of the relationship between church and society; the danger here is that of sectarianism and disengagement with the "real world." Dorothy Day, as a contemporary Catholic, assumes the challenge of the option for the poor in very concrete and ordinary ways that allow her to creatively link spirituality and politics. The problem might be that, in her attempt to distance herself from the dominant Catholic approach (a hierarchical structure and a concern about organizing the whole society), she may lean toward a symbolic but ineffective position that eventually may weaken the outcome of her service to the poor.

The chart below summarizes some of the results of our analysis up to this point.

	Lindbeck	Milbank	Yoder	Dorothy Day
Area	Language	Social sciences	Culture	Politics
Denomination	Lutheran	Anglican	Mennonite	Catholic
Dominant discourse	Particularism-universalism	Naturalism-fideism	Athens-Jerusalem	Liberal-conservative
Alternative	Christian narrative	Supernatural worldview	Bethlehem versus empire	Kenotic revolution
Theological doctrines	From incarnation to eschatology	*Analogia fidei* Supernatural	Christ, the Lord, is our peace	Incarnation eschatology, creation
"Solution"	Christian practices, Christian discourse, dialogue with others	Derivative use within supernatural frame	Authentic transformation of culture	Constructive proposal, civil disobedience, common good
Risk if overemphasized	Mere conservatism	Theocracy	Self-centered sectarianism	"Ornament for capital ism"
Risk if forgotten	"Secular Christianity"	Dilution	Constantinian imposition	Bourgeois religion

At this point, it is important to look at the theological rationale that lies behind the radical proposal developed in this book. I have successively argued for the primacy of particularity versus abstract universality, for a priority of the incarnation that assumes creation, for an understanding of *analogia fidei* that includes within itself *analogia entis,* for a Christological position that grounds an authentic and radical transformation of culture, for a bottom-up revolution, for an ethic of faith understood as "theonomous autonomy." In other words, I am defending a dynamic framework that begins with the particularity of the Christian gospel, but opens itself up to embrace the whole world. Such a proposal is an advantageous way of articulating a radical theology in the face of globalization, with its double challenge of cultural homogenization and economic injustice.

Any reader of this book will have noticed a conscious attempt to build bridges among different theologians. This inclusive and constructive style resonates with Francis Schüssler Fiorenza's theological proposal for a wide reflective equilibrium.[4] Fiorenza understands the task of systematic theology as both hermeneutical and normative, and indicates four interrelated elements of this task: "the reconstructive interpretation of a tradition, the examination of relevant background theories, the consideration of warrants from experience and practice, and the attentive engagement with diverse communities of discourse."[5] These four components provide another way of bringing together the different elements analyzed throughout this book.

I dealt with the hermeneutical reconstruction interpretation of Christian tradition, according to Lindbeck's cultural-linguistic model, in chapter 1. The role of social sciences within theological reflection lay behind the considerations of chapter 2, where our dialogue with Milbank showed the importance of carefully using background relevant theories. Chapter 3 can be read as a practical example of engagement with diverse communities of discourse: in particular, the dialogue with Yoder and the Anabaptist tradition emphasized the importance of Christian communities for social transformation. Finally, the powerful witness of Dorothy Day and the Catholic Worker movement in chapter 4 illustrated the need for "retroductive" (neither deductive nor inductive) warrants from experience. However, as Fiorenza himself acknowledges, this method of broad reflective equilibrium can be too abstract and may neglect a critical consideration of the social location of the theologian. A radical reading of these same issues, as the one espoused in this book, provides a way to avoid those dangers, by grounding the theological task in the daily life of the impoverished peoples.

4. See Francis Schüssler Fiorenza, *Foundational Theology: Jesus and the Church* (New York: Crossroad, 1984), pp. 285-323.

5. Francis Schüssler Fiorenza, "From Interpretation to Rhetoric: The Feminist Challenge to Systematic Theology," in *Walk in the Ways of Wisdom: Essays in Honor of Elisabeth Schüssler Fiorenza,* ed. Shelly Matthews, Cynthia Briggs Kittredge, and Melanie Johnson-Debaufre (Harrisburg, Pa.: Trinity Press International, 2003), pp. 17-45; here, p. 37.

Revisiting Metz's Political Theology

The goal of this section is to provide an integrated reading of the results of the previous chapters through the lens of a European theologian, Johann Baptist Metz. My interest, as stated in the introduction, is twofold: on the one hand, I want to bring together those four authors (Lindbeck, Milbank, Yoder, and Day) in a way that strengthens their valuable contributions and avoids their possible shortcomings. On the other hand, I am interested in articulating a constructive version of a radical proposal that is suitable for the context of postmodern societies, especially Western Europe. For these reasons, the political theology of Metz offers an adequate framework for our discussion.

Reflections on Secularization

Metz dealt with secularization especially during the 1960s. His main reflections on this topic can be found in *Theology of the World*.[6] Once again, the context is important: the Second Vatican Council opened the windows of the church for a promising dialogue with modern society, a dialogue that seemed to have been blocked for about two centuries. The Council's affirmation of religious freedom and of the autonomy of the secular realm is considered to be part of the movement of the contemporary world. Metz regarded secularity, in this sense, as not yet finished (p. 13) but permanent (p. 41), even as a "theologically positive statement" (p. 19). Metz finds himself at ease with the "permanent and growing worldliness" of the world (p. 142). In fact, he suggests that "to Christianize the world is to secularize it" (p. 49) because Christian faith "produces a fundamental secularity of the world" (p. 64). All these affirmations make sense, as long as we keep in mind two aspects: first, a neutral definition of secularity differentiated from secularism; and second, a context that required a reconciliation between the church and modern world, moving away from previous theocratic Christendom mentalities.

Having said that, we need to consider our current situation. I am now

---

6. Johann Baptist Metz, *Theology of the World,* trans. William Glen-Doepel (New York: Herder and Herder, 1969). All parenthetical references in the main body of this section refer to this text.

consciously talking as a Christian theologian of a different generation.[7] For the generation born after the Council, the Second Vatican Council's main innovations are peacefully assumed as the common ground on which we have always lived. We take them for granted and cannot have any sort of nostalgia for previous times. The anthropological turn in philosophy and theology, religious freedom, the separation of church and state, the autonomy of the secular realm, dialogue and engagement with the world, rejection of any kind of privilege or unfair influence of the church, the adulthood of the modern human person, the political implications of our faith, and so on, are all shared assumptions that we do not discuss or contest. Our questions and concerns are of a different kind: given this situation, what is the best way to respond as a church to the challenges of contemporary reality? Is Metz's view of secularity too optimistic, too unilaterally positive, too naïve? What has been the evolution in the past forty years?

I want to reaffirm that I do not consider the possibility or the convenience of going back to a pre–Second Vatican Council situation, regarding legal relationships with the state, ecclesial organization, or the social setting of the church. But, have we not moved toward a situation in which the important issue is to "secularize the world" through ethical coherence? Now that the world has finally reached its adult autonomy, and that Christian difference has disappeared, what do we have to offer? Hasn't this process led to a loss of significance of Christianity for the contemporary world? Has our salt become tasteless (see Matt. 5:13)? It can be said that sometimes the church has assumed secularity in a too passive or uncritical way. As a result, it has lost or weakened its ability to foster alternative worldviews, practices, or relationships that are different from the secular ones. Going back to Metz's categories, if the church considers that its task is "to secularize the world," who will keep alive the dangerous memories of Jesus and all the victims of history? Who will nourish communities in which alternative narrations continue to be shared and re-created? Who will cultivate eschatological hope? Where will asymmetric solidarity be lived? Whatever happened to the eschatological proviso? In sum, how will we embody an alternative against the dominant system of global capitalism?

7. Because I was born in 1968, my whole life has taken place after Vatican II. Strictly speaking, the forty years of difference in age between Metz and myself is the period that sociologists use to define a "generation."

I am well aware that these questions go beyond Metz's theology of secularization, and that he has implicitly reformulated these issues in the following decades.[8] I also know that the reflections of a theologian and the reception of those ideas in the ordinary lives of Christians and communities are two different things. Finally, I also take into account that my criticisms are not only directed to Metz, but are more general, probably even generational. For all these reasons, it is important for us to develop a more detailed consideration of the relationship between church and society in our secular context. As a previous step, we need to analyze Metz's latter and more mature project.

Four Central Categories

In the introduction to the third and final part of his major work on fundamental practical theology, *Faith in History and Society,* Metz writes: "Only together are memory, narrative and solidarity the basic categories for a practical fundamental theology. Memory and narrative do not have their practical character without solidarity, and solidarity does not attain specifically cognitive import without memory and narrative."[9] These three categories of memory-narrative-solidarity are essential to Metz's theological project and have proved to be a fruitful contribution for a contemporary political theology. Matthew Ashley, one of the finest interpreters of Metz's thought in the North American context, has pointed to the temporal dimension of these categories that allows a dynamic interpretation of the human being: dangerous memory grounds us in a past that we remember, solidaristic hope locates us in a community open to the future, and narrative allows us to thematize our present experiences.[10] It is important to realize that the temporality of Metz's anthropology is closely linked to his emphasis on apocalyptic eschatology.[11]

8. See, for example, Johann Baptist Metz, *A Passion for God: The Mystical-Political Dimension of Christianity,* ed. and trans., with an introduction by J. Matthew Ashley (New York: Paulist, 1998).

9. Johann Baptist Metz, *Faith in History and Society: Toward a Practical Fundamental Theology,* trans. David Smith (London: Burns & Oates, 1980), p. 183. Actually I have used the new 2003 translation by J. Matthew Ashley, so far unpublished.

10. See James Matthew Ashley, *Interruptions: Mysticism, Politics, and Theology in the Work of Johann Baptist Metz* (Notre Dame: University of Notre Dame, 1998), pp. 148-53.

11. Ashley, *Interruptions,* p. 165.

This combination of contemporary English-speaking radical theology and German political theology is a fruitful one. Metz helps to integrate the somewhat loose elements present in the authors we have investigated thus far, while the general overview developed in our thesis surfaces some aspects implicit in Metz's theology. For this reason, I develop his categories following an order that maintains continuity with the logic of this thesis (narrative, eschatological reserve, dangerous memory, solidarity), instead of a more directly Metzian one (which would begin with eschatology and then develop memory, narrative, and solidarity). However, this is a merely practical decision that does not affect my interpretation of these categories, since one of my basic points is precisely its dynamic integration.

In accord with liberation theology's method and its emphasis on praxis, Metz has argued for the importance of *narrative* for theology.[12] He is fully aware of theology's performative efficacy, in the sense that narrating or storytelling maintains the capacity to create reality: it is almost a sacramental efficacy. This has a particular significance in the situation of oppressed groups and of the community of followers of Christ. However, we must take into account that Metz is a fundamental theologian and, probably for this reason, he has not developed a narrative theology as such. Instead, he has focused on the task of "defending the cognitive nature of memory and narrative"[13] against instrumental reason. Other German political theologians, especially Dorothee Sölle, have worked more explicitly in the direction of bringing out new narratives.[14] A second aspect we need to consider is Lindbeck's reminder of the importance of the narrative direction; it is not that "believers find their stories in the Bible, but rather that they make the story of the Bible their story."[15] The cross, he continues, is not a figurative symbol of suffering; rather, Christians are invited to live their suffering in a cruciform way. Metz would probably agree with this point, but sometimes the practical reception of his theology has leaned toward a more Gnostic, less powerful understanding of narratives.

The second notion we ought to consider is the *eschatological proviso or eschatological reserve.* With this phrase, Metz affirms that the reign of God

---

12. Metz, *Faith in History and Society,* § 12.

13. Ashley, *Interruptions,* p. 133.

14. See, for example, Dorothee Sölle, *The Silent Cry: Mysticism and Resistance* (Minneapolis: Fortress, 2001).

15. George A. Lindbeck, *The Nature of Doctrine: Religion and Theology in a Postliberal Age* (Philadelphia: Westminster, 1984), p. 118.

(God's hope or God's future) surpasses and relativizes every human achievement. "It brings and forces us constantly into a critical and liberating position towards the social circumstances about us."[16] Again, we find a coincidence between this position and the radical priority of the God of Life affirmed by liberation theology, as well as Milbank's indication that theology functions as a social theory that can criticize any given society. Metz developed this notion during the 1960s, and because of that context, he had a special interest in not breaking the connection to the secular world that the Second Vatican Council had recently reestablished. The eschatological proviso "does not bring about a negative but a critical attitude to the societal present,"[17] he says. This is an important reminder that some authors like Milbank may tend to forget in their negative attitude toward society. However, we must recognize also that the new context of global capitalism forces us to sharpen our negative criticisms. In any case, the eschatological reserve, the primacy of God, and the derivative use of social science mediations function as permanent correctives to our human tendency to become comfortably established in whatever achievement we may have accomplished.

In the third place, *dangerous memory* is a central category that has allowed Metz to develop his theology after Auschwitz as a critical reflection on suffering unto God.[18] The historical reality of Auschwitz as a theological source needs to be actualized in various and new contexts (Ayacucho, Rwanda, Calcutta, or Falluja, for example), because it refers directly to human suffering from the perspective of the victims of history. Given that Jesus Christ was himself unjustly detained, tortured, and assassinated, Christian faith can never be disconnected from the victims. Two aspects need to be stressed here.

On the one hand, the *memoria passionis et resurrectionis Iesu Christi* offers a lens with which to interpret all suffering, violence, and injustice: Jesus not only assumed human nature, but he did so from the social situation of the victims of history; and God's definitive intervention in the resurrection opens our hope for integral liberation. That is why the Eucharist, the memorial of Jesus' paschal mystery, is the center of Christian life. Our broken memories become integrated when we unite them to Jesus' mem-

16. Metz, *Theology of the World*, p. 153.
17. Metz, *Theology of the World*, p. 114.
18. Metz, *Faith in History and Society*, §§ 5, 6, and 11.

ory. On the other hand, these memories are dangerous and subversive. Not only because we recover the memory of the victims of history that the powers would like to cover over and forget, but also because in actualizing those memories we reaffirm our commitment to follow the path of Jesus. As Metz himself writes, and as both Sobrino's reflections on martyrdom and Yoder's insights on Christian witness point out, radical discipleship is and will be seen as "class treason" against bourgeois society and religion.[19]

Introducing our fourth notion, that of *solidarity*, Metz writes: "A practical fundamental theology tries to hold on to solidarity in its indissoluble mystical/universal and political/particular dual-structure, with the goal of protecting universalism from apathy and partial solidarity from forgetfulness and hatred."[20] Solidarity embraces all human beings, especially the most fragile ones. Given the historical situation we live in, Christian solidarity is asymmetric because God opts for the poor (against the modern conception based on ideal reciprocal recognition) and knows absolutely no limits or boundaries, neither geographical nor temporal (it includes solidarity with the dead). In this sense, we refer to a mystical universal solidarity. At the same time, Metz highlights the political and particular dimension of solidarity: Christian solidarity is always concrete, operative, grounded in reality. The preferential option for the poor, and God's calling to an ongoing conversion that breaks class divisions created and maintained by capitalism, are permanent reminders of the political implications of Christian solidarity. Liberation theology has accepted the challenge of being authentically the church of the poor, just as Dorothy Day and the Catholic Worker show a way of doing so in urban settings of wealthy countries.

This section has developed a reading of Metz that, while introducing some corrections in his earlier views, indicates a fundamental agreement between Metz and the authors I have used as interlocutors in this book — which is another way of affirming a general coincidence with my own stance. My task in the following section is to use these insights to develop a general framework to clarify the relationship between church and contemporary society. In so doing we will find some clarifications of relevance for my overall proposal of a radical ecclesiology.

19. Johann Baptist Metz, *The Emergent Church: The Future of Christianity in a Postbourgeois World,* trans. Peter Mann (New York: Crossroad, 1981), p. 15.

20. Metz, *Faith in History and Society,* § 13, p. 3.

Framework for Understanding the Relationship
between Church and Society

In this section I suggest an interpretation of the relationship between church and society that provides a framework for locating the major discussions within Catholic theology. At the same time, it offers the basis for my own proposal. We must simultaneously consider two aspects: the notion of the autonomy of secular realities and the contribution of *la nouvelle théologie* in overcoming the extrinsic understanding of supernatural grace.

With the Second Vatican Council, the church assumes the autonomy of secular or temporal realities, a fact that does not deny the whole world's dependence on God (see *Gaudium et Spes*, 36). The Council also accepts the anthropological unity that de Lubac and others had proposed as the correct interpretation of the relation between nature and the supernatural.[21] The question, then, is how these two aspects are integrated in theological discourse. We can find, accordingly, four possible combinations, as outlined in the chart below.

	Dual vision	Unified vision
Respects autonomy of secular realm	Modern Secular Christianity I	Meta-modern Radical Christianity II
Rejects autonomy of secular realm	Anti-modern Neo-Christendom III	Pre-modern Christendom IV

The first chronological possibility (position *IV* in the chart) is embodied in medieval or *pre-modern* times. The mentality of Christendom offered a unified vision of reality, including political, social, cultural, and economic aspects. All of them are dominated by or integrated under the Christian religious worldview. Of course, one ought to consider various nuances to this assertion, since different tendencies coexisted: for instance, the Thomistic tradition was always more open to the limited autonomy of the secular realm than was political Augustinianism. However, broadly

---

21. Cf., for instance, Henri de Lubac, SJ, "The 'Supernatural' at Vatican II," in *A Brief Catechesis on Nature and Grace* (San Francisco: Ignatius, 1984), pp. 177-90.

speaking, we can consider the Middle Ages as a time dominated by a unified vision of reality that does not adequately recognize the autonomy of a secular sphere.

This autonomy of the secular is one of the main contributions of modern times and the Enlightenment. In that period, however, the church's reaction was one of direct and clear opposition, exemplified by the papal encyclicals against liberalism and the anti-modernist oath. In this sense, position *III* in my chart is *anti-modern,* because it is best understood as a reaction to a new reality. In theological terms, the Neo-Scholastic distinction between nature and supernature fits perfectly into this scheme, because it paradoxically mirrors the modern dualistic view, as de Lubac has shown. The socio-political consequences of this position can be found in the Neo-Christendom and "distinction of planes" models, very influential in the first half of the twentieth century.

With the Second Vatican Council, after centuries of misunderstanding, the church embraces modernity and respects the autonomy of the secular sphere. This framework opens a new era for the relations between church and society. However, this *modern* position (number *I* of my chart) sometimes maintains the inherited nature-grace division. The conflation of these two factors has unintended negative consequences, because it offers a logical stance for secularism. If there are two separate areas of reality and the secular reality is autonomous, the logical consequence is that the religious aspects become superfluous, limited to the private realm and in the process of losing importance. This position has probably been the dominant one in post-conciliar authors, something that can be explained by the cultural context of modern optimism and by the fear of falling back into implicit Christendom mentalities.

Position *II* in the chart combines the autonomy of the secular with a unified vision of reality. This view goes beyond the dualisms of modernity, and for this reason I use the label *meta-modern.* I prefer to avoid the term *postmodern* (because in this context it would be confusing) and also Milbank's more polemical term, *counter-modern.* This view corresponds with de Lubac's position and represents my own view. The main Catholic authors in the discussion (including Rahner, Metz, and liberation theologians), usually read as "position *I,*" are better understood here. At the same time, this view offers a more fruitful socio-political alternative to the liberal-capitalistic system. This position overcomes the shortcomings of the previous ones and provides the basis for a radical political action.[22]

My proposal, then, is an alternative and radical reading of the *meta-modern* position *II* based on nonviolence, the option for the poor, and a positive respect and recognition of pluralism. By doing so, I want to avoid the flaws of Milbank or the *communio* school (currently, the dominant reading of de Lubac, or position *II*) while revisiting the main contributions of liberation theology. One of my underlying principles is an emphasis on the role of the church for social transformation: Christian communities in solidarity with the poor embody an alternative social space in which the nonviolent revolution or integral liberation can take place. I am aware that my view may be at odds with the dominant liberal or conservative discourses, but I think that it is the most accurate reading of the Council and the most adequate Christian response to our reality.

Reconsidering Faith-Justice

What is the contribution of Christian communities to social transformation? How can we articulate the intimate connection between faith and justice in such a way that it is at the same time socially effective and evangelically coherent? What are the structures of plausibility for the strengthening of the mystical-political dimension of Christianity in our postmodern world? I attempt to clarify these questions, in the first place, by analyzing two examples.

In 1974-75, the Society of Jesus (the largest Catholic male religious order) held its very influential Thirty-Second General Congregation, in which it defined its mission as follows: "To engage, under the standard of the Cross, in the crucial struggle of our time: the struggle for faith, and that struggle for justice which it includes" (CG 32, D2, no. 12). In this, the

22. This framework helps to clarify the theological situation in the Catholic field during the late twentieth century. While John Milbank tries to show a sharp distinction between what he calls the German school of Rahner, Metz, and liberation theology ("naturalize the supernatural" or position *modern–I* in our scheme) and the French school of de Lubac ("supernaturalize the natural"), both currents correspond to position *meta-modern–II* of my chart, in the sense that both defend a unified vision of reality and both accept the autonomy of the secular. This is also the official teaching of Second Vatican Council, against the conservative minority during the Council.

Jesuits were following a general trend within the Catholic Church during the decade of the 1970s, with Latin American liberation theology and base communities, European political theology, or the 1971 Synod of Bishops, which declared that justice is an intrinsic element of the Catholic faith. In 1995, the Thirty-Fourth General Congregation of the Society of Jesus reaffirmed its fundamental option for faith and justice, but by that time the language had changed. Faith and justice were explicitly considered in connection with culture and inter-religious dialogue, and "communities of solidarity" were regarded as the main actor in the struggle for justice.[23]

Is there an opposition between the two Congregations? Is CG 34 a "correction" of CG 32? Absolutely not! Then, what happened and how are we to interpret the shift? To put it simply, the experience of those decades and the new global-local context made Jesuits more aware of the complexities of the struggle for justice and the dynamics of contemporary injustice, so deeply rooted in cultural attitudes, values, structures, systems, and relationships. The Thirty-Fourth General Congregation puts it this way: "One of the most important contributions we can make to critical contemporary culture is to show that the structural injustice in the world is rooted in value systems promoted by a powerful modern culture which is becoming global in its impact" (no. 108). An obvious consequence is that, if we need communities of solidarity to overcome injustice, a crucial task is actually to foster such communities. For this reason, the document reads: "In each of our different apostolates, we must create communities of solidarity in seeking justice. Working together with our colleagues, every Jesuit in his ministry can and should promote justice in one or more of the following ways: *(a)* direct service and accompaniment of the poor, *(b)* developing awareness of the demands of justice joined to the social responsibility to achieve it, *(c)* participating in social mobilization for the creation of a more just social order" (no. 68). This need has been one of the conclusions of this book.

The second example I want to consider refers to the context in which theological reflection takes place and is communicated to its wider audience. More specifically, I focus on liberal or progressive theology, for instance, liberation theology. It is somewhat surprising that authors like Jon Sobrino and Pedro Casaldáliga receive attention in the main Spanish

23. See Patxi Álvarez de los Mozos, SJ, *Comunidades de solidaridad* (Bilbao: Mensajero, 2002).

newspaper, *El País*, given its general secularist or anticlerical editorial line, which goes along with its political social-democratic opinions. It could be considered that those theologians are being successful in their attempt to communicate the critical message of the gospel to a broad audience. If that were the case, it would be good news. But I suspect the situation is more complex. Could it be that *El País* is "using" those theologians to criticize yet again the church, to advance secularism one more step? Now if we realize that the owner of that newspaper, Jesús de Polanco, is the third wealthiest person in Spain, and number 210 in the world, worth $2,800 million, can we seriously think that this "progressive" newspaper is favoring the cause of the poor? Should we, as Christians, defend such a strategy that weakens the church and favors secular "progressive" forces?[24] In terms of content, I am personally coming to realize that if there is a litmus test for what a "liberal" or progressive theology means, it is capitalism. The key question is: Do you actually oppose the forces of global capitalism? If you do not, you are just maintaining the oppressive system. And I am afraid that most of the so-called liberal theology falls under this category.

Now it will be more clear why I argue for an ecclesiological priority in our struggle for social change. If the church embodies a radical alternative to the dominant system, it will offer some hope for the victims of history. If it does not, it will simply be playing the game of global capitalism, even if it is a supposedly "progressive" theology. The clear connection between faith and justice (peacefully accepted in church circles) has an obvious parallel in the pair secularization-injustice. If we recognize that faith is intrinsically linked to justice, it cannot be surprising that the opposite relation is also true: secularism advances injustice.[25] The current context of global capitalism (the only dominant social figure of secularism today) is showing this plainly on a daily basis. If we want to oppose those forces, we need to strengthen our Christian communities as the embodiment of a

24. Something similar could be said of the North American academic context. Harvard University, supposedly a "liberal" university, offers a number of well-attended courses on liberation theologies. With an endowment of over $22 billion (larger than the gross national product of Croatia, Iraq, Sri Lanka, Kenya, and 150 other countries), can anyone think seriously that this institution opts for the poor?

25. I am aware of the possible misreading of my proposal as if it were fundamentalist or sectarian, but I hope that the considerations developed in this book help to clarify my own view. See also a clear and intelligent assessment of some of these issues in Phillip D. Kenneson, *Beyond Sectarianism: Re-Imagining Church and World* (Harrisburg: Trinity, 1999).

radical alternative. This implies, as I have argued in this book, a different consideration of language, secular social sciences, culture, and politics. It implies a vision rooted in Jesus Christ. The following section offers a very concrete example of how to flesh out this vision.

Jesuit Refugee Service (JRS) as a Radical Community

Twenty-five years ago, in the context of the "boat people" refugee crisis in Eastern Asia, Father Arrupe, superior general of the Society of Jesus, created the Jesuit Refugee Service (JRS).[26] It was just another example of Arrupe's great vision to respond with evangelical creativity to the signs of the time, often dominated by injustice, violence, and suffering. His personal and institutional interest on the situation of refugees around the globe galvanized the development of a small but significant presence of Jesuits among them. In fact, Arrupe's last public words were addressed to a group of Jesuits working with refugees in Thailand: "I will say one more thing, and please don't forget it. Pray. Pray much. Problems such as these are not solved by human efforts. I am telling you things that I want to emphasize, a message — perhaps my 'swan song' — for the Society."[27]

In these twenty-five years JRS has grown and expanded its presence. It is still a small organization and will probably remain so. Over five hundred workers contribute to the work of JRS at the grassroots level, the majority of whom work on a voluntary basis, including about a hundred Jesuits, eighty-five religious from other congregations and more than three hundred laypeople. These figures do not include the large number of refugees recruited to take part in the programs as teachers, health workers, and others. The central headquarters in Rome hold a staff of ten people, while the worldwide organization covers ten regions in more than fifty countries of the five continents. JRS is present in detention centers in the United States and Belgium, with internally displaced population in Colombia and Chiapas, and in refugee camps in Guinea Conakry, and Burundi. When a

26. With this section, of course, I am not implying that JRS embodies all aspects treated in this thesis, nor that it is an ideal micro-church, nor that it is the best or only example. For instance, the Community of Sant'Egidio offers another good example, with its emphases on prayer, communication of the gospel, solidarity with the poor, ecumenism, and dialogue.

27. Pedro Arrupe, SJ, *Essential Writings,* selected with an introduction by Kevin Burke, SJ, foreword by Peter-Hans Kolvenbach, SJ (Maryknoll, N.Y.: Orbis, 2004), p. 171.

terrible tsunami killed hundreds of thousands of people in Asia in 2006, JRS was already there, in Sri Lanka and in Aceh, Indonesia. Once again, its humble and effective presence in the field, with the people, provided a clear assessment of the needs, a constructive response, and a source of hope.

JRS has defined its mission with three verbs: *to serve, to accompany, to advocate.* It accompanies refugees and forcibly displaced persons, serving them as companions, advocating their cause in an uncaring world. In particular, JRS focuses on forgotten refugees. The mission to *serve* has led to a particular emphases on education. Nowadays, 150,000 children and youth are being educated in JRS-run primary and secondary schools. They constitute a significant part of the 650,000 direct beneficiaries of JRS's work in the refugee camps — for an estimated 2.5 million of total indirect beneficiaries. While working and serving is of course important, one of the main features of JRS is the vital role given to the mission to *accompany* and presence. JRS is a small organization, but its credibility and strength come mainly from its humble sharing of life with the people in the camps. Differences with much bigger NGOs or governmental agencies can be seen in housing, lifestyle, and the pastoral engagement of JRS workers in the camps during the weekends. Finally, JRS has never forgotten its important mission to *advocate* and defend the rights of refugees. Probably the most clear example could be seen at the Nobel Peace Prize ceremony in Oslo on December 10, 1997, when the world watched Tun Channareth of JRS-Cambodia accept the Nobel Peace Prize on behalf of the International Campaign to Ban Landmines (ICBL).

Throughout this book I have argued for the crucial role of radical communities, rooted in Jesus Christ and in the lives of the poor, as an alternative to the dominant system. JRS is such an example of creative communities, in which Jesuits, other religious men and women, and laypersons share their work, their mission, their faith, their commitment to the forgotten refugees, their lives. But anyone who has had any experience with JRS will realize that I am not talking about any ideal of pure and perfect achievements. JRS is a radical example of what sinners can do when they follow God's calling. The obvious weaknesses of JRS are also part of a radical embodiment, one that does not need "perfection" to shine forth.

At the same time, JRS's continued presence and service among refugees is a clear witness of Christian life. Furthermore, JRS has also been blessed with some martyrs *strictu sensu*, whose lives show simply the possible consequences of a radical engagement for the justice that springs from faith. For example, Richie Fernando was a Jesuit scholastic working at Banteay Prieb, the JRS technical school for the handicapped in Cambodia. One student there, Sarom, was considered disruptive and came to the school one day with a hand grenade. Richie Fernando came up behind Sarom and grabbed him. "Let me go, teacher; I do not want to kill you," Sarom pleaded. But he dropped his grenade, and it fell between him and Richie. In a flash Richie Fernando was dead, falling over with Sarom still grasped in his arms, protecting him from the violence he made. It was October 17, 1996. Just twelve days later, Archbishop Christophe Munzihirwa, SJ, was killed in Bukavu, Zaire. While he was not a formal member of JRS, his martyrdom was caused by his strong and public defense of the refugees during the Great Lakes crisis.

In sum, JRS shows a clear and humble example of the kind of church I have been advocating in this book. JRS embodies a radical ecclesiology that gives priority to daily praxis of solidarity, uses social sciences and techniques as a tool to serve and defend refugees, creates a culture of revolutionary nonviolence in the midst of conflict, and stands in solidarity with the poor sharing life with them. JRS illustrates the radical consequences of being rooted in Jesus Christ. This is what every Christian community is invited to live, with creativity, in their own context.

Concluding Remarks: Toward a Radical Ecclesiology

A friend of mine, a religious woman who has spent most of her adult life among poor Muslim peasants in the mountains of Morocco, told me some time ago: "I love to be here, and I am convinced of the fruitfulness of our deep dialogue with Islam on a daily basis. During these years I have learned much about our need to silently surrender to God. But you know what? I *need* to pray directly to Jesus. As a Christian, I feel that need, and I cannot live without it." Her impressive testimony has often made me consider my own need to personally engage Jesus on a daily basis. Moreover, sometimes I think about the similarities between the harsh conditions that Christians endure in many Muslim locations and the severe secular environment of Western European cities. What do we need? I hope this book, with its proposal for a radical ecclesiology, helps us to grasp an answer that ought to be rooted in Jesus Christ.

We need to nourish and strengthen our identity as radical disciples of

Jesus. We need to foster a deep personal relationship with him. We cannot take that for granted; rather, we need to cultivate our spiritual life. For several decades, it seems that we have somehow shied away from this aspect. But now our need for a profound and intense spirituality has become evident. This *mystical* dimension has to be encouraged at the personal and the communal levels. The importance of prayer cannot be overlooked. In particular, liturgy should be rediscovered as a way to embody, in social and visible fashion, the alternative reality that springs from our God. Only when rooted in Jesus Christ can we promote a radical alternative to the dominant system.

I am convinced that we Christians do have an alternative. It is a radical *political* alternative, not in the narrow sense of the term *politics* (limited to political parties, elections, lobbying, policy making, and so on) but in the broad sense of polis, the city, the public space, the common good. This political concern of the *ekklesia,* the church of the poor, necessarily will lead to the struggle for justice. The current phase of global capitalism only adds urgency to the call for a radical alternative. At the same time, we must remember that *politics* is also related with the word *polemos,* conflict, battle, struggle. In the midst of conflicts, violence, and war, Christians must embody a much needed nonviolent alternative. When the ideologues of the empire are renovating a "theological coverage" of their interests, a theo-political alternative must be fleshed out. In the face of global capitalism and imperial wars, we need a radical alternative of peace and justice, based on the poor and on revolutionary nonviolence. We need to be the church that embodies such an alternative.

Thus, a radical political ecclesiology has evident *ecclesial* dimensions as well. We need to face the challenge of internal coherence. As we pray in every diaconate ordination, we beg that every disciple of Jesus Christ hears as directed to her or him: "Believe what you read, teach what you believe, and practice what you teach." If we want to be a radical alternative to the world (and, as I have argued in this book, this is what God wants from us and this is what we need) we ought to embody alternative practices, relationships, and structures. We need to embody an alternative to the logic of the dominant system. The prophet Isaiah said it clearly, "they shall beat their sword into plowshares . . . they shall learn war no more" (Isa. 2:4). When we live that way, "all the nations shall stream" to us (Isa. 2:2). Or as Jesus himself put it, we are the salt of the earth and the light of the world. But if we do not live the radical alternative we are supposed to embody, then we become absolutely worthless (Matt. 5:13-14).

PART TWO

Initial Meditation

The first part of this book (with its convergent perspectives drawing from language, culture, politics, and the social sciences) has led us to the conclusion that we urgently need to develop a radical theology, one centered on the lived experience of the church. The Christian community, firmly rooted in Jesus Christ, proposes a radical alternative to the system that now dominates our world. In this second part I draw out the implications of this conclusion by developing a radical ecclesiology structured around the notion of the body of Christ. Each chapter in this part analyzes an aspect of the ecclesial and social implications that derive from Eucharistic communion. First we examine some significant examples of how the body of Christ has been experienced and understood in the course of history. The second chapter then interprets the ecclesial sacraments as communal practices that form, nourish, strengthen, and heal the body that is engendered as a radical alternative to the established order. Third, we turn our attention to the mystically committed experience of the body of Christ as it was lived out faithfully by four privileged witnesses of the twentieth century. The fourth and final chapter develops in more detail the implications of my proposed ecclesiology on the level of daily life, politics, economics, and culture.

Before beginning my treatment of these topics, however, I offer a more contemplative focus. To do so, I draw on the following meditation of José Ramón Rodríguez Martín,[1] which grows directly out the experience of

---

1. José Ramón Rodríguez Martín, "Cuerpo humano: lectura martirial de 1 Corintios 12, 12," at www.servicioskoinonia.org/martirologico/textos/cuerpo.htm.

many Latin American Christian communities. It is entitled "Human Body: A Martyrial Reading of 1 Corinthians 12.12":

The human body, though it is formed of many parts,
is only one body. So also Christ (1 Cor. 12:12).
    Your body, our body,
must have the deep, imperturbable, serene,
accusing, and consoling eyes of Óscar Romero.
    Your body, our body,
must manifest the constant smile of Héctor Gallego.
    Your body, our body,
needs the spirit of struggle, the defiance,
and the coherence of Ernesto Guevara.
    Your body, our body,
requires the tenderness, the affection,
and the simplicity of Teresa of Calcutta.
    Your body, our body,
must keep on acquiring the mind, the ability to analyze,
the intelligence, and the wisdom of Ignacio Ellacuría.
    Your body, our body,
needs the unlimited capacity for loving
  — even those who most hurt us — of Martin Luther King.
    Your body, our body,
must be radically faithful, like Francis of Assisi.
    Your body, our body,
desires the constancy, the tenacity,
the evangelical stubbornness of Dom Helder Câmara.
    Your body, our body,
longs to be strong and indefatigable,
as was Fray Bartolomé de Las Casas.
    Your body, our body
must know how to search inward for love,
which must then be projected outward toward others, like Augustine.
    Your body, our body,
to stay alive needs the capacity for peaceful struggle,
and active nonviolence of Mahatma Gandhi.
    Your body, our body,
needs nothing to hide our face

like the ski mask that covers that of Marcos,
but it does long to have his passion for justice,
for dignity, and for fighting against forgetfulness.
    Your body, our body,
must seek to draw close, as Bishop Leónidas Proaño
did to the Indians of Ecuador.
    Your body, our body,
must be strong and tough of heart
in order to pour out its life as did Lucho Espinal.
    Your body, our body,
is the instrument for building the kingdom,
and must surrender its hands and its voice, if need be,
as did Victor Jara.
    Your body, our body,
following the banner of Augusto César Sandino,
will come to a courageous end, because our cause is that of God.
    Your body, our body,
must exhale a hunger for truth,
such as that came forth from Bishop Gerardi.
    Your body, our body,
must shout out words of anger and words of hope,
like the poems of José Martí.
    Your body, our body,
must be filled with the utopian dream and consciousness
of Emiliano Zapata.
    Your body, our body,
must give firm and compelling testimony,
as did Bishop Angelelli.
    Your body, our body,
must know how to remain always at the side of the dying
and to be always pardoning, as was Joan Alsina.
Father,
we don't want to keep being shelled
by the cannons of wealth and power;
we want carnations to stop up their barrels.
Father,
we don't want to keep working from sun to sun,
only to have the boss rob us of our sweat,

our food, our money, our labor;
we want the dignity to fight for what is ours.
Father,
we don't want the wind to blow any stronger through our houses
and to snuff out our candle of hope for a future that now seems so
dim;
we want a fierce fire that always burns bright.
Father,
we don't want to keep seeing our people disappearing,
being killed, tortured, and eliminated,
while those responsible just keep on watching TV in their Christian
suburb.
Father,
we don't want to go on that way,
and we know that you don't want it either,
but until the Utopia of your Reign is finally present among us,
until justice and love overwhelm the idols of capital,
until every person feels the pain of others who are suffering,
until every woman becomes indignant at the injustice done to the rest,
    we will keep on shouting,
    we will keep on pleading,
    we will keep on denouncing,
    we will keep on dreaming,
    we will keep on working,
    we will keep on declaring
    that you behold the suffering of your children
    and are coming forth in might to liberate them (Exod. 3:7).

5. Sources for the Root

Following a classical method in theology — seen especially in Roman Catholic circles — this chapter suggests three different approaches to the three basic sources for my project in radical ecclesiology: Scripture, tradition, and ecclesial teachings. While the conversation partners in the first part of this book were mainly non-Catholic authors, the reader will notice a more explicit Roman Catholic perspective in the second part. However, both parts are harmonically interpenetrating. For this reason I ask of the non-Catholic reader patience with the general scheme and terminology used in the following pages. In fact, this chapter does not offer a complete and systematic development of what those sources could unfold for Catholic theology.[1] Rather, I simply present three partial sketches that may throw some light on our topic. In other words, I do not intend to offer a comprehensive survey of these sources, but merely seek to illustrate the issue with a few significant examples.

This chapter seeks to clarify some of the social implications of the Eucharist, as it has been desired, lived, and formulated by a number of Christian communities throughout history. Specifically, the first section provides an analysis of Paul's first letter to the Corinthians, following an approach drawn from the social sciences. The second section sweeps forward over a thousand years to thirteenth-century Liège, Lower Countries, and studies the Eucharistic praxis of a group of creative communities of

---

1. See a splendid survey, based on patristic sources, in Jean Marie R. Tillard, OP, *Flesh of the Church, Flesh of Christ: At the Source of the Ecclesiology of Communion,* trans. Madeleine M. Beaumont (Collegeville, Minn.: Liturgical, 2001).

women who lived in solidarity with the poor. Another historical leap, in the third section of this chapter, introduces the reflections of the twentieth-century pontifical magisterium. It is only in this analogical and flexible sense that this chapter follows the classical theological scheme of Scripture, tradition, and magisterium.

The Body of Christ in First-Century Corinth

In recent years, a social science–based reading of Saint Paul's letters to the Corinthian community has gained strength. What can we learn from this research for our ecclesial understanding and praxis of the Eucharist? There are a number of relevant aspects that arise with this perspective that can nourish our spiritual and ecclesial life. This section analyzes Paul's notion of the body of Christ, as well as its socio-political implications. Contributions from the fields of sociology, cultural anthropology, archaeology, economics, and political science will help us to grasp the diverse aspects of the body of Christ as it was lived in Corinth — and as Paul understood it.

The Notion of Body: Terminological Clarification

Scholars agree that Paul did not invent the term *body (sōma)*, but he was "apparently the first to apply it to a community within the larger society and to the personal responsibilities of people for one another rather than for their civic duties."[2] For instance, Gosnell Yorke offers a summary of the history of research regarding the different sources of the notion of body in the Pauline corpus. He finds nine hypotheses, some drawing on extra–New Testament sources (Hebrew Scriptures, rabbinic Judaism, Gnosticism, and Greco-Roman philosophy) and intra–New Testament ones (Paul's Christophanic encounter, Paul's Eucharistic Christology, Paul's nuptial theology, and Paul's theology of baptism).[3] The novelty of Pauline theology stems from the fact that, against a corporate-institutional approach, Paul

2. Robert Banks, *Paul's Idea of Community: The Early House Churches in Their Cultural Setting*, rev. ed. (Peabody, Mass.: Hendrickson, 1994), p. 66.
3. Gosnell L. O. R. Yorke, *The Church as the Body of Christ in the Pauline Corpus: A Reexamination* (Lanham, Md.: University Press of America, 1991), pp. 1-10.

emphasizes the communitarian and personal aspects included in the notion of body, stressed by his Christological and ecclesial experience.

It is important to recognize that, in the Pauline corpus, the term *sōma* bears a comprehensive meaning that includes four aspects: the bread, Christ's body, the church, and the body of the Christian.[4] No reductive interpretation will be able to acknowledge the full richness of meanings included in this Pauline expression. For example, this helps us understand the different meanings of body in the phrase "discerning the body" (1 Cor. 11:29). As Dale Martin says, "Greco-Roman constructions of the body were significantly different from our own. Categories and dichotomies that have shaped modern conceptions of the body for the past few centuries — dichotomies like natural/supernatural, physical/spiritual (or, for those embarrassed by the spiritual side of the pair, physical/psychological) — did not exist in the ancient world as dichotomies."[5] For this reason, Paul sees no sharp distinction between public and private, and, accordingly, he is able to link both aspects under the notion of body.

The Weak and the Strong: A Sociological Approach

Conflicts between "the weak" and "the strong" within the Corinthian community are well known. Sociological approaches suggest that these differences regarding ways of doing and thinking are based on social stratification in the midst of that same community. Gerd Theissen's seminal work,[6] although criticized, continues to provide the general framework for analysis and interpretation. Specifically, we can assume three basic conclusions as our starting point. First, Hellenistic Christian communities were neither a proletarian movement nor a phenomenon of wealthy and powerful classes. Second, there was a clear internal social stratification within the Corinthian church, which leads Theissen to interpret the conflicts among

4. Dale B. Martin, *The Corinthian Body* (New Haven and London: Yale University Press, 1995), pp. 194-95. On this issue I agree with Martin's integral interpretation, against Yorke's reductive one, which avoids any mystical or metaphorical association between the body of the church and the body of Christ (Yorke, *The Church as the Body of Christ in the Pauline Corpus*, pp. 7, 49, 61, and 120).

5. Martin, *The Corinthian Body*, p. 3.

6. Gerd Theissen, *The Social Setting of Pauline Christianity: Essays on Corinth*, ed. and trans. with an introduction by John H. Schütz (Philadelphia: Fortress, 1982).

the weak and the strong as class-specific: the more liberal positions of the strong correspond to the upper classes, while the lower strata maintain more conservative ideas. Third, Paul responds to this social conflict from a theological perspective, and proposes "benevolent patriarchalism" as his solution: this "love-patriarchalism allows social inequalities to continue but transfuses them with a spirit of concern, of respect, and of personal solicitude."[7] Paul's position, then, is seen as moderate social conservatism, a creative solution with historical effectiveness.

The first two conclusions — pluralism and social stratification — seem to describe adequately the Corinthian context,[8] but there is a danger of reading them in a functionalist and static way. The issue is not only the degree to which the Christian community was similar to its surrounding society, but — more important — how community and society diverged. In other words, Theissen seems to describe the initial conditions, but it is essential to explore how that social stratification was transformed in the midst of the community.[9] At this point, the so-called new consensus faces serious criticisms with important implications for ecclesial praxis.

It is evident that, in this social context and in the face of the existent divisions, Paul seeks the unity of the Corinthian community. The issue is to know how he does it and what his horizon is. Margaret Mitchell has shown that Paul effectively uses a curious rhetorical strategy: he initially identifies himself with the strong and then asks them to give up their own interests for the sake of the weak.[10] By doing so, Paul pursues a strategy of status reversal, siding with the weak, directing his criticisms primarily toward the strong, and then overturning the normal expectations of upper-class ideology. While traditional "homonoia" speeches invoke a unified,

7. Theissen, *The Social Setting of Pauline Christianity,* p. 139.

8. These claims are assumed, among other authors, by Wayne A. Meeks, *The First Urban Christians: The Social World of the Apostle Paul,* 2nd ed. (New Haven and London: Yale University Press, 2003 [orig. ed., 1983]), leading to the so-called new consensus.

9. Similar criticisms have been pointed out by C. K. Robertson, *Conflict in Corinth: Redefining the System* (New York: Peter Lang, 2001), p. 15, and Antonio González, *Reinado de Dios e imperio. Ensayo de teología social* (Santander: Sal Terrae, 2003), pp. 201-47. Interesting background information can be found in Ekkehard W. Stegemann and Wolfgang Stegemann, *The Jesus Movement: A Social History of Its First Century,* trans. O. C. Dean Jr. (Minneapolis: Fortress, 1999), and Rodney Stark, *The Rise of Christianity: A Sociologist Reconsiders History* (Princeton, N.J.: Princeton University Press, 1996).

10. Margaret M. Mitchell, *Paul and the Rhetoric of Reconciliation: An Exegetical Investigation of the Language and Composition of 1 Corinthians* (Tübingen: J. C. B. Mohr, 1991).

stable cosmos, Paul defends an alternative status system according to which the strong are weak and the weak are strong. The crucified Christ (1 Cor. 1:23-25) is the central icon of the gospel, the paradigm of the radically different value system of a new realm.[11]

Therefore, on the basis of this rhetorical strategy and this theological conviction, Paul modifies a Greco-Roman mentality that (built on the notion of body) aimed at maintaining social hierarchy by telling lower social classes they should remain under the powerful. Paul's ability consists precisely in using the same rhetorical instrument (the unity of the body) to achieve radically different objectives. Whereas the upper classes sought to maintain the status quo and to defend their own interests, Paul turned the social situation upside down in order to defend the weak and the poor.

At this point we also see that the social horizon toward which Paul leans is not a conservative "benevolent patriarchalism" that maintains social inequalities.[12] It is precisely this ideology that Paul denounces, unmasks, and corrects. It may be excessive, or anachronistic, to say that Paul defended a radical egalitarianism. However, we can affirm that he did foster alternative and radically inclusive relationships.[13] Paul's central argument aims to transform unequal relationships by creating, in the midst of the Christian community, an alternative social space in which the weak ought not to be oppressed by the dominant hierarchical social structure.

Purity System: Cultural Anthropology Approach

Cultural anthropology suggests some perspectives for a better understanding of the problems Paul addresses in his first letter to the Corinthians. From among the many issues involved, I select the two that I consider most interesting: the system of purity (especially vis-à-vis the physical body) and the system of patronage (more directly connected to the social body). These two cultural-anthropological approaches shed light on and deepen our understanding of this issue.

First of all, let us consider the meaning of the cultural code of purity

11. Martin, *The Corinthian Body,* pp. 60-103.

12. This a central element of Martin's criticism to Theissen. See Martin, *The Corinthian Body,* pp. 42, 76, 103, 135, and 196.

13. See John H. Elliott, "Jesus Was Not an Egalitarian: A Critique of an Anachronistic and Idealistic Theory," *Biblical Theology Bulletin* 32 (2002): 75-91.

in Paul's correspondence to the Corinthian community. This is treated in an analysis of body and pollution. As Jerome Neyrey has rightly noted, the greatest challenge for a holy body is pollution and the most dangerous risk for a whole body is division.[14] Here we find the core of Paul's position in the Corinthian conflict, especially if we bear in mind that physical-biological dimensions cannot be separated from socio-political ones. While Paul favors "body control" and defends the primacy of the community over the individual, his opponents favor relatively limited body control and honor individualism. Both the argument and the underlying worldview reflect the central importance of the notions of purity and pollution in a Hellenistic cultural context.

Furthermore, it is important to bear in mind that the Greco-Roman worldview basically used two interpretative models, in both the medical and the socio-political realms. The first model, imbalance etiology, interprets health as stability (in the biological and the social bodies). This model was preferred by the powerful social classes. The second model understood illness as invasion. This model flows from a much more vulnerable social situation vis-à-vis threat from external forces.[15]

During the Corinthian conflict, while "the strong operate by a logic of balance, with its relative lack of concern about pollution or invasion, Paul operates by a logic of invasion"[16] in face of what he considers an external cultural invasion. For example, Paul regards incest as a scandal that threatens the community (1 Cor. 5); he opposes eating meat that has been sacrificed to idols (1 Cor. 8); and he remains implacable against the divisions that take place during the Eucharistic celebration (1 Cor. 11). Paul argues from a threefold persuasion. First, he says that the body of Christ is a real body, structured and differentiated. Second, he considers the church a system that defines group identity from a needed purity and boundaries. Third, Paul is convinced that the Eucharist expresses and strengthens community identity, internal consistency, and external borders. Obviously, Paul does not defend a Puritan, or merely rigorist, view based on individual ethics. Rather, he struggles to guarantee that the alternative — a Christian community — can endure in the midst of the pervasive cultural system.

14. Jerome H. Neyrey, SJ, "Body Language in 1 Corinthians: The Use of Anthropological Models for Understanding Paul and His Opponents," *Semeia* 35 (1986): 129-70.

15. Martin, *The Corinthian Body*, pp. 159-160, and 197.

16. Martin, *The Corinthian Body*, p. 163.

The second issue that we examine using cultural anthropological methods is the patronage system. It is well known that honor was among the key cultural values in Hellenistic society. In particular, Paul uses what anthropologists call "patron-client relationships" to explain God's relationship to the community of believers. He accepts a God of order and purity who clarifies social and communal relationships, but also (given Christ's centrality, which inverts social values, relationships, and mentalities) a God of disorder and alteration who deeply modifies those same relationships.[17]

Again we find the subversive Pauline vision that, while grounding Christian community in the body of Christ, proposes alternative relationships to the dominant patronage system. The conflict with the "super apostles" (see 2 Cor. 11:13), already seen in several disputes of 1 Corinthians, refers to Paul's opposition to a group of local leaders who tried to make use of their social and economic patronage within the Christian community.[18] The "strong" of the community are not simply the wealthy or the morally relaxed. They are the ones who aim to employ their privileged social position to attain community leadership. They are the ones who, in order to strengthen their social status, do not hesitate to establish marriages of convenience (1 Cor. 5), to present legal battles in secular courts (1 Cor. 6), to participate in banquets and sacrifices that take place in pagan temples (1 Cor. 8–10), to promote exclusions and differences in the Lord's Supper (1 Cor. 11), or to uncritically follow the path of ecstatic spirituality (1 Cor. 12–14).

However, the Christian community was a small minority in Corinth. For this reason, their members were surrounded by the regular practices of that chaotic harbor city. They lived the daily problem of their multiple and overlapping memberships in the social network: neighborhood, leisure, family, friends, jobs, worship. Is there a unifying principle or identity that gathers those diverse social interactions? Many members of the community "saw themselves *primarily* as patrons, clients, masters, slaves, Jews, gentiles, males, [and] females" with the logical effect that "their roles as fellow believers in Christ were relegated to a secondary status."[19] Against this

17. Jerome H. Neyrey, SJ, "Patronage and Honor, Order and Disorder: God in 1 Corinthians," in *Render to God: New Testament Understandings of the Divine* (Minneapolis: Augsburg Fortress, 2004), pp. 144-90.

18. John K. Chow, *Patronage and Power: A Study of Social Networks in Corinth* (Sheffield: Journal for the Study of the Old Testament Press, 1992).

19. Robertson, *Conflict in Corinth,* p. 181.

view, Paul defends the primacy of Christian identity, based on a twofold strategy: "the redefinition of the overall system as the *ekklesia* and the reconfiguration of interrelationships from collegial to familial terms."[20] Paul is well aware that this is the only way not to fall under the oppressive net of the patronage system: it is crucial to build, to nourish, and to strengthen alternative relationships and a strong communal identity. This is precisely what the notion of the body of Christ provides.

The Physical Space of the House: An Archaeological Approach

The way in which the Corinthian community celebrated the Eucharist intrigues scholars. Jerome Murphy-O'Connor has formulated the best-known hypothesis, based on the archaeological excavations at Anapogla (Corinth), suggesting that the community used to meet in the villa of some of the wealthy families of the community.[21] These relatively ample houses had a courtyard and a *triclinium* (dining room). Yet, archaeological data suggest that the space (approximately 70 m² of courtyard and 40 m² of dining room space) would be insufficient for all of the participants gathered for the Lord's Supper (approximately fifty regular members and a few guests). This fact may explain the conflict of 1 Corinthians 11: since everyone could not fit in the allotted space at the same time, some of them had to eat before the others. However, the scandal Paul critiques is that the wealthy (the house owners and their friends who were blessed with more leisure time that in turn allowed them to gather earlier) failed to wait for the poor, who were restricted by a less flexible working schedule. The Corinthian community functioned as if there were first- and second-class believers. The former ate warm and well-prepared dishes while reclining, while the latter came in late and ate cold leftovers while sitting. "One goes hungry and another becomes drunk" (1 Cor. 11:21). This situation tears the fabric of the body of Christ and so, says Paul, it is impossible to celebrate the Eucharist.

Murphy-O'Connor's explanation is clear and consistent. However, it remains a hypothesis based more on intuition than evidence. For example,

20. Robertson, *Conflict in Corinth*, p. 228.
21. Jerome Murphy-O'Connor, OP, *St. Paul's Corinth: Texts and Archaeology*, 3rd ed. (Collegeville, Minn.: Liturgical, 2002), pp. 175-98.

some recent archaeological excavations near the eastern section of Corinth's theater provide data for alternatives to this dominant hypothesis. Here investigators have discovered multilevel structures, with shops and workshops on the ground-floor level and living space for the craftsmen and their families on the upper floors. On the one hand, this fact could explain the access of poor persons to meat consumption in the *taberna*. On the other hand, the same findings suggest a new gathering space for the Christian community. They would not need to go to a wealthy family's villa. Instead, they could gather for worship in those workshop-dwellings with space for about fifty people. This new hypothesis offers a better explanation of the incident at Troas in which a young man named Eutychus fell down from a third-floor window while celebrating the Eucharist (Acts 20:7-9).[22]

This particular approach is an invitation to continue searching for new hypotheses with creativity, to make use of our own imagination, and to analyze everything critically. For example, although the alternative to Murphy-O'Connor's proposal is based on solid archaeological data, it still forms part of a wider movement that highlights the role of economics in the various conflicts within the Corinthian community. Let us now consider that economic dimension.

The Wealthy and the Poor: The Economic Approach

In recent years, a number of scholars have criticized the so-called sociological new consensus growing around Theissen, Meeks, and others, particularly with respect to the assumption of an unequal social stratification within the Christian community. This new current of thought affirms that Pauline communities were poor, their members overwhelmingly urban plebs. This contrasts with an earlier vision that regarded the Christian community merely as a mirror of the larger society. That vision awarded a key role to well-off families. The new line of interpretation not only offers a more accurate view of Corinth's socio-economic reality, but it also avoids the elusive use of the sociological notion of social status.

---

22. This paragraph draws on David G. Horrell, "Domestic Space and Christian Meetings at Corinth: Imagining New Contexts and the Buildings East of the Theatre," *New Testament Studies* 50 (2004): 349-69.

Justin Meggitt[23] is one of the main authors of this new tendency, which has generated a vibrant scholarly discussion.[24] His view may be summarized in two basic points. First, he says that Pauline Christians were poor people, members of the great mass of the urban population, living near the threshold of basic subsistence.[25] Second, Meggitt claims that this poor Christian community generated through their daily practices a very effective survival strategy — a creative combination of economic mutualism, self-sufficiency, almsgiving, and hospitality. This system responded to a very real need, helped to solve deep problems of subsistence, and provided for relative well-being. It may also help to explain the numeric expansion of Christianity among the masses of the empire.[26]

This economic mutualism is connected with egalitarian reciprocity, although it does not necessarily mean complete social homogeneity. The debate between Meggitt and Theissen has led the latter to abandon his notion of benevolent patriarchalism, because, while it is true that mutualism does not necessarily entail egalitarian relationships, it does imply the breaking of a hierarchically structured scheme (a point that Martin does not seem to incorporate). In any case, what seems clear is that this alternative social system rests on a participatory and corporal Christology (an expression of the body of Christ), with theological, spiritual, and sacramental roots. The importance of baptism and the Eucharist in forming the social body of mutual aid is evident. In other words, Corinth's Christian community did not interpret sacraments as mere symbolic rituals but as channels that create a new reality.

23. Justin J. Meggitt, *Paul, Poverty, and Survival* (Edinburgh: T&T Clark, 1998).

24. See Dale B. Martin, "Review Essay: Justin J. Meggitt, *Paul, Poverty, and Survival*," *Journal for the Study of the New Testament* 84 (2001): 51-64; Gerd Theissen, "The Social Structure of Pauline Communities: Some Critical Remarks on J. J. Meggitt, *Paul, Poverty, and Survival*," *Journal for the Study of the New Testament* 84 (2001): 65-84; Justin J. Meggitt, "Response to Martin and Theissen," *Journal for the Study of the New Testament* 84 (2001): 85-94; and Gerd Theissen, "Social Conflicts in the Corinthian Community: Further Remarks on J. J. Meggitt, *Paul, Poverty, and Survival*," *Journal for the Study of the New Testament* 25, no. 3 (2003): 371-91.

25. See an interesting attempt to measure the degree of poverty in Pauline communities in Steven J. Friesen, "Poverty in Pauline Studies: Beyond the So-Called New Consensus," *Journal for the Study of the New Testament* 26, no. 3 (2004): 323-61. His methodology and result, however, are quite arguable, as the articles by Barclay and Oakes show, in that very issue of the journal.

26. On the connection between mutual aid and Christianity's growth, see chapters 4, 5, and 9 in Stark, *The Rise of Christianity*.

An Alternative to Imperial System: Political Approach

Richard Horsley and other authors have analyzed Corinth's Christian community from the perspective of power relationships and their political meaning. These scholars argue that Pauline communities were able to form a social movement as a network of local cells.[27] These communities were to a certain extent autonomous. Given the fact that Christians were clearly a minority, there was a great overlap of the various social subsystems and a stable interaction with non-believers. Borders were porous and, for Paul, that was part of the real problem: not division in itself, but how this division weakened the reality of the Christian alternative. Accordingly, Paul's main task was to redefine ecclesial borders and to reconfigure communal relations as a familial body. For example, consider the refusal to partake in banquets with meat that had been sacrificed to idols. This strengthened the Christian identity as an alternative community within the larger Corinthian society, where such banquets were an essential piece of the social, economic, cultural, and relational system.

As I mentioned — and as 1 Corinthians 8–10 shows — the community embodied economic relationships that were poles apart from the dominant ones in imperial Roman society. The example of the collection of Pauline communities (in Antioch, Asia Minor, and Greece) for the benefit of the Jerusalem community shows that this Pauline network had an international concern that sharply contrasted with the empire's fiscal policies. It is clear, then, that Paul's objective in 1 Corinthians was to construct alternative communities over and against the dominant society.

It may be useful to nuance these sharp claims and to recognize, with Wayne Meeks, that there were "gates in the boundaries"[28] of Pauline communities. There was some tension between measures that strengthened internal cohesion (such as staying apart from society), and the desire to foster acceptable relations with non-Christian neighbors. In any case, it is undeniable that Pauline communities were convinced that being part of the body of Christ gave them a clear identity, different social practices, a relatively autonomous economic organization, and, finally, a humble but real alternative to the oppressive imperial system.[29]

27. Richard A. Horsley, "1 Corinthians: A Case Study of Paul's Assembly as an Alternative Society," in *Paul and Empire: Religion and Power in Roman Imperial Society,* ed. Richard A. Horsley (Harrisburg, Pa.: Trinity Press International, 1997), pp. 242-52.

28. Meeks, *The First Urban Christians,* pp. 105-7.

29. In this sense, I am in complete disagreement with the conclusions of Elizabeth A.

Conclusion

This section has demonstrated the interplay between the Eucharist, the church, and the socio-political reality. Building on several complementary approaches from the social sciences (sociology, archaeology, cultural anthropology, economics, and politics) we have deepened our knowledge of the meaning of the body of Christ in first-century Corinth's Christian community. This section does not argue for unilateral readings that forget or overlook the Christological, the mystical, and the personal aspects of the Eucharist. However, it does invite the integration of our spiritual and ecclesial lives. Note that we are talking about texts that Christian tradition has always considered as revealed by God — and, therefore, normative for the identity and the praxis of every follower of Jesus Christ. For this reason, we cannot fall into a "spiritualistic spirituality." To do so would go against the very essence of the Eucharist. Furthermore, we cannot limit ourselves to some moral consequences for individual behavior. Rather, we must look at the unavoidable communal aspects. As we have seen, living the socio-political dimension of the Eucharist means strengthening the Christian community and reshaping it as an alternative to the dominant system — whether imperial Rome, Hellenism, or twenty-first-century global capitalism.

The Body of Christ in Thirteenth-Century Liège

This section offers a complementary vision to the one just presented. While keeping the focus on the understanding and practice of the body of Christ, we move from ancient to medieval times, from ancient Greece to Belgium. We analyze a case study of some Christian communities that were able to link their Eucharistic life with an effective solidarity with the poor in the body of Christ. However, we must first consider the theological context in which that experience unfolded. This section concludes with some general remarks that transcend our historical case and are widely valid for all Christians.

Castelli, "Interpretations of Power in 1 Corinthians," in *Michel Foucault and Theology: The Politics of Religious Experience,* ed. James Bernauer, SJ, and Jerome Carrete (Hampshire: Ashgate, 2004), pp. 19-38.

Theological Models and Aspects of the Body of Christ

In a classic study Henri de Lubac examined the evolution of the term *body of Christ* in theology, spirituality, and praxis during the early centuries of Christianity.[30] He showed that at the turn of the first millennium the patristic model that dominated the first thousand years of Christianity was abandoned. The main historical and theological conclusion of *Corpus Mysticum* is that Christian faith implies an intimate connection between the mystical body and the real body of Christ — and the total body of Christ includes "real" and "mystical" elements found in both the Eucharist and the church.

De Lubac shows that this vision was central in first-millennium ecclesial praxis and throughout patristic theology. However, between the ninth and the eleventh centuries the move from symbolic to dialectical thought, and the subsequent split between mystical and rational reflection, profoundly modified the understanding of the body of Christ.[31] A division between the real and the mystical body evolved, separating the Eucharist and the church and creating a rift that still persists. Let us look more carefully at this change.

Gary Macy has shown that Eucharistic theology has always moved between two tendencies — the realist and the spiritual.[32] The first, or realist, tendency derives from Saint Ambrose and is also called corporal, metabolic, or "capharnatic" (because of its literal reading of the discourse on the bread of life at Capernaum, in John 6). The second, or spiritual, tendency draws on Saint Augustine and is also called symbolic or "stercoranist" (because of its reading of Matt. 15:17). Both currents coexisted for centuries in a fruitful and harmonic dialogue, each one comprising the complementary feature highlighted by the other.

The first discussion of this issue, more implicit than explicit, took place at the Abbey of Corbie in France around 833 CE. The monastery received a consultation regarding the sense of the Eucharist. Pascasius Radbertus, one of the monks, leaned toward a realist position. Ratramnus,

---

30. Henri de Lubac, SJ, *Corpus Mysticum. L'Eucharistie et l'Église au Moyen Age. Étude historique,* 2nd ed. (Paris: Aubier, 1949).

31. De Lubac, *Corpus Mysticum,* pp. 248-77.

32. Gary Macy, *The Theologies of the Eucharist in the Early Scholastic Period: A Study of the Salvific Function of the Sacrament according to the Theologians c. 1080–c. 1220* (Oxford: Clarendon, 1984).

his colleague, offered a more symbolic explanation. Both positions, though, coexisted in relative harmony. However, a problem arose when, at the Council of Quierzy (838 CE), Amalarius of Metz was condemned for dividing — in his reflection — sacrament, church, and the body of Christ in heaven and on earth. Two centuries later in 1050, when (according to de Lubac) dialectic thought had displaced symbolic, the controversy reached its apex with the condemnation of Berengar of Tours, who stood accused of maintaining spiritual-symbolic positions. Lanfranc of Bec's reaction, during the next decade, led to a more accurate theological formulation of sacramental realism similar to Pascasius's thought.[33]

Beyond these controversies, a wider view reveals three primary schools of thought in medieval Eucharistic theology.[34] First, there is the realist school, emphasizing the real presence of Christ in the Eucharist, in particular under the species of bread and wine. The second, or mystical, school highlights the personal relationship of the believer with Christ. The third school, sometimes called "ecclesial," remembers and develops the presence of Christ in the community of the church as the real body of Christ. It is critical to appreciate that what is considered erroneous is the separation of these three lines of interpretation. In other words, the key is to maintain a union of these three perspectives of Eucharistic reality.

William of Auxerre was a thirteenth-century author who integrates in an illuminating way the three positions. Although unifying approaches (with different emphases that do not deny the other positions) are common for medieval authors, we must remember de Lubac's conclusion: as the medieval age advances, there is a growing rift between the different dimensions of the body of Christ. Let us now consider the movements that arose in this theological and ecclesial context.

The Feast of Corpus Christi and the Beguine Movement

The feast of Corpus Christi started in the thirteenth century, most likely as a popular reaction to a theology and a praxis that — as I have just described — gradually isolated the Eucharist from the people. First, the chal-

---

33. For a survey of medieval authors, with abundance of original texts, see Darwell Stone, *A History of the Doctrine of the Holy Eucharist*, vol. 1 (London: Longmans, Green, 1909).
34. Macy, *The Theologies of the Eucharist*, pp. 44-131.

ice for laypersons was abandoned. It then became increasingly rare to receive communion. Later, the elevation of the host was introduced to (at least) guarantee a "visual communion." In this context, new forms of piety emerged (including the procession of the Corpus) to compensate for decreased lay participation in the Eucharist.

This explanation is consistent with the fact that tenth- and eleventh-century theological views needed some time to impregnate ecclesial praxis and daily spirituality. Furthermore, there is a historical element that is not always taken into consideration: the social context in which this situation arose. More specifically, I refer to the beguine movement, a Eucharistically rooted and socially engaged movement in service of the poor — a movement that emerged precisely during this period. We focus our discussion on a concrete geographical area.

The city of Liège, located in the current territory of Belgium, played a fundamental role in the birth, the development, and the expansion of the feast of Corpus Christi. Robert de Turotte, bishop of Liège, first established the feast in 1246. In 1261, Pope Urban IV (originally from Liège) expanded it to the universal church.[35] It is not by chance that this city became the center of this movement of liturgical, spiritual, ecclesial, and social renewal. Let us first consider some theological issues that will help us understand the environment of this region.

Already in the twelfth century, around the 1110s, Liège had become a center of theological defense of the real presence of Jesus Christ in the Eucharist. Distinguished authors, such as Alger of Liège, led the way.[36] William of Saint-Thierry (d. 1148), a native of Liège, was one of the finest proponents of what we have called the mystical current. He was probably the most "Greek" of twelfth-century Western theologians. It seems evident that the development of Eucharistic devotions needs, at least, a firm conviction of two basic beliefs: (1) the real presence of Christ in the Eucharist, and (2) the real possibility of a personal encounter with Christ. Both beliefs were lived out — together — in the religious environment of Liège. However, the picture is incomplete: we must turn now from the theological context and consider the social context.

---

35. Herbert Grundmann, *Religious Movements in the Middle Ages: The Historical Links between Heresy, the Mendicant Orders, and the Women's Movement in the Twelfth and Thirteenth Century, with the Historical Foundations of German Mysticism*, trans. Steven Rowan, introduction by Robert E. Lerner (Notre Dame: University of Notre Dame Press, 1995 [German orig. ed., 1935]), p. 140.

36. Macy, *The Theologies of the Eucharist*, pp. 49-50 and 67.

It has been proved that the main impulse for the feast of Corpus Christi came from some mystical women, in particular Juliana of Cornillon (also known as Juliana of Liège). In 1208, she experienced a profound Eucharistic vision while she was serving the poor lepers in one of the city's hospitals. After that event, she devoted the last fifty years of her life to foster an embodied charity and Eucharistic spirituality. Liège was not only the diocese where the first group of beguines was formed (around 1170) but also one of the most vibrant centers of the beguinage. It is estimated that by 1240 there were some 1,500 beguines in the city of Liège, forming a socio-religious movement with deep Eucharistic roots. Community life, service to the poor, manual work, prayer life with direct access to the Gospels in vernacular languages, lay creativity, and urban character were some of the essential features of this group of women.[37] It is precisely in this socio-religious context that there first arose a need for a public devotion to the sacrament of human-divine communion. Hence, it does not seem to be mere chance that Pope Urban IV, who helped to spread the devotion to Corpus Christi, also approved the rule for the beguines.

By way of a provisional conclusion, we can say that the example of thirteenth-century Liège demonstrates the connection between a new form of Eucharistic participation and the development of a socio-charitative renewal movement in service of the poor. The combination of both elements illustrates, on the one hand, a popular and intuitive response to an increasingly speculative Eucharistic theology that was less relevant to daily life. On the other hand, the combination points to the permanent Eucharistic call for a way of life based on radical sharing.

Social Implications

Inspired by the analytical framework suggested by Raymond Williams,[38] I define three positions in twelfth- and thirteenth-century Liège: the dominant tradition, the emergent tradition, and the residual tradition. These

37. Miri Rubin, *Corpus Christi: The Eucharist in Late Medieval Culture* (Cambridge: Cambridge University Press, 1991), pp. 166-67. See also Ernest W. McDonnell, *The Beguines and Beghards in Medieval Culture: With Special Emphasis on the Belgian Scene* (New Brunswick, N.J.: Rutgers University Press, 1954).

38. Raymond Williams, *Marxism and Literature* (Oxford: Oxford University Press, 1977), pp. 121-27.

three positions are different in their social location, in their relationship to power, in their theological understanding (in both Eucharistic and ecclesial issues), and in their ways of conceiving social transformation.

The dominant tradition can be identified with the feudal model, which penetrated every social reality. Linked to the dominant sectors of society, it religiously legitimated social stratification and inequality. Master-serf relationships controlled all aspects of social (economic, political, and cultural) life, influencing its institutional and relational dimensions. Obviously, ecclesial life and theology, too, reflected and legitimated this frame of relationships. This dominant position also exerted influence over Eucharistic life, which then became more and more elitist, privatized, and distant from the people.

As a logical reaction to this situation, the socio-ecclesial movement of Cathars and Waldensians developed what I have called an emergent tradition. These groups appeared during the twelfth century. The presence of the Waldensians in Liège in 1202 has been documented.[39] Cathars and Waldensians maintained an essentially anti-hierarchical attitude. However, they also became strongly anti-Eucharistic, since the Eucharist was the central symbol of medieval society.[40] They tried to reform the church and society, based on an apostolic lifestyle and Christian poverty, but they were more individualistic than communitarian. Interestingly, by the mid-twelfth century Bernard of Clairvaux had denounced the fact that significant elements within the emergent nobility were sympathetic to these movements because they hoped to enrich themselves with the goods of the church.[41]

We are now in a position to explain the theological roots of this situation. We have seen that the evolution of Eucharistic theology and ecclesial praxis led to a split between the different aspects of the body of Christ

39. Malcolm Lambert, *Medieval Heresy: Popular Movements from the Gregorian Reform to the Reformation,* 3rd ed. (Oxford and Malden, Mass.: Blackwell, 1992), p. 78. On pp. 38 and 65, Lambert addresses the possibility of a Cathar presence in Liège, and he concludes that these groups of Manichean tendency cannot properly called Cathars until the twelfth century.

40. Rubin, *Corpus Christi,* pp. 12 and 347-50. Macy, *The Theologies of the Eucharist,* notices that realist (pp. 56-58), mystical (pp. 88-93), and ecclesial tendencies (pp. 114-18 and 131) were opposed to Cathars and Waldensians, forming in this point a consensus that was later supported by the Fourth Lateran Council.

41. Grundman, *Religious Movements,* pp. 7-30.

(between the real Eucharistic body and the ecclesial mystical body). It seems consistent to say that the interest of the dominant feudal groups centered on the real presence of Christ in the bread and wine — a strategy that would limit its transforming action to a limited space at a specific time, all under a sacral character. Emergent groups, such as the Cathars and the Waldensians, were particularly interested in the social and ecclesial body, which they wanted to transform along more egalitarian lines. However — precisely because of their theological context — they did not have the necessary tools to synthesize both elements. For this reason they tilted toward heretical views on Eucharistic issues, denying the real presence of Christ.

Was there another possibility — an alternative to the dominant feudal and emergent sectarian positions? In fact, the beguinage embodied this third way, this residual tradition. The beguine movement offered an alternative that rested on both orthodoxy and orthopraxis. On the one hand, they firmly believed in the real presence of Christ in the Eucharist, they promoted its public cult through the feast of Corpus Christi, and they encouraged a deep spirituality with Eucharistic roots. On the other hand, they accepted the consequences of their faith in the real presence of Christ in the poor as a call to solidarity and to the transformation of social reality. Furthermore, they never moved along these two lines separately. Rather, their activities expressed their dedication to one and the same faith in the only and real body of Christ, with its different dimensions.

We can see in the beguinage an example of a radical and practical ecclesiology, rooted in Jesus Christ, full of socio-politically transforming implications. It would be excessive to consider the beguinage a proletarian movement, forgetting the fact that its social origins were often related to the incipient bourgeois class.[42] However, it would also be misguided to overlook the social dynamics generated by the beguine movement: knowing where their members came from is one thing; knowing where they went is quite another. The beguinage truly embodied a community of social *declassment* based on the gospel. For this reason, they promoted a real and radical dynamic of social transformation.

---

42. Grundman advises against this error (*Religious Movements*, pp. 14, 17, 69-74, and 231-35).

Conclusion: Waiting for Juliana of Cornillon and the Beguines?

I am now in a position to offer some conclusions. Let me begin by quoting two contemporary texts from the field of political philosophy. Alasdair MacIntyre concludes his influential *After Virtue* saying that "this time however the barbarians are not waiting beyond the frontiers; they have already been governing us for quite some time. And it is our lack of consciousness of this that constitutes part of our predicaments. We are waiting not for Godot, but for another — doubtlessly very different — St. Benedict."[43] The second text comes from two radical authors in the anarchist tradition, Toni Negri and Michael Hardt, who also conclude their book *Empire* with a surprising ecclesial-religious reference to waiting for a new saint Francis of Assisi: "Once again in postmodernity we find ourselves in Francis's situation, posing against the misery of power the joy of being. This is a revolution that no power will control — because biopower and communism, cooperation and revolution remain together, in love, simplicity, and also innocence. This is the irrepressible lightness and joy of being communist."[44]

Are we waiting for Benedict of Nursia and Francis of Assisi in order to rediscover the meaning of our lives and a decent social configuration? Are we waiting for Juliana of Cornillon and for the beguinage? It would be ridiculous to fall into this sort of nostalgia. However, it is possible for these bright examples to shed some light on our times. What these individuals did was to embody what they believed. By doing so in a radical way, they generated a new social reality.[45] Once again we see that a deep experience of the body of Christ, without divisions, offers a true dynamic of social transformation. My conclusion, then, is twofold: (1) we cannot break the body of Christ and limit his power; and (2) a life rooted in Jesus Christ has

43. Alasdair MacIntyre, *After Virtue: A Study in Moral Theory,* 2nd ed. (Notre Dame: University of Notre Dame Press, 1984), p. 263.

44. Michael Hardt and Antonio Negri, *Empire* (Cambridge, Mass.: Harvard University Press, 2000), p. 413.

45. Although we have focused our attention on the case of the beguines in thirteenth-century Liège, it is also evident that the Benedictine monastic movement reshaped Europe and that mendicant orders (specially Franciscans and Dominicans) provided a viable alternative to the incipient and growing capitalism. Note that in all these examples, we find a powerful spirituality with Eucharistic roots, which develops itself in new and innovative social forms.

powerful and radical consequences in all areas of reality. With these results we can now move on to the final section of this chapter, which again means advancing several centuries in history.

The Body of Christ in Twentieth-Century Rome

Despite the beguines and other movements, the dominant model continued to overshadow the ecclesial landscape throughout the second millennium.[46] The theological evolution vis-à-vis the Eucharist also manifested in the *societas perfecta* ecclesiology, heir to a vision of society linked to the feudal system. The First Vatican Council (1870) endorsed this ecclesial model, which endured until the twentieth century. It is also important to note that during the decades that preceded the Council — in theological writings and in preparatory documents — this ecclesiology of the perfect society was not the only one. It coexisted with other views.

In the magisterial teachings of Pope Leo XIII, we find a juxtaposition between the church as the perfect society and the church as the body of Christ. It is not by chance that the same pope who inaugurated Catholic social doctrine with his encyclical letter *Rerum Novarum* (1891) also wrote another encyclical (*Mirae Caritatis*, 1902) focused on the Eucharist as the sacrament of unity in the church. Once again, we find here the unavoidable ties among the Eucharist, the church, and social transformation.

The 1920 to 1940 period brought "the awakening of renewal forces in the field of ecclesiology."[47] This involved several related elements: a growing and vital sense of community, a Christocentric spirituality, a developing laity within the church, a liturgical renewal, a deepening interest in biblical studies, and an ecumenical movement. One of the convergent lines of these elements was the maturation of an ecclesiology of the body of Christ — in part a reaction to the notion of the church as perfect society.

46. See John Driver, *Radical Faith: An Alternative History of the Christian Church* (Kitchener, Ont.: Pandora, 1999). At this point I want to thank Mennonite theologian John Driver. We met in the summer of 2004, an encounter that became not only a fruitful theological conversation, but also a deep experience of Christian fellowship.

47. See Ángel Antón, SJ, *El misterio de la Iglesia. Evolución histórica de las ideas eclesiológicas*, vol. 2 (Madrid: Biblioteca de Autores Cristianos, 1987), pp. 507-62. It is also interesting to consult Joseph J. Bluett, "The Mystical Body: A Bibliography 1890-1940," *Theological Studies* 3 (1942): 260-89.

For instance, Pope Pius XI in his encyclical *Quadragesimo Anno* (1931) articulated the social implications of this doctrine of the body of Christ: "If the members of the body social are, as was said, reconstituted, and if the directing principle of economic-social life is restored, it will be possible to say in a certain sense even of this body what the Apostle says of the mystical body of Christ: 'The whole body (being closely joined and knit together through every joint of the system according to the functioning in due measure of each single part) derives its increase from the building up of itself in love'" (no. 90). However, it was undoubtedly Pope Pius XII who, with his encyclical letter *Mystici Corporis Christi* (1943), provided an official endorsement to the ecclesiology of the body of Christ.

Around the Encyclical Mystici Corporis Christi *(1943)*

The model of the church as a perfect society, dominated by a juridical and formalist perspective, seemed to be worn out and incapable of responding to the new situation. Alternatively, the ecclesiology of the body of Christ was gaining strength, clarity, and presence, and by the 1940s-1950s it was the primary ecclesial doctrine in the church.[48] During this period there were several interpretations of the mystery of the church as the body of Christ, including the understanding of the church (1) as a living organism, (2) as a community united by personal bonds, (3) as part of the "total Christ," and (4) as a mystical body. Let us look more carefully at these different perspectives.

The organic and vital perspective understood the church as a living organism animated by the Holy Spirit. This tendency was influenced by the notion of continuous incarnation formulated by Johann Möhler and Mathias Scheeben in the nineteenth century. However, its excessive anti-intellectual character occasionally led to a type of spiritual biologicism and a false mysticism. For instance, Karl Pelz's work, *The Christian as Christ* (1939), argued — without further clarification — for a *corporal* presence of Christ within the believer.

A second perspective, the personalist, highlighted the personal union in Christ between God and the human being along with a strong ethic of fraternal communion. Romano Guardini and Karl Adam were distin-

---

48. For this section, see Antón, *El misterio de la Iglesia*, pp. 563-675.

guished members of this group. Beyond this, a third perspective developed the Augustinian notion of *Christus totus* and expanded it to embrace all humanity. The main contribution of this current was probably the patristic foundation for the theology of the body of Christ, especially as developed by Emile Mersch. Its most radical move was dissociating the spiritual reality and the institutional reality of the same church. A fourth perspective, sometimes called "corporative," is represented by Erich Przywara and Sebastian Tromp. The pope clearly preferred this particular line of interpretation.

In 1937 the first volume of Tromp's ecclesiological trilogy was published.[49] In it he articulates an understanding of the church as an organism vivified by the Spirit and with Christ as its head. Furthermore, he identifies the mystical body of Christ with the Roman Catholic Church. Tromp himself helped write Pope Pius XII's encyclical *Mystici Corporis Christi* (1943). His influence was so evident that some observers lamented that a pontifical document had assumed "even the minimal details of the doctrine of a particular theologian."[50]

In any event, the encyclical sought to respond to a twofold ecclesiological danger. On the one hand, it was a reaction against the rationalism and the naturalism that limited ecclesial reality to its legal, sociological, visible, and institutional aspects. On the one hand, Pius XII warned against certain exaggerated forms of ecclesiological mysticism and quietism that blurred the line between God and God's creatures, eventually leading one to overlook human cooperation with the Spirit's action. In a more positive and constructive way, the encyclical developed four intertwined theses: (1) the church is a "body"; (2) the church is the body "of Christ"; (3) the church is the "mystical" body of Christ; and (4) this ecclesial understanding implies a deep union of all members with Christ and among themselves. Out of this doctrinal framework, *Mystici Corporis Christi* fleshed out some pastoral implications, including the bond between the legal church and the church of love, the complementary character of the different aspects inside the one ecclesial reality, and the need to love this mystical body.

We see, therefore, that the encyclical's vision is consistent with the

---

49. Sebastian Tromp, SJ, *Corpus Christi quod est Ecclesia. Introductio generalis* (Rome: Pontificia Universitas Gregoriana, 1937).

50. Antón, *El misterio de la Iglesia*, p. 630.

ecclesial life and theology of the first millennium, except for the terminological shift that insists on the "mystical" body instead of the "real" body of Christ. Moreover, by linking legal elements to the practice of charity, the pope demanded coherence in ecclesial structures. He thus issued a call for a permanent conversion of those very structures so that they could truly reflect the exercise of charity at the intra-ecclesial level and in the socio-political realm.

Finally, it is important to note that the ecclesiology of the body of Christ was a powerful stimulus for praxis in a socially engaged church. This favored the poor. Besides the examples of Virgil Mitchel and Dorothy Day, already mentioned in the first part of this book, we can now refer to two more witnesses. First, the previously named theologian Emile Mersch who, beyond his very important theological reflection in this regard,[51] literally offered his life serving the poor, the body of Christ. He died in 1940 while helping to care for the wounded in World War II. Second, Chilean Jesuit Saint Alberto Hurtado, promoter of Christian trade unions and founder of Hogar de Cristo, sought to provide housing for poor families. In 1950, Hurtado delivered a powerful lecture entitled "The Mystical Body: Distribution and Use of Wealth."[52]

The Synthesis of the Second Vatican Council (1962-65)

Just as the image of the church as *societas perfecta* dominated Catholic ecclesiology for decades, and just as the notion of body of Christ later assumed a similar monopoly, theological reflection from the 1940s onward began to actively incorporate new dimensions, images, and categories regarding the church. These new currents of ecclesiological thought grew and matured, so that their influence during the Second Vatican Council would be evident. There were two main lines of reflection in this period (between 1940 and 1960): the ecclesiology of the people of God and the church as radical sacrament. Let us consider them in some detail.[53]

---

51. Emile Mersch, *Le Corps Mystique du Christe. Études du Théologie historique* (Paris: Desclée de Brouwer, 1933) and *Morale et Corps Mystique* (Paris: Desclée de Brouwer, 1937).

52. The complete text can be found in Alberto Hurtado, SJ, *Un fuego que enciende otros fuegos. Páginas escogidas* (Santiago: Editorial Universidad Católica de Chile, 2004), pp. 163-65.

53. Antón, *El misterio de la Iglesia*, pp. 676-831.

By 1940 M. D. Koster had already described the church as the people of God. However, his reactive attitude in radical opposition to the ecclesiology of the body of Christ and the excess of some of his contentions prevented him from having a greater influence. Much more nuanced were the contributions of Lucien Cerfaux in the field of biblical studies, Joseph Ratzinger in patristic theology, A. Schaut in liturgical theology, and Michael Schmaus in dogmatic theology. These figures opened the way toward a synthesis involving the dominant model from *Mystici Corporis Christi*.[54] The people of God ecclesiology highlights the historical-salvific dimension of the church, makes us remember its eschatological orientation, deepens the social rearticulation of the church as an effect of divine grace, and opens new possibilities for ecumenical encounter.

The ecclesiology of the church as radical sacrament entered contemporary theological conversation thanks to Otto Semmelroth, who was able to recover patristic and medieval data, and to build on them.[55] The same may be said of Karl Rahner, Joseph Ratzinger, and Hans Urs von Balthasar, although each introduces particular terminology. In fact, these authors agree in privileging Christ as God's proto-sacrament, from which flow the reality of the church as radical sacrament or original sacrament (*Ursakrament* in Semmelroth's expression) — and, eventually, the specific sacraments. This is a truly Christian way of looking at the world as sacramentally structured by Christ's grace. I cannot analyze here the deep transforming consequences that the classical distinction between *res* and *sacramentum* implies for this vision of the church as radical sacrament; and I cannot explore the suggestions that arise when considering the church from the double aspect of sign and instrument.[56]

It is clear that all of these currents converged in the Second Vatican Council, most especially in *Lumen Gentium*. It is well known that after the initial chapter on the mystery of the church, the Council devoted the entire second chapter to the church as the people of God. With this option, the theological development of the previous decades was explicitly assumed.

54. See Ángel Antón, SJ, "Hacia una síntesis de las nociones 'cuerpo de Cristo' y 'pueblo de Dios' en la eclesiología," *Estudios Eclesiásticos* 44 (1969): 173-75.

55. Otto Semmelroth, SJ, *Church as Sacrament*, trans. Emily Schossberger (Notre Dame: Fides, 1965).

56. See an interesting ecumenical perspective, from a Mennonite position, in Neal Blough, "The Church as Sign or Sacrament: Trinitarian Ecclesiology, Pilgrim Marpeck, Vatican II and John Milbank," *Mennonite Quarterly Review* 78 (2004): 29-52.

By changing the order of the chapters from previous schemes, the Council underlined the prominence of the people of God before its own hierarchical constitution (an issue treated in chapter 3). Already in the first paragraph of the constitution, though, we read that "the Church is in Christ like a sacrament or as a sign and instrument both of a very closely knit union with God and of the unity of the whole human race" (*LG* 1). Later on, it will be said that Christ by the Spirit "established His Body which is the Church as the universal sacrament of salvation" (*LG* 48). All of number 7 of *Lumen Gentium* is devoted to a description of the church as the body of Christ. The Second Vatican Council harmonically uses the primary theological notions that twentieth-century ecclesiology had developed: the body of Christ, the people of God, and the radical sacrament.

Theological reflection after the Council has tried to clarify whether there is a primacy among these models of the church.[57] Most especially, it has attempted to elucidate the way they are related. Some scholars highlight the dominant role of the people of God (in *Lumen Gentium* an entire chapter versus a single numbered section devoted to the body of Christ). Others argue that the key notion is the mystery of the church (noted in chapter 1 in which we find the numbered section on the body of Christ — apart from the rest of the images mentioned in *LG* 6). Still other scholars, following the insights of Michael Schmaus in systematic theology and of Heinrich Schlier in Bible studies, have developed a Trinitarian ecclesiology that considers the church as the people of God the Father, the body of Christ, and the temple of the Holy Spirit (cf. *LG* 2-4).[58]

This variety of approaches shows that the Second Vatican Council offers a complex and nuanced vision of the church: simultaneously balanced and radical. It is balanced because it keeps in creative tension the various aspects of the ecclesial reality (*LG* 8: "one complex reality which coalesces from a divine and a human element"). It is radical because it is rooted in Jesus Christ and his kingdom (*LG* 5) without denying the consequences derived from it (a poor and humble church: *LG* 8). To that end, *Lumen Gentium* retrieves tradition and thereby offers a deep proposal for the contemporary church.

---

57. Avery R. Dulles, SJ, *Models of the Church,* expanded ed. (Garden City, N.Y.: Image, 1987).

58. For instance, see Bruno Forte, *The Church, Icon of the Trinity: A Brief Study,* trans. Robert Paolucci (Boston: St. Paul Books and Media, 1991).

Combining these various aspects and theological currents may not lead to a simple equilibrium, but rather to a creative synthesis. This is achieved when we consider the central idea of the Second Vatican Council's ecclesiology: the term *communion*.[59] Following Walter Kasper, it can be said that considering the church as *communio* includes five essential aspects: (1) a communion with the Trinitarian God; (2) the basic meaning of communion, a participation in God's Life through Word and sacraments; (3) the church as *communio* — unity with a healthy and creative tension between local and universal church; (4) the communion of believers, understood as the participation and co-responsibility of everyone; and (5) communion as mission to be sacrament for the world.

To conclude this section, I underscore two important elements for my global project in this book. First, we see that the term the *body of Christ* is now present in a more nuanced way without the monopolies or unilateral claims of previous times. It has not disappeared. Rather, it is reconfigured within the powerful notion of *communio* — which has deep and clear Eucharistic resonance. Second, we find again that there is no possible dichotomy or separation between communion and mission, between *koinonia* and *diakonia*. The church will be truly itself only if it comprises both poles. As long as it does so — rooted in Jesus Christ — its own ecclesial life will be a locus for radical transformation of our world.

Communion Ecclesiology at the Turn of the Century

Pope John Paul II launched the preparation for the great jubilee year 2000 with an apostolic letter, *Tertio Millennio Adveniente* (1994). In it, among other things, he invited the faithful "to lay greater emphasis on the Church's preferential option for the poor and the outcast" (no. 51). Furthermore, he announced that "the Year 2000 will be intensely Eucharistic" (no. 55). Following three years of preparation dedicated to Jesus Christ, to the Holy Spirit, and to the Father (and after the jubilee year as such), another apostolic letter, *Novo Millennio Ineunte* (2001), closed the cycle by

59. Walter Kasper, "The Church as Communion: Reflections on the Guiding Ecclesiological Idea of the Second Vatican Council," in *Theology and the Church* (New York: Crossroad, 1989), pp. 148-65.

collecting the central features of the process. We should keep in mind three concrete examples and three central notions.

The examples include the purification of memory and the church's public request for forgiveness (no. 6); the vibrant example of saints, martyrs, and witnesses to the faith (no. 7); and the struggle to overcome the problem of the international debt of materially poor countries (no. 14). The three global principles are the conviction that Eucharistic life is the best antidote to our world's dispersion (no. 36); the challenge to promote a spirituality of communion (no. 43); and the impulse for a new creativity and resourcefulness in charity (nos. 49-50). Even this brief summary indicates how deep the letter's content is, and how relevant it is for Christian communities.

Thus we come to 2003 — to the last encyclical letter published by John Paul II, *Ecclesia de Eucharistia.* It is divided into six chapters: (1) the mystery of faith; (2) the Eucharist builds the church; (3) the apostolicity of the Eucharist and of the church; (4) the Eucharist and ecclesial communion; (5) the dignity of Eucharistic celebration; and (6) the school of Mary, "woman of the Eucharist." Given the variety of topics presented, and given the limited space we have here, I limit myself to a brief selection of and commentary on the dimensions more directly related to the main concerns of this book.

First, it is important to underscore the aspect of personal relationship with the Lord Jesus. We could call this the mystical dimension of the Eucharist. "The Church has received the Eucharist from Christ her Lord not as one gift — however precious — among so many others, but as *the gift par excellence,* for it is the gift of himself" (no. 11).[60] In the Eucharist, we receive in a real and free way the radical self-giving of God in Christ for the sake of human beings. A little later, the encyclical insists: "The Eucharistic Sacrifice is intrinsically directed to the inward union of the faithful with Christ through communion; we receive the very One who offered himself for us. . . . Jesus himself reassures us that this union, which he compares to that of the life of the Trinity, is truly realized. *The Eucharist is a true banquet,* in which Christ offers himself as our nourishment" (no. 16). It is precisely at this Eucharistic banquet that we Christians enter into communion with our Lord. This is the foundation of our ecclesial communion. That is

---

60. In the following paragraphs, all emphasis is in the official original text. As in all Vatican documents, I am using the Internet edition from www.vatican.va.

why we can talk rigorously about a Eucharistic ecclesiology of communion rooted in Jesus Christ, as the second chapter of the encyclical asserts: "the Eucharist builds the Church."

With this we avoid the risk of understanding the mystical dimension of the encounter with Jesus Christ in a private or intimate way. This is the second aspect I need to highlight. The pope reminds us of the "universal and, so to speak, cosmic character" of the Eucharist (no. 8). We could even talk about the wedding of God and humanity, a sort of cosmic nuptials anticipated in the Eucharistic celebration. We should never forget that "the Eucharist is always in some way celebrated on *the altar of the world*. It unites heaven and earth. It embraces and permeates all creation" (no. 8). No one and nothing remain outside this Eucharistic reality and dynamic.

We come now to the third element. Eucharistic participation, argues the pope, "increases, rather than lessens, *our sense of responsibility for the world today*" (no. 20). Concretely, this same numbered section of the encyclical mentions the urgency to work for peace, to struggle for justice and solidarity among the peoples, to advocate for human life in the midst of this world's contradictions, and to opt for the weakest, the poorest, the most destitute. By participating in the Eucharist believers are "committed to changing their lives and making them in a certain way completely 'Eucharistic'" (no. 20). In fact, says the text, there is a twofold movement within the same Eucharistic dynamism: on the one hand, the transfiguration of personal and community existence, and, on the other hand, the commitment to transform the world according to the gospel.

The fourth aspect for our consideration is this: the encyclical asserts that Eucharistic communion strengthens the unity of the church as the body of Christ and explicitly mentions its "*unifying power* of participation in the banquet of the Eucharist" (no. 23). Beyond devout considerations, the pope points to the powerful implications of this reality: "The seeds of disunity, which daily experience shows to be so deeply rooted in humanity as a result of sin, are countered by the *unifying power* of the body of Christ. The Eucharist, precisely by building up the Church, creates human community" (no. 24). At the Eucharist and within the Eucharistic community we find, then, an efficient force for unification — a force opposed to and counterbalancing the powers of violence, injustice, and exclusion in this world of global capitalism. In summary, "the Eucharist creates *communion and fosters communion*" (no. 40).

Conclusion

This chapter has articulated a firm conviction and reality: the life of the church acquires its radical character insofar as it is rooted in Jesus Christ; and this experience of the body of Christ implies a deeply transforming power. We have seen this in Corinth, in Liège, and in Rome. We have grasped it with a social-science approach to the Bible, with a historical and theological analysis of the medieval period, and with a reading of some contemporary papal encyclicals. We have discovered it through Scripture, tradition, and magisterial teachings. Ecclesial communion generates social communion. A life rooted in Jesus Christ means a radical transformation of all reality. Eucharistic dynamism embraces each Christian's personal life. It embraces ecclesial life. It embraces the world's life. United to Jesus Christ, we believers are called to be the body of Christ, to be a sacrament of communion and liberation for the life of the world. This is the topic of the following chapter.

6. The Sacraments as a Radical Alternative

In this chapter I take a further step in our exploration of the practical implications of living as persons rooted in Jesus Christ. Concretely, I investigate how such life unfolds in the realm of liturgy and how the sacraments, as Christian practices par excellence, nourish a radical alternative to the dominant system. To that end, I especially stress the social dimension of the sacraments,[1] but without denying other aspects. Before entering into this topic, however, I make some prior clarifications, with the help of two simple examples.

In the summer of 2004 there took place in Barcelona a "Symposium on Intercultural and Interreligious Liberation Theology," which concluded with a declaration on the ethical principles and the practices of liberation in different religions. The five concrete practices of liberation proposed for all religions were the following: (1) democratizing the multilateral world organizations, especially the United Nations; (2) democratizing the internal operating structures of the religions themselves; (3) establishing a close relationship between the World Parliament of Religions and the World Social Forum; (4) promoting peace as something inseparable from justice, by means of interreligious dialogue, political negotiation, and active nonvio-

---

1. Henri de Lubac, SJ, *Catholicism: Christ and the Common Destiny of Man,* trans. Lancelot C. Sheppard and Elizabeth Englund, OCD (San Francisco: Ignatius, 1988). This work continues to be a fertile reference point for its solid scholarship, its manner of "accumulative" argumentation, and the vigor of its theological and social intuition. An interesting proposal that stresses the liturgical matrix of Christian ethics can also be found in Stanley Hauerwas and Samuel Wells, eds., *The Blackwell Companion to Christian Ethics* (Malden, Mass.: Blackwell, 2004).

lence; (5) struggling vigorously to eliminate patriarchy both within the religions and outside of them.[2] The five proposals are clearly laudable and necessary. We might well ask ourselves, however, questions such as the following: What specifically do these practices consist in? What should the religions specifically do to work toward a more just world? How can the force of liberation-oriented religions best be channeled and utilized? If these questions are not discussed seriously, then theology becomes totally superfluous because it is saying nothing that is not said already in discourses that are in turn ethical, political, or social.

For contrast, let us look at a second example. Some years ago Mennonite theologian John H. Yoder offered a short but powerful book on political sacramentology with the felicitous title of *Body Politics*.[3] His reflection centers on the question of whether the church, if it really is a social body presenting an alternative to the dominant system, should function through communal practices that are equally alternative. The five practices that he proposes are: (1) the discipline of "binding and unbinding," linked to conflict resolution and reconciliation; (2) breaking bread together: the Eucharist as an economic act; (3) baptism and the new humanity: ethnic inclusiveness; (4) the fullness of Christ, or the multiplicity of gifts; (5) the open assembly and the shared word. Clearly, in each case a traditional Christian practice is proposed and the socio-political implications contained therein are drawn out.

The contrast between the two approaches is evident. The first example betrays a certain skepticism or ignorance regarding the transformative potential of the sacramental practices of Christianity (or those of other religions). As a result, recourse is had directly to secular political language (democratization or struggle against patriarchy), with the double danger of diffusing the specifically theological contribution and of remaining at the level of blandly generic ideas (promoting peace, democratizing structures). The second perspective, in contrast, appears convinced that there is a liberating force (concealed, but real) in the sacramental praxis bequeathed to us by tradition. It recognizes that great principles and noble

---

2. The text of the declaration may be found in the appendix of Juan José Tamayo and Raúl Fornet-Betancourt, eds., *Interculturalidad, diálogo interreligioso y liberación. I Simposio Internacional de Teología Intercultural e Interreligiosa de la Liberación* (Estella: Verbo Divino, 2005), pp. 299-303.

3. John H. Yoder, *Body Politics: Five Practices of the Christian Community before the Watching World* (Nashville: Discipleship Resources, 1992).

desires must become incarnate in concrete, real, shared practices. It perceives that the creation and the strengthening of the alternative social body is really the most effective contribution toward waging the struggle against every oppressive empire. Furthermore, it acknowledges that the church is called precisely to engage in that struggle, and that it has within itself the resources necessary for nurturing an alternative truly grounded in hope.

As I show in this chapter, my own proposal clearly resonates more with this second way of seeing sacramental reality and its socio-political implications. It should be noted, all the same, that my own perspective is that of a Catholic theologian. As regards the sacraments there are significant differences among the different Christian denominations and there are many nuances of meaning that we will not be able to go into in this short treatment. Even the name turns out to be problematic. Yoder, for example, avoids both the term *sacrament* (proper to Catholic theology) and the term *ordinances* (typical of Anabaptist theology) and uses instead the more neutral term *practices* in order to allow for a more open, ecumenical reflection. For my part, I habitually use the word *sacrament,* but I hope that such usage does not present an insurmountable barrier for Christians of other denominations.

Furthermore, I assume the traditional Catholic doctrine that holds there are seven sacraments: baptism, confirmation, Eucharist, penance, anointing of the sick, priestly orders, and matrimony. At the same time, though, in accord with canon 3 of the Council of Trent, I maintain that there are differences of dignity and importance among the sacraments.[4] In fact, a longstanding ecclesial tradition has argued for a hierarchy among the sacraments, as regards both their origins and their effect; for such a tradition baptism and Eucharist are considered to be the principal sacraments.[5] In this way a path is opened to certain ecumenical accords, while at the same time attention is paid to the wealth of the sacramental tradi-

---

4. "If anyone says that these sacraments are so equal to one another that one is not in any way of greater worth than another, anathema sit." In *The Christian Faith in the Doctrinal Documents of the Catholic Church,* ed. and rev. J. Neuner, SJ, and J. Dupuis, SJ (New York: Alba House, 1982), p. 371, no. 1313 (DS 1603).

5. See Yves Congar, OP, "La idea de sacramentos mayores o principales," *Concilium* 31 (1968): 24-37. Something similar is expressed by José I. González Faus, SJ, *Símbolos de fraternidad. Sacramentología para empezar* (Barcelona: Cristianismo y Justicia, 2006). Without denying the sevenfold tradition, he speaks of two sacraments and five living metaphors.

tion and to its many possibilities for engendering practices that strengthen the ecclesial body.[6]

This chapter, therefore, treats the seven sacraments, but in a differentiated manner. In so doing I develop the thesis that the sacraments are privileged practices through which the radical alternative of Christ's body finds true expression, incarnation, and deployment.

Forming the Body

We begin our reflection, then, with the two sacraments of initiation. In order to speak of a body, any body, it is first necessary to form that body. The sacraments of initiation are oriented to constituting the body of Christ. As with all the sacraments, they are the gratuitous action of God's grace (pardon the redundancy), but they are also actions that are visible, efficacious, operative, and corporal. Christian theology has always insisted that the final result (the *res* of the *sacramentum,* in medieval terminology) of the sacrament of baptism is the unity of the church. In this part I argue, in four steps, that baptism (and confirmation) are oriented to forming a body rooted in Jesus Christ and that this process has radical consequences for the life of the world.

Baptism and the Paschal Mystery

Since I cannot develop fully the wealth of the theology of baptism, I concentrate on its central core, which is the connection between the baptism of Christians and the death-resurrection of the Lord Jesus. Although there are many elements associated with baptism (purification, pardon of sin, illumination, being clothed in Christ, the seal of the Spirit, recalling Jesus' own baptism), the core of all of them is clearly to be found in the profound Christological-paschal meaning that baptism had in the theology and the praxis of the first Christian communities. To be baptized was to be incor-

---

6. This is perhaps the moment to indicate that my connection to the Anabaptist-Mennonite tradition, which has appeared at various moments in this book, has taken the form of involvement with the base group Bridgefolk, which defines itself as a meeting place or movement of sacramentally minded Mennonites and peace-minded Roman Catholics.

porated into Christ, to be submerged into the mystery of his life, to be introduced into the kenotic movement of death-resurrection: "We were buried therefore with him by baptism into death, so that as Christ was raised from the dead by the glory of the Father, we too might walk in newness of life" (Rom. 6:4). The significant ethical consequences that derive from this incorporation into Christ are evident in this text: first comes the indicative (rooted in Christ, we are new creatures), and then appears the imperative (we must live in a radically new way).[7]

This deep linkage of baptism with the paschal mystery appears also in Mark's Gospel, concretely in the episode in which James and John ask Jesus for a privileged place in his kingdom. The Lord responds to their request with a question that clearly links baptism and the cross: "Are you able to drink the cup that I drink, or to be baptized with the baptism with which I am baptized?" (Mark 10:38). With the image of the cup or the drink Jesus is referring to his passion and death, his radical giving of self, and he clearly links it to baptism, which was by immersion, though the "submersion" of Jesus' dead body in the earth was also part of the baptismal imagery used by the early Christians, as the above quote from Romans shows.

This same idea is found reflected in one of the mystagogical catecheses of Cyril of Jerusalem in the fourth century. Explaining the baptismal symbols, he states: "After this you were conducted to the sacred pool of divine Baptism, as Christ passed from the cross to the sepulchre you see before you. . . . You dipped thrice under the water and thrice rose up again, therein mystically signifying Christ's three days' burial." Further on: "Let no one imagine, then, that Baptism wins only the grace of remission of sins plus adoption, as John's baptism conferred only the remission of sins. No; we know full well that Baptism not only washes away our sins and procures for us the gift of the Holy Spirit, but is also the antitype of the Passion of Christ."[8]

The connection, then, between Christian baptism and the paschal mystery seems quite clear, but let us examine it in a bit more detail in the following section, by analyzing a text that is clear, powerful, and engaging.

---

7. On the interrelation between indicative and imperative, see Gabino Uríbarri, SJ, *El mensajero. Perfiles del evangelizador* (Bilbao: Desclée de Brouwer, 2006), pp. 136, 157-58, and 173-75.

8. *Mystagogical Lecture II,* nos. 4 and 6, trans. Anthony A. Stephenson, in *The Works of Saint Cyril of Jerusalem,* vol. 2, trans. Leo P. McCauley, SJ, and Anthony A. Stephenson (Washington, D.C.: Catholic University of America Press, 1970), pp. 163-66.

The Baptismal Hymn of Philippians 2:5-11

The hymn cited by Paul in his letter to the Philippians is well known as a powerful passage with deep reverberations for Christian life, which it understands as identification with Christ through radical self-emptying (kenosis) and constant service to others. Biblical scholars have shown clearly that it is a pre-Pauline hymn of baptismal origin. It is also fairly well recognized that it is a hymn strictly speaking, that is, a poetic composition used in the liturgy. Since 1928, when Ernst Lohmeyer proposed his division of the text into six stanzas of three lines each, a variety of alternative readings have been suggested. While recognizing that the question is still open, I follow here the argument of Ralph P. Martin,[9] which enjoys great credibility and appears to me to be most coherent, in both its literary analysis and its pragmatic understanding of the text's use in the community's worship. Besides, we will see that Martin's interpretation is one that allows for a full unfolding of the text's powerful social implications.

Martin founds his thesis on the classical *parallelismus membrorum* of Hebrew literature. He proposes a division of the hymn into six paired phrases that resemble antiphons and could be sung by two choruses. He suggests the following reconstruction:

I. v. 6: [He], though he was in the form of God,
   did not count equality with God a thing to be grasped,
II. v. 7: but emptied himself
   [taking the form of a servant]
   being born in the likeness of men.
      III. v. 8: And being found in human form
         he humbled himself and became obedient unto death
         [even death on the cross].
      IV. v. 9: Therefore God has exalted him
         and bestowed on him the name which is above every name,
V. v. 10: that at the name of Jesus
   every knee should bow,
   [in heaven, on earth and under the earth]

---

9. Ralph P. Martin, *A Hymn of Christ: Philippians 2:5-11 in Recent Interpretation and in the Setting of Early Christian Worship* (Downers Grove, Ill.: InterVarsity, 1997). This is already a classic study, originally published in 1967 and with two subsequent editions (1983 and 1997) that update the research.

VI. v. 11: and every tongue confess
   that Jesus Christ is Lord
   [to the glory of God the Father].

Martin explains and justifies the suppressed clauses enclosed in brackets, but we cannot go into that question, since it can be analyzed adequately only by studying the Greek text. The arguments in favor of a baptismal context for this hymn can be condensed into five. First, the formula "Jesus is Lord" (v. 11) comes from an ancient creed and is considered to be the confession of faith that was required for baptism. Second, the "name theology" (vv. 9, 10) is a trait proper to the rites of Christian initiation. Third, the term *form* (*morphē*, v. 6), related to or identified with *eikōn*, alludes to the fact that Christians are conformed to Christ in baptism in such a way that Christ "takes form" in the believer. Baptism, then, becomes the place where soteriology and ethics meet. Fourth, the hymn refers to the broader context of the formula of exorcism, that is, to the victory of the name of Jesus over the demonic forces of evil. And fifth, the proposed distribution of the stanzas allows us to envision the liturgical use of the passage in the three steps of the baptismal rite.[10]

Martin himself recognizes that his interpretation is not neat or linear, but requires the nuanced interrelation of different clues and the exercise of a certain intellectual cross-fertilization. Even so, his explanation appears to be the most complete and coherent; it is the best argued and has the best explanatory power. In sum, he claims that this hymn resounded in the ears of the Philippian community as a solemn and effective reminder of their own baptismal metamorphosis in Christ and of their new alliance against the powers of this world.[11]

Reading the hymn of Philippians in a baptismal key and, reciprocally, understanding baptism as participation in the descending movement of Jesus Christ *(kenōsis)* turn out to have extremely important consequences: if such interpretations have validity, then the church is by essence and by definition constituted as a kenotic body. The socio-political implications of this affirmation are only too evident in a society structured according to the totally opposed movements of dominion, power, oppression, social as-

10. See José Luis del Palacio Pérez-Medel, "La fuente bautismal y el catecumenado," published as an appendix in Louis Bouyer, *Arquitectura y liturgia* (Basauri: Grafite, 2000).
11. Palacio, "La fuente bautismal y el catecumenado," pp. 292-94.

cent, meritocracy, violence, and injustice. In fact, a recent study has shown clearly that in Philippians Paul is at once defending a redefinition of the social order and attacking the social stratification of the Roman empire, basing his argument precisely on the kenotic humbling of Christ.[12]

Social Implications

If I may be allowed to play a simple word game in the Greek language, we might say that only *kenōsis* makes possible *henōsis*. Only through despoilment and descent *(kenōsis)* is it possible to form a unified communion-society (*henōsis*, unity). The church is a social body which — by God's grace — incarnates this self-emptying, this kenotic "downward mobility," in order to make way for a new reality that is structured around love. This body, and no other, is the one that is formed through baptism.

Let us hear, further, what the author of the letter to the Ephesians has to say: "But now in Christ Jesus you who once were far off have been brought near in the blood of Christ. For he is our peace, who has made us both one, and has broken down the dividing wall of hostility, by abolishing in his flesh the law of commandments and ordinances, that he might create in himself one new man in place of the two, so making peace, and might reconcile us both to God in one body through the cross, thereby bringing the hostility to an end" (Eph. 2:13-16). Although this text refers directly to the overcoming of the divisions between Jews and gentiles, the saving work of Christ has universal value and therefore can be applied to any other human situation where division reigns.

In Christ Jesus every wall that separates persons and human groups has been broken down. In him we are one single people. Christ is our peace and our reconciliation. In him all hatred, oppression, death, discrimination, injustice, and exclusion are overpowered. Thanks to Christ, the law, the commandments, and the "old man" with his worn-out mentality finally disappear. Thanks to him, we Christians by baptism constitute a new people, a social body that provides a true alternative to the dominant logic and the powers of this world.

The letter to the Galatians reminds us that, thanks to baptism, we be-

12. See Joseph H. Hellerman, "The Humiliation of Christ in the Social World of Roman Philippi," *Bibliotheca Sacra* 160 (2003): 321-36 and 421-33.

come incorporated into the saving dynamic of God, who dissolves all divisions. "For as many of you as were baptized into Christ have put on Christ. There is neither Jew nor Greek, there is neither slave nor free, there is neither male nor female; for you are all one in Christ Jesus" (Gal. 3:27-28). This type of argument is quite frequent in the Pauline writings and in other parts of the New Testament. We might even say that what happens in baptism is not simply an "incorporation" (which in itself would be extraordinary if really lived out), but a true "con-corporation" of the whole church in a mysterious unity.[13] Paul describes it thus: "By one Spirit we were all baptized into one body — Jews or Greeks, slaves or free — and all were made to drink of one Spirit" (1 Cor. 12:13).

Now someone might object that all such theoretical musings are quite pious, but it remains to be known whether they correspond to the reality actually lived by the Christian communities. By way of example, Wayne Meeks asks, from a sociological perspective, how the Pauline communities actually celebrated baptism,[14] and he concludes that one of the principal images in the baptismal celebration and the community's understanding of baptism is the motif of dying and rising with Christ. Furthermore, he stresses that all the central themes associated with baptism are grouped together into opposing pairs: death/life, dying/rising, descending/ascending, burial/enthroning, old man/new man, body of flesh/body of Christ, divisions/unity, denuding/vesting, vices/virtues, powers of this world/Christ Jesus as Lord of the universe. Finally, Meeks notes that the ritual process of baptism manifests two almost symmetrical movements: one descending, toward being "buried" in the water, which symbolizes the separation of the one to be baptized from the external world; and the other ascending, and marking the baptized person's integration into a new reality, a new social body, an alternative space.

Pastoral Considerations

We come now to two interrelated questions, infant baptism and the sacrament of confirmation, which have great relevance for ecumenical dialogue

13. The original expression is from Pascasio Radberto ("Totius Ecclesiae mira unitate concorporatio") and is cited by de Lubac, *Catholicism*, p. 62. Even before that, Cyril of Alexandria had insisted that "we are con-corporated into Christ, not just among ourselves."

14. Wayne A. Meeks, *The First Urban Christians: The Social World of the Apostle Paul*, 2nd ed. (New Haven and London: Yale University Press, 2003), pp. 150-57.

and pastoral praxis. I have already stated that I will not treat in this book the complexities of the theological differences and agreements in the ongoing ecumenical dialogue. I do not intend to do so in this case either, but I do feel it necessary to mention at least some of the elements involved in these practices.

The basic problem concerning infant baptism may be stated thus: if we link baptism with participation in the death/resurrection of Christ and the beginning of a new life marked by a radical following of the Lord, then how can the baptism of small children be justified? That is, how can a baby assume the responsibilities inherent in a new life in Christ? Another matter of concern is the practice of confirmation, which is an independent sacrament but closely related to baptism. We know that it in fact developed out of the post-baptismal rites (imposition of hands and anointing with scented oils) and has always been understood as one of the sacraments of initiation. Some scholars, however, suspect that it was a late-arriving sacrament, which, in order to endow itself with content, had to rob meaning from the fullness of baptism. Such is not really the case, for the sacrament of confirmation allows the community to stress (in a vital context of greater Christian maturity) other aspects of Christian initiation, such as the gift of the Holy Spirit, the ecclesial and especially episcopal element, the vocation to mission, and the continuing nature of the catechumenal process.

In this sense, both the Reformation churches and the Orthodox and Latin churches tend to highlight the unity of the Christian initiation, at times speaking of a single initiatory sacrament, at other times offering baptism, confirmation, and first communion in the same ceremony. The Baptist churches, and especially the heirs of the Radical Anabaptist Reformation, tend to obviate the problem through their consistent practice of baptism of adults and their non-recognition of the sacrament of confirmation. The theological reflection of the Catholic Church, for its part, especially in the second half of the twentieth century, has led to a revalorization of the catechumenal process, a rediscovery of the baptism of adults, and a more nuanced understanding of the meaning and the implications of infant baptism. Attention should especially be called to the new *Ritual for the Christian Initiation of Adults* (1972), which is now considered the typical and normative road to baptism, though not the only one. We are still far from tapping into all the practical possibilities that are enclosed in the *Ritual*,[15] which is indeed a true treasure.

15. See Aidan Kavanaugh, OSB, *The Shape of Baptism: The Rite of Christian Initiation*

What is really important is to affirm simultaneously both the radicality of the new life in Christ, marked by a kenotic descent, and the logical need for gradual growth in that movement of service-oriented kenosis.[16] In my opinion, the Catholic Church possesses more than sufficient resources to work out a creative combination of infant baptism and adult confirmation, along with a vigorous community praxis of accompanying the young people involved. In so doing, we will indeed make progress in forming a true body of Christ that offers real alternatives to the dominant system. Although with clear theological differences, my proposal is not far removed from the Mennonite practice of "dedicating children" (in a non-sacramental rite) and reserving baptism exclusively for young people or adults. In both kinds of practice we have two rites that express both the radical change and the gradualness of the process.

Going beyond the intricacies of sacramental theology (which exceed my discussion here, as I have said), we now come to a most interesting and crucial pastoral question. How do we form the body of Christ in a post-Christian situation? How do we accompany new members in their dynamic process of becoming incorporated into the church? How do we live out this ecclesial "con-corporation," on the assumption that the basic subject of baptism is never just the individual baptized (whether child or adult), but the community as such?[17] What implications does all this have for our pastoral praxis?

Only if the Christian community is itself involved in a descending, kenotic process that leads to participation in Christ's death-resurrection, will that community be able to receive into its bosom new members and properly introduce them to this alternative body. Such precisely is the task of the godparents, who are assigned to guide the catechumens throughout the whole process of initiation (*Ritual of the Christian Initiation of Adults*,

---

(New York: Pueblo, 1978); Dionisio Borobio, *Catecumenado para la evangelización* (Madrid: San Pablo, 1997); and José Luis del Palacio Pérez-Medel, *El catecumenado postconciliar de adultos, forma privilegiada de la evangelización permanente de la iglesia local: estudio del catecumenado en el Concilio Vaticano II y en el ritual de iniciación cristiana de adultos. Tesis doctoral* (Madrid: Universidad Pontificia Comillas, 1998).

16. In the rest of this section, I follow Gerald W. Schlabach, ed., *On Baptism: Mennonite-Catholic Theological Colloquium 2001-2002* (Kitchener, Ont.: Pandora, 2004), especially the lead essay by Catholic theologian Frederick C. Bauerschmidt, "Baptism in the Diaspora" (pp. 16-61) and the response by Mennonite theologian Thomas Finger (pp. 63-79).

17. The expression is from Bauerschmidt, "Baptism in the Diaspora," p. 45.

no. 11). The aim of the process is not so much learning a few articles of faith; it is rather more like learning a profession: it requires time, teachers, practice, learning new habits (and unlearning others!), and being introduced into the community.[18] For this reason everyone in the community should become involved in the initiation process, by showing through their own lifestyle that there is another, very different way of experiencing and understanding the world: the whole community gives witness through alternative practices and communal habits that become concrete in relationships, dynamics, structures, and institutions that are firmly rooted in Jesus Christ and radically different from those that prevail in the world.

Once again, to prevent this proposal from being simply a declaration of good intentions, I would suggest structuring the catechesis for confirmation (or for adult baptism, as the case may be) as a process truly oriented toward forming followers of Jesus Christ. We might think in terms of what the anthropologists call "rites of passage," which have a triple moment of separation, transition, and reunion. That is to say, the process requires a certain dose of rupture, an element absent in most present-day catechesis. Such rupture would involve well-planned, challenging activities that might include elements such as the following: serious commitment to the poor (whether in daily life or in more intense periods, such as collaboration with the Catholic Worker movement or with the Jesuit Volunteer Corps), deeper experience of prayer life (perhaps through the Ignatian Spiritual Exercises or experiences of contemplative monastic life), active participation in a vibrant liturgical program, or practicing active nonviolence as a type of "alternative military service" (on this point, the Christian Peacemakers Teams offer a good model and an opportunity for getting involved). All such activities would make sense and be successful only insofar as the participants were well accompanied in the process, and the community as such, rooted in Jesus Christ, was embarked on a similar process of kenotic descent.[19]

18. Bauerschmidt, "Baptism in the Diaspora," p. 41. Along this same line there are interesting practical suggestions in Stanley Hauerwas and William H. Willimon, *Resident Aliens: Life in the Christian Colony* (Nashville: Abingdon, 1989), pp. 104-7.

19. Within the Catholic Church, one interesting experience is the Neo-catechumenal Way. Its evangelizing fruits are undeniable, although its excessive spiritualism and lack of social commitment continue to be worrisome, as well as the fact that it is frequently the cause of division within the church itself. See Ricardo Blázquez, *Las comunidades neocatecumenales. Discernimiento teológico,* 3rd ed. (Bilbao: Desclée de Brouwer, 1988), and Juan José

Nourishing the Body

Once the body is formed, it is necessary to nourish it so that it stays alive. The sacrament of the Eucharist is the Christian practice whose aim is nourishing the body, which is done precisely by receiving the body of Christ. Since a Eucharistic vein runs through this book from beginning to end, the present section simply uses the particular sacramental perspective to complement what has been said in other parts of the text.

Eucharist, Divinization, and Social Transformation

"He who eats my flesh and drinks my blood has eternal life. . . . He . . . abides in me, and I in him," says Jesus in his discourse on the bread of life in the synagogue of Capernaum (John 6:54, 56). The theme of the Eucharist as food that gives energy for life has been a constant in Christian experience throughout the centuries. Receiving the Lord and entering into communion with him supposes a profound transformation of our personal, ecclesial, and social reality. Quite rightly has it been said that the doctrine of Eucharistic transubstantiation cannot be limited to the gifts of bread and wine, but must also include all things and all persons.[20] Without risk of exaggeration, we may say that when we participate in the Eucharist, we are transformed into the body of Christ.

In the fourth century Cyril of Jerusalem was already explaining to the catechumens that "the body is given to you in the form of bread, and the blood is given to you in the form of wine, so that in partaking of the body and blood of Christ you become con-corporal and con-sanguine with him. Thus do we come to be bearers of Christ, by infusing his body and his blood into our members. In this way, as the apostle Peter said, we come to be participants in the divine nature."[21] In other words, the Eucharist makes us con-corporal with the Lord, makes us into "Christophers" (bearers of Christ) and bestows on us his own divine being. This divinization

---

Calles Garzón, *El camino neocatecumenal: un catecumenado parroquial,* 2nd ed. (Salamanca: Universidad Pontificia de Salamanca, 2005).

20. See the solid and suggestive reinterpretation of transubstantiation offered by Manuel Gesteira, *La eucaristía, misterio de comunión* (Salamanca: Sígueme, 1992), pp. 421-575.

21. *Mystagogical Lecture IV,* no. 3, in *The Works of Saint Cyril of Jerusalem,* vol. 2.

(*theosis* in Greek) is a direct effect of the Eucharistic food, as the Eastern Christian tradition has especially stressed. Specifically, the connection that some modern Russian theologians make between *theosis* and *sobornost* is noteworthy for the social implications of the Eucharist that it highlights. The notion of *sobornost* refers to an organism of love that keeps the individual and society in equilibrium, affirming the absolute value of the person and at the same time the absolute value of communion. In this way the individualist atomism of purely formal democracies is overcome, since, in accord with *sobornost,* all social bonds are freely accepted and established on the basis of service.[22]

Even though such questions are interesting, I cannot treat them here. In this section I adopt a more limited focus, restricting the discussion to presenting some aspects of the relation between Eucharist and divinization as found in Saint Augustine, the most important of the Western fathers. Thus I hope to make clear the convergence between the Eastern and the Western traditions, beyond terminological differences. While one tradition speaks of *theosis,* or divinization, the other uses notions like grace, justification, or filiation, but the meanings are similar. At the same time, the Eucharistic aspect of social transformation that comes about will also become evident.

I should first explain that Augustine uses a Neo-Platonic philosophical framework, but he reformulates and modifies it substantially. This can be seen clearly in the Augustinian use of the concept of participation, which is totally rethought according to the Christian category of incarnation: what for the philosophers was an ascending effort to reach divinity is recognized in the believer as a descending initiative of God himself in Jesus Christ.[23] The human transformative process in its personal and socio-ecclesial levels is sustained by the inwardly Trinitarian structure of reality. The bishop of Hippo, in his treatise *De Trinitate,* states that we humans

22. For an introduction, see Catherine de Hueck Doherty, *Sobornost: Eastern Unity of Mind and Heart for Western Man* (Notre Dame: Ave Maria, 1977). It is also interesting to consult Myroslaw I. Tataryn, *Augustine and Russian Orthodoxy. Russian Orthodox Theologians and Augustine of Hippo: A Twentieth Century Dialogue* (Lanham, Md., and Oxford: International Scholars Publication, 2000), especially pp. 57-61, 84, and 126.

23. This point is made clearly by David D. Meconi, SJ, "The Incarnation and the Role of Participation in St. Augustine's 'Confessions,'" *Augustinian Studies* 29 (1998): 61-75; and by Gerald Bonner, "Augustine's Conception of Deification," *Journal of Theological Studies* 37 (1986): 369-86.

should imitate the unity of divine love, both in our relations with God and in our inter-human relations. He then adds: "it is by his gift that we are one with each other; with him we are one spirit, because our soul is glued on behind him."[24] Joseph Lienhard not only has emphasized the importance of the verb *agglutinare* (bind) in Augustine's writing, but has also pointed out that the subject of this verb is the Holy Spirit, as the true bond that keeps believers united among themselves and with the Trinity.[25] A real transformation is brought about in fact, but this is not achieved by human means: "The good of such desirable transformation is conferred on us by God's grace."[26] In fact, when human beings enter into this new relation with the Trinitarian God and allow themselves to be transformed by him, they discover a new and surprising reality: "True freedom is holy bondage *(pia servitus)*."[27] This is truly the liberty of the bond of love, the revolutionary depths of the dialectical kenosis-*theosis*, emptying and fulfilling.

There is no doubt that for Augustine the Eucharist is the privileged space in which this transformation becomes operative, and the Christian community is the concrete social form of the new reality. For that reason he structures his reflections around the body of Christ, as, for example, when he states that Jesus Christ himself "has linked us all together as members of his own body, bound to one another by the tender bond of love."[28] Once again, we find in this text that the initiative and the power correspond to God's grace, but that its effects are real and are manifested in a new space or social body. "Just as you see that the bread which was made is one mass, so may you also be one Body by loving one another, by having one faith, one hope, and one undivided charity. . . . We receive [his

---

24. Augustine, *The Trinity*, introduction, translation, and notes by Edmund Hill, OP (Brooklyn, N.Y.: New City, 1991), book VI, chapter 1, number 7, p. 209.

25. Joseph T. Lienhard, SJ, "'The Glue Itself Is Charity': Ps 62:9 in Augustine's Thought," in *Augustine: Presbyter Factus Sum, Collectanea Augustiniana*, ed. Joseph T. Lienhard, SJ, Earl C. Muller, SJ, and Roland J. Teske, SJ (New York: Peter Lang, 1993), pp. 375-84.

26. Augustine, *Trinity* XV, 3, 14, p. 406.

27. Augustine, *The Enchiridion on Faith, Hope and Love*, trans. J. B. Shaw, with an introduction by Thomas S. Hibbs, and an appendix by Adolf von Harnack (Washington, D.C.: Regnery, 1996), p. 37 n. 30.

28. Augustine, "Tractatus 65 on John's Gospel," no. 3. CCL 492, quoted in *Liturgy of the Hours*, vol. 2, p. 789. Spanish edition in San Agustín, "Tratado 65 sobre el Evangelio de Juan," in *Obras Completas. Tomo XIV*, ed. Fr. Vicente Rabanal, OSA (Madrid: Biblioteca de Autores Cristianos, 1957), p. 361.

body] together, and we drink [his blood] together because we live together."[29] As Gerald Bonner points out, the city of God and the earthly city are necessarily intertwined in history, but the Eucharist anticipates the plenitude of God's kingdom, in which all evil, all injustice, all pain, and all sin will finally disappear.[30] This anticipation is a gift of the free initiative of divine grace, but it takes on a socially visible body in the new type of bonds and relationships that are formed in the church, the body of Christ. Let us examine this a bit more in detail.

The Eucharist as Anticipation of the Future Kingdom

Love of one's enemies offers an especially significant example of how the Eucharist announces, incarnates, and testifies to the transformed reality, for such love reveals the new reality precisely in the most conflictive aspect of our social relations. Augustine addresses this issue in his *Eighth Homily on 1 John:*

> Let your desire for him [your enemy] be that together with you he may have eternal life: let your desire for him be that he may be your brother. And if that is what you desire in loving your enemy (that he may be your brother) when you love him, you love a brother. You love in him, not what he is, but what you would have him be.[31]

In the *Tenth Homily* he adds, "You are to love all men, even your enemies — not because they *are* your brothers, but in order that they may be."[32] Love anticipates reality: it makes into a brother one who is (still) an enemy. That is, when we receive God's love, it transforms us personally and propels us to love to transform our social reality. That is, not only are we

29. Augustine, "Sermon 229 for the Easter Season, On the Sacraments of the Faithful," in *Sermons on the Liturgical Seasons,* trans. Sr. Mary Sarah Muldowney, RSM (New York: Fathers of the Church, 1959), p. 202.

30. Gerald Bonner, "Augustine's Understanding of the Church as a Eucharist Community," in *Saint Augustine the Bishop: A Book of Essays,* ed. Fannie LeMoine and Christopher Kleinhenz (New York and London: Garland, 1994), pp. 39-63.

31. "Homilies on the First Epistle of St. John, Eighth Homily," in Augustine, *Later Works,* selected and translated with introductions by John Burnaby, vol. 8 (Philadelphia: Westminster, 1955), pp. 323-24.

32. Augustine, "Homilies on the First Epistle of St. John, Eighth Homily," p. 344.

transformed passively, but the transformation changes the reality. The Eucharistic anticipation has revolutionary consequences, as long as it is embodied in a particular and historic community. Since the daily practice of Eucharist involves precisely nourishing that body, Augustine can play with the two different meanings of body of Christ, bread and community, and can say to those who are going to participate in the Eucharist: "If you are the body and the members of Christ, then there on the Lord's table is the very mystery that you yourselves are, and you receive the mystery that you are."[33] In another sermon he states: "If you have received him worthily, you are yourselves that which you have received."[34] The dual aspect of the body of Christ, as Eucharistic bread and as ecclesial community, involves still another duality that is proper to the transformative dynamism of which we are speaking, namely, between present reality and future reality.

The last texts cited indicate how the Eucharist anticipates the eschatological fullness, a topic that brings us to our final reflection in this section, on the temporal structure of the sacrament. We know that there is only one sacrifice and only one Eucharist (that of Jesus Christ, who offers himself once and for all: *ephapax,* Heb. 7:27), but, since the church is the body of Christ, all reality becomes assumed into its transforming dynamism, and this happens in quite ordinary ways. The power contained in such theological notions as transubstantiation or memorial resides in the fact that the Eucharist really does graft us into eschatological time.[35] While the famous expression of Oscar Cullmann, "already but not yet," preserves a lineal timeframe, the true Christian vision (Eucharistic-eschatological) overflows such a schema. To cite one example, in the Johannine account of Jesus' appearance to the disciples by the lakeside, the meal begins with the expression "Jesus comes" (John 21:13), which is an echo of the prayer "Come, Lord Jesus" (*Maran atha:* Rev. 22:20) and of the "I will come to you" that Jesus repeats at the Last Supper (John 14:3, 28). All the time dimensions — past, present, future — are thus touched by the transforming reality of Christ. As de Lubac puts it well, the Eucharist involves a dynamic relationship among the three facets of memorial, anticipation, and presence. The mystery of the Eucharist and the church includes the triple di-

33. Augustine, "Sermón 272," in *Obras Completas. Tomo XXIV,* ed. Fr. Pío de Luis, OSA (Madrid: Biblioteca de Autores Cristianos, 1983), p. 767.

34. Augustine, "Sermón 227," in *Obras Completas. Tomo XXIV,* p. 285.

35. Gabino Uríbarri, SJ, "Escatología y eucaristía. Notas para una escatología sacramental," *Estudios Eclesiásticos* 80 (2005): 51-67.

mension of the past as *memoria passionis,* the future as glorious anticipation of the kingdom, and the present as real body.[36] The three aspects are woven intimately together and must be kept in dynamic tension.

This theological intuition has been taken up, expanded, and deepened by several contemporary authors. Louis-Marie Chauvet, for example, has developed a potent fundamental sacramentology through dialogue with current philosophical thought (philosophy of language, phenomenology, anthropology, hermeneutics). Chauvet posits that God, human beings, and the sacraments are related together in a dynamic, not merely lineal, fashion. The sacramental symbols are thus linked to the biblical word and to ethical praxis in a fresh, original way. Fundamental to Chauvet's proposal is the dynamic of the gift, that is, the gratuitous irruption of God's grace as the engine of the whole saving sacramental process. Religious practices, especially the sacraments and perhaps above all the Eucharist, dispose the believer both to receive the gift and then to return it again as a newly incarnate gift. I synthesize his proposal in the chart below.[37]

Gift	Reception of gift	Return of gift
Scripture	Sacrament	Ethics
Body of Christ, historical and glorious	Body of Christ, sacramental	Body of Christ, ecclesial
Gift of God	Reception of the gift	Return of the gift ("counter-gift")
Faire grâce	*Rendre grâce* Oblation and thanksgiving	*Vivre-en-grâce* The community's life-in-grace
Past	Present	Future

In this way, the gift of God, which assumes the history of salvation and above all the life of Jesus Christ (past), becomes real in the present thanks to the sacraments, which in turn thrusts us toward the future of a life radically renewed in Christ. The Christian community thus shines (in the

---

36. Henri de Lubac, *Corpus Mysticum* (London: SCM, 2006), pp. 67-88 and 295-339.

37. Louis-Marie Chauvet, *Symbole et sacrement: une relecture sacramentelle de l'existence chrétienne* (Paris: Ed. du Cerf, 1990), p. 285. The author here offers a dynamic schema that I have adapted in my chart.

present) before the world as the social space that proclaims the gratuity of the gift over against the dominant commercial mentality, and this happens precisely because the church is engaged with the inherited tradition (past) that anticipates the eschatological future of the kingdom. Although we cannot delve deeper into the matter now, the social implications of this fact have been explored by Bruce Morrill in his analysis of the connection between the Eucharistic anamnesis and the *memoria passionis* emphasized in the political theology of Johann Baptist Metz.[38] Suffice it to recall that the Eucharist, in light of all I have said, is a powerful communal practice that configures and nourishes a social body that seeks to be an alternative to the dominant system. In this sense, we Christians hear also the words spoken to the prophet Elijah: "Arise and eat, else the journey will be too great for you" (1 Kings 19:7).

Strengthening the Body: Matrimony and Priestly Ordination

I treat together in this section two sacraments geared to strengthening the body of Christ. Both matrimony and ordained ministry are signs of God's love for humanity and instruments for giving visible corporal expression to God's fecundity, but this will happen only insofar as we live truly as body, on a basis of complementarity. In the church there are different charismas and styles that we must integrate together in love so that we can manifest that love to humanity. Concretely, there can be said to be two poles in love: one that is intensive and another that is extensive. Love always assumes radical commitment to and deep affection for the people at our side. This is lived above all in matrimony. Love here is intensive. There are other people, however, who live this same reality but stress the extensive aspect of love. The ministers ordained for the community manifest the universal and all-embracing quality of love; they show that the Christian community cannot close itself off in intensive love but must grow into a body of extensive love. Such an emphasis is seen most clearly in the Catholic Church, through the intimate connection between ordained ministry and celibacy. However, the intensive-extensive polarity of love is not limited only to that aspect.

---

38. Bruce T. Morrill, SJ, *Anamnesis as Dangerous Memory: Political and Liturgical Theology in Dialogue* (Collegeville, Minn.: Liturgical, 2000).

The gist of the matter is in the complementarity. God's love wants to embrace all human beings intensely, with no one left out: God loves both intensively and extensively. As a result, either we Christians will learn how to harmonize these two poles, the intensive and the extensive, or else the church will be incapable of making present the full force of God's affection for humanity. If we do succeed in constituting a body that truly incarnates both intensive and extensive love, then the reality of our world will end up quite different. We will not simply carry out charitable actions that can easily become individualistic and superficial, but we will discover the force of a political charity that transforms unjust structures at all levels.

Accordingly, I first examine how the experience of the sacrament of Christian matrimony involves, on the basis of intensive love, a subversion of the family values dominant in our society. Then I analyze how the ordained ministry, sealed by the sacrament of orders, implies a subversion of the sacral values that dominate the sacerdotal horizon of religions.

Matrimony and the Subversion of Family Values

Matrimony is a peculiar sacrament, because it presents a twofold aspect that does not exist in the other sacraments. On the one hand, marriage is a gift of creation and therefore a natural human reality, but on the other, it is an image of God's fidelity manifested in Christ and so assumes also a sacramental character. Thus, the institutions of marriage and family that are present in all cultures acquire a specific meaning, form, and orientation in Christianity that reach the point of constituting what is called the "domestic Church" (*Lumen Gentium*, 11). In this way, the natural institution is strengthened through a sacramental grounding in the promise and active presence of God's Spirit, so as to make more evident the horizon of fecundity and fidelity that helps define matrimony.

What, then, is the basic meaning of matrimonial commitment? We Christians call it a sacrament precisely because the commitment of the spouses, in the body of Christ, is rooted in God's promise. As Hannah Arendt has said so wisely, the ability to make promises is a specifically human faculty that allows people to order the future and free it from chaos.[39]

39. Drawing on the thought of Hannah Arendt, Michael Sandel, and Daniel Bell, I and Juan Guerrero have reflected on promise, "co-promise" and bonds in Juan A. Guerrero, SJ,

Furthermore, from the Christian point of view, every promise is in reality a co-promise, or commitment (the Spanish word for commitment is *compromise*). When we promise something, we create a bond with somebody else. This is obvious in the case of matrimony, but not only with regard to the couple that is getting married. The couple makes a public commitment in the presence of the whole community, but the community itself also commits itself to them and thus expands and strengthens the bonding beyond just the couple.

Some analysts have pointed out that in the modern world constitutive bonds have become eroded as a result of the predominance of instrumental and sentimental bonds, even in the realm of matrimony and the family. The clearest example may be seen in sentimental matters, since we are much influenced by the romantic ideal and are little aware of what a recent invention it is. The important thing in life, we are told, is to be in love. Such a conception makes it very difficult for us to keep promises, since the promises will retain their meaning only as long as does the sentiment I had when I made them. It is no wonder that contemporary society is so characterized by successive polygamy. We should not, therefore, think of Africa when we hear these words of Pope Benedict XVI: "Monogamous matrimony corresponds to the image of the monotheistic God. Matrimony based on an exclusive, definitive love becomes the icon of the relation of God with his people, and conversely, God's way of loving becomes the measure of human love" (*Deus Caritas Est,* no. 11). Permanent, monogamous matrimony is based on the promise of the one, true God. Obviously, affirming and living this in today's world is something countercultural.

While it may seem relatively simple to detect the error in applying exclusively sentimental bonds to matrimony, a more complicated (but perhaps more important) matter is exposing the influence of instrumental bonding. Although in principle few people defend matrimony as simply an agreement based on practical interests, there was possibly some truth in the Marxist critique that viewed the puritanical family of the nineteenth century as an effective cell for reproducing the mechanisms of production capitalism. What is curious is that now at the start of the twenty-first century supposedly progressive forces are defending family models of a plural, fragmented nature, models that without a doubt serve to nourish and re-

and Daniel Izuzquiza, SJ, *Vidas que sobran. Los excluidos de un mundo en quiebra* (Santander: Sal Terrae, 2004), pp. 115-96.

produce consumer capitalism.[40] We have passed, then, from conceiving the family as a unit of production to conceiving it as a unit of consumption, but we are still constrained by an instrumental mindset.

The Christian vision of the sacrament of matrimony is, of course, quite different. It is characterized by constitutive bonds which, rooted in Jesus Christ, offer a radical alternative to the traditional modern or postmodern models.[41] In this sense, we should take note of the contradiction that exists in certain types of conservative discourse, which employs a rhetoric of defense of Christian family values, but does not realize that such values are in fact values of liberal capitalism and the nineteenth-century bourgeoisie. Jesus of Nazareth never defended the modern nuclear family — among other reasons, because he had no experience of it. Neither, however, did Jesus accept the traditional model of the extended family that was prevalent in his time. Rather, with great liberty, he lived out and proposed brand-new forms of family relations: "Here are my mother and my brothers! For whoever does the will of my Father in heaven is my brother, and sister, and mother" (Matt. 12:49-50). For Christians, family is not an absolute value, but is clearly subordinated to the kingdom of God; this is in clear contrast to the dominant cultural system.[42] The church, which is Christ's body and God's family, is precisely the social space that incarnates this new reality. The sacrament of matrimony is for that reason an indispensable ecclesial practice that strengthens the body of Christ and subverts the established order.

On the basis of this argument, we can now proceed to some final reflections on alleged attacks against the family and the consequent policies in defense of the family. Quite interesting is the apostolic exhortation *Familiaris Consortio,* published by John Paul II in 1981, which denounces that "in many regions, because of the extreme poverty caused by unjust or

40. A similar critique, using arguments drawn from secular economics and feminism, can be found in Nancy Folbre, *The Invisible Heart: Economics and Family Values* (New York: The New Press, 2002).

41. See Rodney Clapp, *Families at the Crossroads: Beyond Traditional and Modern Options* (Chicago: InterVarsity, 1993). Also, Agustín Domingo Moratalla, *Ética de la vida familiar. Claves para una ciudadanía comunitaria* (Bilbao: Desclée de Brouwer, 2006), pp. 33-57, offers a clear historical framework and a sensible proposal for the "relational family."

42. Cf. Santiago Guijarro, *Fidelidades en conflicto. La ruptura con la familia por causa del discipulado y de la misión en la tradición sinóptica* (Salamanca: Universidad Pontificia de Salamanca, 1998).

inadequate socio-economic structures, young people are not in a position to get married as they should"; the document therefore asks that "the society and the public authorities support legitimate matrimony through a series of social and political interventions, such as guaranteeing a basic family wage, arranging for housing fitting for family life and creating suitable possibilities for work and life" (no. 81). In keeping with the pope's statements, we might ask ourselves what is really causing the breakup of the family in our society. If we ask ourselves honestly and do not limit ourselves to an ideologized rhetoric, we will discover, among other things, the following factors: labor flexibility and geographic mobility; structural injustice that makes migration and the separation of nuclear families necessary (along with restrictive migratory policies that make family reunification difficult); an economic situation that makes two incomes necessary to sustain a household, in part because of poverty, in part because of the pressure of fictitious needs; a rhythm of life that is full of tension, rush, and exhaustion — all for the sake of consumerism (the economic driving force of advanced capitalism); real estate speculation that makes housing difficult to obtain. These factors are not just matters of economic policy, but have a direct effect on an ordinary family's lived reality.[43]

In this regard, other kinds of political decision, such as monetary assistance to families, free school books, or maternity leave, while they are important, are relatively minor matters. Likewise, it should be recognized that laws that decriminalize abortion or that permit divorce or homosexual marriage, while they clearly do not support family, are not in themselves breaking up the family. What is most important to emphasize here is the need for us to present an alternative perspective on family and marriage, without giving in to alarmism or frivolous proposals. Once again we must affirm that Christian morality applies first of all to Christians and not to society as a whole. That is, our main task is to foster communal practices and community spaces in which it becomes possible to live in a different way: in matrimonial fidelity, in intergenerational dialogue, in wholehearted support of life in all its manifestations, in active solidarity with the impoverished. Most definitely, if we Christians find our primordial identity in the body of Christ, then we must not ever allow the state to define and control our reality.

43. See Comisión Permanente de la HOAC (Hermandad Obrera de Acción Católica), *Un trabajo digno para la familia. Una familia para la vida.* Reflexión para el día de la HOAC, Madrid 2006.

Before concluding this section, I would like to explain that a fundamental difference exists between a rigorist posture and a radical one. In these pages I am arguing that the radicality of the gospel implies a marked contrast with the norms of the prevailing society, but I by no means wish to defend positions that are exclusive, closed, or rigorist. As Johann Baptist Metz points out, "rigorism proceeds rather from fear, while radicality is born of the liberty of Christ's call."[44] The radical alternative embodied in Christian matrimony is not at odds (quite the contrary!) with mercy, flexibility, and compassionate comprehension of the diverse circumstances and situations of human fragility. We therefore affirm a radical Christian ethics that is compatible with the "pastoral gentleness" that the gospel calls for.[45]

Ordained Ministry and the Subversion of Sacral Values

The sacrament of orders is intimately linked to the church's ministries, charisms, and services and therefore to whatever ecclesiological conception we employ. Thanks to baptism, the whole community of believers participates in the unique priesthood of Christ, so that all that I said in the section about baptism may serve as a general framework for what I discuss here. That common priesthood, in which all the baptized share, is expressed visibly in the ministerial priesthood of certain members of the community. This ordained priesthood includes three grades (episcopacy, priesthood, diaconate) and exists precisely for the service of the whole body of Christ, to help that body to take form in accord with the grace of baptism.

When, with Jesus, the novelty of God's kingdom broke into history, it brought about a radical subversion of sacral values, which until then had dominated the understanding of how humans related to God. Specifically, with Jesus and the rise of Christianity there comes about an authentic upheaval of religious priesthood. The quite profound and nuanced study of

44. Johann Baptist Metz, *Jenseits bürgerlicher Religion. Reden über die Zukunft der Christentums* (Munich and Mainz: Kaiser/Matthias-Grunewald-Verlag, 1980), p. 18. English edition, *The Emergent Church: The Future of Christianity in a Postbourgeois World,* trans. Peter Mann (New York: Crossroad, 1981).

45. See, for example, Marciano Vidal, CSsR, *El matrimonio, entre el ideal cristiano y la fragilidad humana. Teología, moral y pastoral* (Bilbao: Desclée de Brouwer, 2003). While good, this book does not emphasize sufficiently the radical pole of the Christian alternative.

the recently named Cardinal Vanhoye shows this well. He quite aptly describes how the letter to the Hebrews "blows to pieces" the schemas of ancient priesthood.[46] At the same time, we must also recognize a perhaps unexpected twist. Despite the rupture and the novelty (or precisely because of them!), the author of the letter to the Hebrews is able to affirm convincingly that Christ is the one and only true priest. A truly revolutionary change is brought about in the manner of understanding cult and priesthood. The ritual aspect retires to the background, and existential self-donation becomes the core of Christian priesthood. The one and only true priesthood is that of Jesus Christ. For that reason, argues Vanhoye, we should avoid two types of backtracking: we Christians cannot remain attached to the ancient priesthood (a temptation of the Catholic right?), but neither can we prescind from a truly sacerdotal expression of our Christian reality, as if we had not really assimilated the New Testament conception of priesthood (a temptation of Protestantism and the Catholic left?).

We thus come to the second aspect I wish to highlight in this section, namely, that the key to Christian ministry is radical service and self-donation to the very end. "I am among you as one who serves," says Jesus in the so-called service *logion* of Luke 22:27, a text that may be read in parallel with the words of the institution of the Eucharist: "This is my body which is given for you" (Luke 22:19). In both cases we find a threefold structure: first, the person of Jesus ("I am," "my body" = my person); second, service and handing-over ("one who serves," "given for"); third, "among you," "for you," that is, on behalf and in the midst of humankind. As Manuel Gesteira has pointed out, a combined reading of these texts, along with the washing of the feet (John 13) and the hymn from Philippians (Phil. 2), allows us to discover a rich relationship linking ser-

---

46. Albert Vanhoye, SJ, *Prêtres anciens, prêtre nouveau selon le Noveau Testament* (Paris: Éditions du Seuil, 1980), p. 10: "Sa conception du sacerdoce et du sacrifice ne peut absolument pas se réduire aux schémes anciens. Elle les transforme profondément et les fait éclater de tous côtés." In this book there appear a multitude of similar expressions: the first Christians do not see even "the least relation between Jesus and the institution of priesthood"; there is an "absolute contrast," "a radically new way" of being priest, "an unprecedented conception of priesthood." The fullness of Christ manifests "the aspect of rupture," "is of a different order," is "overcoming" the earlier stage. Jesus is the most radical of the ancient prophets "because he attacks simultaneously the whole system of the law" with a "radical rejection of all the ritual sacrifices"; he is a "totally different" priest. Likewise, there is also "an enormous difference" between Paul's ministry and the ancient priesthood. In sum, "there was a true rupture between the new faith and the ancient priesthood."

vice, Eucharist, kenosis, and ministry.[47] The consequences of this connection are so evident that there is no need to expand on them; rather, they need to be lived out with radicality.

Strictly speaking, then, in the church there are no priests. There is only one priest, Christ, and he is a priest in such a way as to shatter all the old priestly models. All of us Christians, incorporated into Christ through baptism, constitute a priestly people. Only in a derived, analogical, and tenuous sense can the leaders of the Christian community be called "priests." The ordained ministers we call priests serve to help the whole church live out the radicality of this existential priesthood. From this point of view, the ordained ministries are at the service of the common priesthood, not the other way around. These ministries constitute, in Pauline terminology, a "ministry of reconciliation" (2 Cor. 5:18) carried out by "ministers of a new covenant" (2 Cor. 3:6) — reconciliation and new covenant realized in the life-death-resurrection of Jesus Christ.

Entering into our third and final theme in this section, we note that theology has traditionally envisioned two poles in the understanding and grounding of Christian priesthood. In the words of Gisbert Greshake, "in *persona Christi* the priest represents the head of the Church; in *persona ecclesiae* he represents the body of Christ built up and filled by the Holy Spirit."[48] The priesthood, then, has a twofold foundation, Christological and ecclesiological. Although theological reflection has at times emphasized one aspect more than the other, even to the point of eclipsing one or the other, it is clear that an adequate theology of the Christian priesthood requires that it be closely linked with both Christ and the church, simultaneously if also differently. The aim of such theology is to help in the formation of an ecclesial body that recognizes Jesus Christ as its only head, without any type of clericalism. This twofold character, Christological and pneumatic-ecclesial, is at the heart of Christian ministry and is strictly related to one of the most important conclusions of the previous chapter, namely, that in the Eucharist there can be no separation of the diverse aspects and dimensions of Christ's body, which is real and mystical, ecclesial and Eucharistic, in the bread and in the poor.

We must proceed further, however, for this dogmatic type of reflection

---

47. Gesteira, *La eucaristía, misterio de comunión,* p. 50 n. 98 and p. 140.

48. Gisbert Greshake, *The Meaning of Christian Priesthood,* 2nd ed., trans. Peadar MacSeumais, SJ (Dublin: Four Courts, 1993), p. 88.

encompasses important consequences of a socio-ecclesial, political nature. Obviously, we cannot avoid the fact that ministry and priesthood have some relation with the distribution of power within the community. To ignore this would be an irresponsible exercise of naïve spiritualization. We must admit, then, that the priesthood has to do with power in the church, and I hold (hopefully without being idealistic) that in the believing community power has meaning only if it takes the form of service. Many authors, to defend this position, lean toward the pneumatic-ecclesial pole of the priesthood and seek to ground ministry in the community's initiative. Emphasis is thus placed on the horizontal or vertically ascending dynamic of the choice, the formation and the ordination of priests: the initiative and the primacy are with the community, in which the Spirit dwells. The Christian community in this way manifests egalitarian relationships, modifies the ordinary uses of power, and offers a contrast to the dominant authoritarianism.[49]

Giving exclusive or excessive emphasis to the ecclesial pole, on the other hand, and forgetting the Christological foundation is an error that impedes the radicalization of the Christian alternative. For if we insist only on horizontal relationships and a balanced distribution of power, what new contribution is the believing community offering over and above what is offered by other egalitarian groups in our world? Though it may seem paradoxical, our affirmation of the vertically descending dimension of the Christian priesthood has far more radical implications. Jesus Christ is the only Lord, the only master of the entire universe, the source of all power. Jesus Christ despoiled himself of his lordly condition, lived a life totally devoted to the service of others, and was brutally nailed to a tree trunk. The Christian priesthood represents *that* Christ; we are therefore not discussing merely certain organizational aspects of how power is distributed in a human community. Rather, we are talking about the revelation of God in Christ, the head of the ecclesial body. For that reason, the Christological foundation of the Christian priesthood, precisely because of its vertically descending character, has powerful consequences for changing the way we understand and organize power in the world. As I

49. In this paragraph I develop some of the proposals of Edward Schillebeeckx, OP, *Ministry: A Case for Change* (London: SCM, 1981) and of José Ignacio González Faus, SJ, *Hombres de la comunidad. Apuntes sobre el ministerio eclesial* (Santander: Sal Terrae, 1989). The reality of the matter is quite nuanced, but in general the balanced posture of Greshake allows for an understanding of the more radical consequences.

have mentioned already, the root offers a more radical subversion than do the rhizomes alone.

In order for this to become truth and not so many empty words, ecclesial praxis must obviously be consistent with the theology that we are formulating. Thus Greshake states: "Looked at in this way, priesthood essentially signifies 'vicariousness,' 'representation'; it always occupies only the second place to the Lord, whose will is to come himself in priestly service to mankind."[50] The minister personally empties himself out in order to manifest Jesus Christ, and he devotes himself totally to the service of the brothers and sisters — such is the synthesis of the Christian priesthood.

We end here, having seen in this section how the sacrament of matrimony and the sacrament of orders nourish the body of Christ and, in so doing, incarnate a way of relating that is different from the world's ways. I make a final comment regarding the complementarity that necessarily exists between these two ecclesial charismas. Interestingly, we find this convergence mentioned in reflections on the priesthood as well as in reflections concerning matrimony and maternity. Greshake insists on the need to distinguish the different emphases that are evident in the ministerial priesthood and the common priesthood. The accent of ministry is found in a "concentrating" type of activity, that is, in its mission of gathering the community together and keeping it united in the ecclesial *communion*. The accent of the common priesthood, for its part, is rather on an "ec-centric" type of action, the *missio*, the impregnation of the world with the gospel.[51] In similar fashion, a lay woman theologian, married and with children, says that Christian love unfolds between a "concentrated" pole and a "de-centered" pole, which are given a privileged form of incarnation in matrimony and the celibate state.[52] No doubt, these two poles or accents are both necessary for fully forming the true body of Christ.

---

50. Greshake, *The Meaning of Christian Priesthood*, p. 74.

51. These lines are missing in the English version, but they refer to pages 118-20 of the German original edition, which correspond to pages 142-43 of the Spanish version. See Greshake, *The Meaning of Christian Priesthood*, p. 71.

52. María Dolores López Guzmán, *Donde la maternidad se vuelve canto. Apuntes para una teología de la maternidad* (Santander: Sal Terrae, 2006), pp. 79-81.

Healing the Body: Reconciliation and Anointing of the Sick

In this section we look at the two final sacramental practices, both of which have to do with the process of healing the body. The sacrament of reconciliation and the sacrament of anointing of the sick make present in the midst of the Christian community the healing power of God in two very concrete existential situations: sin and sickness. Both these states are related to the weakness of the body of Christ, whether in the moral sphere or on the physical plane. It would be appropriate, therefore, to speak of these two sacraments as community practices that incarnate the healing of the weak body and the healing of the weak bodies. Studying both sacraments together in the same section allows us to avoid dualisms and to emphasize more strongly the integral character of Christian anthropology. It is not that one sacrament is directed to the soul and the other to the body, nor is it that one is individual and the other is communal. Rather, we know that the human organism is a psychosomatic and spiritual unity and that when one member of the body suffers, the whole body suffers. Therefore, God's action in and through the community aims at an integral liberation/ healing.

In the Face of Sin: Healing the Weak Body

Moral evil, sin, and pardon are unavoidable realities that introduce us to the deepest chambers of the human condition. According to Hannah Arendt, the capacity to forgive and to ask for forgiveness is a properly human ability, which allows us to order the past, which has been fragmented by our faults. Just as the capacity to make promises allows an ordering of the future and a liberation from chaos, so forgiveness makes it possible to begin anew when we have fallen short in our promises and commitments. It is quite understandable, then, that the Christian community has, from its very origins, offered practices that allow this human dynamic to operate in a joyful and liberating manner.

Any examination of the life and praxis of Jesus that does not consider his nearness to pain, fragility, sin, and forgiveness would be not only incomplete, but quite incomprehensible. The Gospels tell of the kingdom's irruption into history in the person of Jesus Christ, through a series of signs that are basically the manifestation of God's healing force.[53] Jesus cures the sick, drives out demons, and pardons sins, all at the same time. The liberation is integral and total; it awakens amazement in those who behold it and provokes accusations of blasphemy. "Who can forgive sins but God alone?" (Mark 2:7), exclaim the scribes after the healing of the paralytic in Capernaum. Jesus always maintains a compassionate proximity to the reality of evil, always sees from the viewpoint of the most vulnerable, always plumbs the deepest levels, all the way to the nadir of sin. For that reason his healings have a tangible physical effect, but they go further than that: they are linked to faith ("your faith has saved you," he says frequently) and to the forgiveness of sins. When he sends forth his disciples, he gives them the same power of healing, of casting out demons (Mark 6:13), and of forgiving sins (John 20:23).

In continuity with the praxis of Jesus, the church has always had a community practice that is oriented to healing the weak body or, said differently, aimed at making sacramentally tangible God's response to the fact of sin. The ways of celebrating the practice have varied, as have the names employed to denominate it: sacrament of mercy and pardon, of reconciliation, of penance, of conversion, of confession.[54] Such terms are not to be understood in any exclusive sense, but rather give evidence that we are dealing with a profound reality that can hardly be contained in a single expression. From the viewpoint of this book, we may state that it is a sacrament that expresses and realizes God's healing love with regard to the wounds in the body of Christ (in its dimensions of being a glorious, Eucharistic, ecclesial, personal, and cosmic body).

All things considered, forgiveness constitutes one of the most powerful and revolutionary actions that we can bring about or even imagine, for if sin fractures our own personal project, our human solidarity, and our relationship with God, then forgiveness repairs and restores those relationships. And not only does it allow us to return to the starting point, but it carries us to a more advanced situation, where those relationships are warmer, closer, and more consistent. Forgiveness includes a large measure of madness, pure excess, and profound mystery. For that very reason pardon is a properly divine action, the expression of a gratuitous gift, evi-

---

53. Manuel Gesteira, "'Christus medicus'. Jesús ante el problema del mal," *Revista Española de Teología* 51 (1991): 253-300.

54. These are the five expressions found in the *Catechism of the Catholic Church*, nos. 1423-24. See also the theological analysis in Fernando Millán Romeral, *La penitencia hoy. Claves para una renovación* (Bilbao: Desclée de Brouwer, 2001), pp. 99-143.

dence of God's overflowing love (*per-don:* superabundant gift). At the same time, pardon is a specifically human action, insofar as the human being is *imago Dei*. Once again, we discover that living rooted in Jesus Christ introduces us into a dynamic of radical consequences. We are called to reproduce in our lives Jesus' own love, the love that pardons everybody, even our enemies, to the very end. This crucified and crucifying pardon has profound repercussions in our own personal liberation, in the renovation of our interpersonal relations, and in the transformation of our sociopolitical reality.[55]

As John Paul II points out in his 1984 apostolic exhortation *Paenitentia et Reconciliatio,* we live in "a broken world" (no. 2) that is "longing for reconciliation" (no. 3). The exhortation discovers here the anthropological and sociological link to an ecclesial practice that may offer a suitable response to this situation. The necessary distinction between the broader level of reconciliation and the more narrow level of sacramental reconciliation does not confine the latter to the sacral sphere, but actually opens it up to the full dimensions of reconciliation. Similarly, the exhortation stresses the real existence of "social sin" (no. 16), which of course does not exclude personal sin, but is not either merely a sum-total of personal sins: we may speak quite precisely about "structures of sin" (*Sollicitudo Rei Socialis,* 36).

In this context we should be especially mindful of the ecclesial dimension of the sacrament, which was described well by the Second Vatican Council: "Those who approach the sacrament of Penance obtain pardon from the mercy of God for the offense committed against Him and are at the same time reconciled with the Church, which they have wounded by their sins, and which by charity, example, and prayer seeks their conversion" (*Lumen Gentium,* 11). Three important elements in this text are the ecclesial repercussion of sin, the church's accompaniment of the sinner, and the ecclesial reconciliation that the sacrament brings about even as it grants God's pardon. Accordingly, the new *Ritual for Penance* of 1974 offers several modalities for celebrating the sacrament, indicating clearly that the second formula, called B, "manifests most clearly the ecclesial nature of penance" and should therefore be preferred. The possibility of using for-

---

55. See Robert J. Schreiter, *Reconciliation: Mission and Ministry in a Changing Social Order* (Maryknoll, N.Y.: Orbis, 1992) and *The Ministry of Reconciliation: Spirituality and Strategies* (Maryknoll, N.Y.: Orbis, 1998).

mula A is not denied, but the communal modality is affirmed to be the "principal analogue" of the sacrament.[56]

The significance and the implications of this fact are evident. If sin supposes a rupture in communion with God and with other people, then reestablishing communion will require the action of God and the ecclesial community. If sin is a wound in the body of Christ, then the body will be involved in the healing of that wound: it is a wound that affects not only the Lord, who continues to suffer in his body, but also the church community as such and the sinner, who likewise needs to be healed.

I find quite attractive, therefore, Dionisio Borobio's proposal for restoring penance as a process that involves all of the community.[57] Such a procedural structure would allow us to relate more closely everyday reconciliation and sacramental reconciliation, to grow creatively as a reconciled and reconciling community, and to renew sacramental praxis in keeping with our tradition. The three phases include: first, recognizing the situation of sin and separation; second, deepening the experience of conversion through the practice of satisfaction, which today has lost most of its force; and third, recovering full ecclesial communion thanks to reconciliation. Borobio indicates that this process is compatible with the three modalities found in the Ritual, but he suggests also that we should explore a Lenten process of penitential reconciliation, organized in a dynamic series of celebrations that might be considered a "form D" of the sacrament. Although the same author points out some possible difficulties, I would like to end this section by stressing the advantages of this proposal: it emphasizes the ecclesial dimension; it allows attention to be paid to satisfaction or reparation of the fault, so important in social sin; it links together splendidly both tradition and the contemporary situation; it makes possible community involvement in broader processes of social reconciliation and conflict resolution; and it opens up ways to an authentic, profound mystagogical experience.

56. For the ecclesial dimension of the sacrament, both in the post-conciliar renovation process and in the development of his systematic-pastoral proposal, see Millán, *La penitencia,* pp. 23-72 and pp. 173-203.

57. Dionisio Borobio, *La penitencia como proceso. De la reconciliación real a la reconciliación sacramental* (Madrid: San Pablo, 2005), pp. 117-207, with practical material and pastoral examples from different communities in Europe and Africa.

In the Face of Sickness: Healing the Weak Bodies

Recent practice of the sacrament of the anointing of the sick has suffered a pendulum movement from an almost magical kind of wonderworking to a trivialization that tends to avoid the reality of death. For centuries primacy was given to a theological conception and sacramental praxis that were centered on "extreme unction," which stressed the need to die in God's grace in order to save one's soul and avoid the pains of hell. Because of excesses in this regard the sacrament was closely associated with moribund, sometimes unconscious patients, and the emphasis frequently was on individual salvation. Such a framework was not always free of a certain amount of social control on the church's part. The logical reaction to such distortions of the sacrament led to emphasizing other, more positive elements, especially with the Council reforms. The celebrative dimension and the community aspect were recovered, the dramatic "prelude to death" aspect was downplayed, and a more integral vision of the sacrament was rediscovered. All these elements are summed up in the name *anointing of the sick.*

The new conceptions coincide with a change in the social situation of sick people, especially in the rich countries of the North. Life expectancy has increased, and chronic illnesses (cancer, diabetes, AIDS in the rich countries) have become common, so that sickness as such is more present in the society, but has lost much of its destructive force. It might be said that sickness is more familiar and more trivial. The anointing of the sick has also been affected by this context, as is seen, for example, in many parishes and communities that celebrate the sacrament periodically, even once a month. "Extreme" anointing has become "habitual."

Another contextual element is also quite important: the rationalization and professionalization of health care. Even though there is still room for traditional healers in postindustrial society, in reality the great majority of people have good reason to trust in health care personnel and the medical system for treating and curing their illnesses. Very few persons, including Christians, hope for a miracle from God, trust in the tangible efficacy of prayer, or confide in the curative power of the sacrament of anointing. Should such anointing, then, be relegated to a merely empty rite or a devout practice? I am convinced that it should not, and in the rest of this section I briefly suggest three simple ways to renew our understanding and our practice of the sacrament of anointing.

In the first place, we must undertake a spiritual consideration that sinks its roots into anthropological reality. Beyond the medical advances, beyond the types of sickness and their treatment, beyond the expectancies of life in a given socio-economic context, the fact is that human beings must come to grips with a process of decay that leads to death. Such a process may be experienced in a resigned, a defeatist, or a painful manner, or it may be experienced as an invitation to enter more deeply into the mystery of life. Pierre Teilhard de Chardin has possibly been the person who has treated this point with the greatest clarity, depth, and Christian sensibility, as when he spoke of the "divinization of passivities" and, more concretely, of the "passivities of diminution."[58] He was speaking of the passive, patient dimension of life, of the flotsam of our existence, which is not limited to our sicknesses, but does find in them an especially acute form. In the midst of our struggle against evil, our apparent defeat at its hands, and its definitive transfiguration, we are carried through a process that leads to full communion by way of that same diminution. Living this truth is not easy, nor do the advances of medical science (or even the psychological aids) really help us to enter into those rough patches of our existence. The sacrament of the anointing of the sick offers the possibility of converting fragility, diminution, and sickness into an occasion for encountering God at a deeper level, for diving into mystical experience, and for grasping the healing power of the Lord's mysterious working. When I spoke of baptism at the beginning of this chapter, I talked about the descent that is involved in being submerged with Jesus Christ into the depths of life. There I emphasized the active element of our own commitment, but now we are called on to appreciate the more passive dimension of that same reality. It would be most unfortunate if we were to reduce the sacrament of anointing of the sick to a merely superficial rite and failed to take advantage of all its force and depth, simply because of our diffidence or lack of courage in facing up and attending to this aspect of human existence.

Our second reflection concerning the sacrament is aimed at avoiding the excessive professionalization of our experience of health and sickness. If we were to fall into this modern error, we would be favoring a separation of the religious sphere from the medical dimension, which is incompatible with an integral Christian anthropology and leads to a radical privatiza-

---

58. Pierre Teilhard de Chardin, SJ, *The Divine Milieu: An Essay on the Interior Life* (New York: Harper, 1960), pp. 45-66.

tion of faith. Rather than such restrictive conceptions, I would like to argue here for a more integral vision. To that end I would suggest linking the sacrament of healing of the sick with our reflection about lay ministries.[59] By lay ministers I do not mean only those who pastorally attend to the sick (hospital chaplains and visitors), but I refer also to the wide gamut of health professionals who are committed Christians and who experience their profession as a true ecclesial vocation (for example, doctors, nurses, caretakers, psychologists, or educators who attend to drug addicts). They are the ones who on a daily basis accompany the sick, and they do so out of a sense of Christian vocation and professional expertise. It would be absurdly negligent for the church not to take this reality into consideration and not to endow it with greater meaning by empowering it and expressing it creatively in sacramental form. I am well aware that simply suggesting something is only the first step toward making it a reality, especially in our secularized society and in our oversized health care facilities, but the opportunities offered here are important and could open up other fertile areas, as regards both integral care of the patients and effective support for lay mission in the field of health. An especially interesting example is care of the elderly, given that a good number of the people who are actually caring for the elderly are Latin American immigrants. Simplifying a bit, I have joined together here two of the most fervent groups of the church in Spain (the elderly and Latino immigrants); they often participate together in the daily Eucharist, they share together many hours, much life, and much service. Nevertheless, we still do not seem to have found the formula for bestowing a ritual-sacramental meaning on this reality. The praxis of the sacrament of anointing seems to be going in another direction, but in fact the sacrament offers both groups (elderly and caretakers) a wide range of possibilities for rediscovering a new dimension of existence, grounded in the power of God that heals the body in the body of Christ.

Finally and much more briefly, I would like to say that our changed experience of the sacrament of anointing of the sick and of sickness itself should not make us lose sight of the horizon of death. It is well known that our culture tends to avoid the presence of death and camouflages it in diverse ways (linguistic, physical, social). Ecclesial praxis certainly should

---

59. In this regard, see Bernard Sesboüé, SJ, ¡No tengáis miedo! Los ministerios en la Iglesia hoy (Santander: Sal Terrae, 1998), pp. 163-66; and Dionisio Borobio, Misión y ministerios laicales. Mirando al futuro (Salamanca: Sígueme, 2001), pp. 215-59.

not fall into that kind of one-sided error. Perhaps it would be good, therefore, to keep the name *extreme unction* precisely for those dramatic, extreme end-situations, which of course should also be accompanied by the believing community. Thus there might well be some wisdom in a differentiated use of two names for the sacrament: *anointing of the sick* for everyday situations of old age, chronic sickness, progressive deterioration, and acceptance of the passivities of diminution; and *extreme unction* for the ultimate situation that looks more directly toward death. It is important to resist the culture of death, not by closing our eyes to this reality, but by creating alternative spaces in which people can experience, in the body of Christ, the new, mysterious dimensions of life.

Conclusion

As we come to the end of this survey of the seven sacraments, I simply wish to stress once again the importance of communal practices as signs and instruments of the formation of a new social reality. In so saying, I do not wish to fall into the sort of reductionism that limits the religious to a simple social function. Rather, I have stated clearly that the sacraments are an initiative of divine grace and an expression of our ecclesial way of being. In the following chapter I develop more explicitly the mystical dimension of sacramental praxis. Right now, however, my main point is that that same gift of God and that same ecclesial communion inevitably involve a true social, cultural, economic, and political transformation. As many observers have acknowledged, it is precisely the practices of social groups that affect the social order, whether by reproducing it, modifying it, legitimizing it, or even subverting it.[60]

In the Christian case, these sacraments include a complex of practices that root us firmly in Jesus Christ and that therefore have consequences that are radically transformative of reality. As Chauvet says, "it is impossible to separate the divine *kenosis* from the *kenosis* that must take place in ourselves: our corporality changes as it becomes transformed into the site for this *kenosis*."[61] The same author points out that God's subversion of the

60. Cf. Graham Ward, *Cultural Transformation and Religious Practices* (Cambridge and New York: Cambridge University Press, 2005).

61. Louis-Marie Chauvet, *Symbol and Sacrament: A Sacramental Reinterpretation of*

social order requires us to pass from discourse to body, from concept to symbol, from orthodoxy to orthopraxis, from ideas to practices. That is why it is so important for us to cultivate communal signs in the body of Christ, signs that are at the same time instruments for forming, nourishing, strengthening, and healing that same body. As we do so, a new reality burgeons and blooms, the reality of the kingdom.

Christian Existence, trans. Patrick Madigan and Madeleine Beaumont (Collegeville, Minn.: Liturgical, 1995), p. 509.

7. Mystical Roots, Radical Witnesses

Christianity consists in the divine shaping of the whole human being, in the *deiformation,* or *divinization,* of humanity, according to Spanish philosopher Xavier Zubiri, who connects with Eastern tradition. Zubiri also holds that this transformation manifests itself as mystical corporeity: it is an "incorporation [that] takes place in the life of each individual, in the structure of history, and in all nature."[1] This chapter seeks to develop this insight and this experience under the guidance of four outstanding witnesses, who will help us to grasp the mystery of the body of Christ from a deeper perspective: from what we could call its mystical roots.

Once again, my approach is limited and partial; I do not pretend to encompass all the nuances and dimensions of this mystery. In order to deepen our understanding of the reality of the body of Christ ("reality is the body of Christ," we read in Col. 2:17), I invite readers to contemplate the profoundly radical lives of four twentieth-century witnesses. Each one of them underscores a particular aspect of the reality of Christ's body, so that the complementary character of their approaches will reveal the unfathomable richness of this mystery of radical communion.

These witnesses present us with four distinct and complementary atti-

---

1. Xavier Zubiri, *El problema teologal del hombre: cristianismo* (Madrid: Alianza/ Fundación X. Zubiri, 1997), p. 71. We read something similar in William Johnston, *Being in Love: The Practice of Christian Prayer* (New York: Fordham University Press, 1999), p. 30: "Conversion to the Body of Christ is the key to the Christian religion."

tudes. Their specific contribution to the overall purpose of this book consists in helping us to articulate a mystical or spiritual theology. As Hans Urs von Balthasar poignantly stated:

> Prayerful theology does not mean "affective theology" as opposed to theology so called, and strictly scientific. The antithesis is merely superficial, and invalidated by the exact and very often abstract studies of Anselm and Albert, not to mention Thomas. . . . In those days, men were quite clear as how theology should be written: it should reflect both the unity of faith and knowledge and the attitude of objectivity allied with one of reverence and awe. Theology was, when pursued by men of sanctity, a theology at prayer; which is why its fruitfulness for prayer, its power to foster prayer, is so undeniable.[2]

This chapter, thanks to the testimony and the experience of four witnesses truly rooted in Jesus Christ, is an invitation for us to live radically in the body of Christ; it is an invitation to holiness. First, we see how the life of Mother Teresa of Calcutta places us with the *broken body* of Christ, in the lives of the poorest persons on earth. We will then be exposed to the experience of the *silent body* of Christ, following the path of Charles de Foucauld, whose life was marked by self-giving, dispossession, humility, and poverty, all in radical silence. A third stage leads us to Pierre Teilhard de Chardin's reflections, which will help us to widen our sight and broaden our hearts, by opening ourselves to the universal dimensions of the *cosmic body*, the total Christ. Finally, we consider the words and the life of Salvadoran martyr, Archbishop Oscar Romero, whose testimony will help us to grasp the mysterious power of the *transfigured body* of Christ in his paschal dynamic of death and resurrection.

Broken Body: Mother Teresa of Calcutta

"The contemplative and apostolic fruitfulness of our way of life depends on our *being rooted in Christ* our Lord by our deliberate choice of small and simple means for the fulfillment of our mission and by our fidelity to humble work of love among the spiritually poorest, identifying ourselves

---

2. Hans Urs von Balthasar, *Explorations in Theology*, vol. 1, *The Word Made Flesh*, trans. A. V. Littledale and Alexander Dru (San Francisco: Ignatius, 1989), pp. 207-8.

with them, sharing their poverty and insecurities until it hurts."[3] This quote from Mother Teresa of Calcutta offers a good starting point for this chapter. It shows both how a life devoted to the poor is rooted in Christ, and how such a mystical experience has radical and practical consequences.

Mother Teresa of Calcutta is one of the clearest examples of what Christian charity is all about. Her life embodies a direct, radical, and untiring service to the poorest of the poor. From the streets of Calcutta, India, her presence grew to embrace the poor in Europe, Africa, and the Americas. While it may be true that she did not directly address the structural dimension of poverty in the twentieth century, her life is widely recognized as a powerful gospel witness, demanding dignity for every human being. In this section, we will get some glimpses into her spiritual life, articulated around the notion of the broken body of Christ.

First, we need to acknowledge the powerfully integrated synthesis that moved Mother Teresa's life, as she herself stated: "In Holy Communion we have Christ under the appearance of bread. In our work we find him under the appearance of flesh and blood. It is the same Christ."[4] And she continues: "The Mass is the spiritual food that sustains me, without which I could not get through one single hour in my life; in the Mass we have Jesus in the appearance of bread, while in the slums we see Christ and touch him in the broken bodies, in the abandoned children."[5] Everything I articulated theologically in previous chapters is now shown in a new shape, revealed with all the strength of a life fully devoted to the poor and with the simplicity of true personal experience. With sharp clarity Mother Teresa refers to the mutual identification of the various aspects of the body of Christ, as we have just quoted: "It is *the same* Christ." Her words and her experience are connected to the ecclesial tradition of Eucharistic realism: "*Actually* we are touching Christ's body in the poor."[6] She cannot doubt the real presence of Christ in the Eucharist and in the poor, and she refers to it without hesitation. She narrates a specific example:

---

3. Mother Teresa, *Essential Writings,* selected with an introduction by Jean Maalouf (Maryknoll, N.Y.: Orbis, 2001), p. 71. Emphasis added.

4. Mother Teresa of Calcutta, *A Gift for God: Prayers and Meditations* (San Francisco: HarperSanFranscisco, 1996), p. 76.

5. Mother Teresa, *A Gift for God,* p. 76.

6. Mother Teresa, *A Gift for God,* p. 39.

A girl came from outside India to join the Missionaries of Charity. We have a rule that the very next day new arrivals must go to the Home for the Dying. So I told this girl: "You saw Father during Holy Mass, with what love and care he touched Jesus in the Host. Do the same when you go to the Home for the Dying, because it is the same Jesus you will find there in the broken bodies of our poor." And they went. After three hours the newcomer came back and said to me with a big smile — I have never seen a smile quite like that — "Mother, I have been touching the body of Christ for three hours." And I said to her, "How? What did you do?" She replied: "When we arrived there, they brought a man who had fallen into a drain, and had been there for some time. He was covered with wounds and dirt and maggots, and I cleaned him and I knew I was touching the body of Christ."[7]

The young novice had very profoundly understood that Jesus Christ was not being devious when he said, "I was sick and you visited me" (Matt. 25:36).

Someone might think that this kind of vision stems from the devout idealism typical of a naïve novice. Nothing would be further from reality. Mother Teresa's radical life and her daily experience led her to express a tangible realism, such as when she recognizes that "sometimes it is more difficult to work with the street people than with the people in our homes for the dying, because the dying are peaceful and waiting; they are ready to go to God. You can touch the sick and believe, or you can touch the leper and believe, that is the body of Christ you are touching, but it is much more difficult, when these people are drunk or shouting, to think that this is Jesus in that distressing disguise. How clean and loving our hands must be to be able to bring that compassion to them!"[8] For this very reason, Mother Teresa says, it is necessary to come back again and again to the source of compassion, to the contemplation of the same Lord Jesus who purifies our sight and our whole life.

"Our lives are woven with Jesus in the Eucharist, and the faith and the love that come from the Eucharist enable us to see him in the distressing disguise of the poor, and so there is but one love of Jesus, as there is but one person in the poor — Jesus."[9] Mother Teresa insists on explaining a

7. Mother Teresa, *A Gift for God,* pp. 56-57.
8. Mother Teresa, *Essential Writings,* pp. 136-37.
9. Mother Teresa, *A Gift for God,* pp. 35-36.

daily practice that unifies the diverse aspects of the body of Christ: "This is why our life needs to be closely linked to the Eucharist. We begin our day with the Holy Mass and Communion, and we finish the day with an hour of adoration, which unites us with Jesus and with the poor in whom we offer our services."[10] She then justifies a decision that conveys quite an unusual logic: "In our congregation, we used to have adoration once a week for one hour, and then in 1973 we decided to have adoration one hour every day. We have much work to do. Our homes for the sick and dying destitute are full everywhere."[11] Notice the type of argument used, most probably quite opposite to the one we normally use in similar situations: since there is a lot of work to be done, we increase the time we devote to contemplation. Only from a deep belief in the real identity of the body of Christ in the Eucharist and in the poor can this gospel logic be understood.

In light of this, we can now fully appreciate a very important and concrete aspect of Mother Teresa's vision, which her life highlights with astounding clarity: the suffering dimension of the body of Christ in the midst of human history. "If we really understand the Eucharist, if we really center our lives on Jesus' body and blood, if we nourish our lives with the bread of the Eucharist, it will be easy for us to see Christ in that hungry one next door, the one lying in the gutter, that alcoholic man we shun, our husband or our wife, or our restless child. For in them, we will recognize the *distressing disguises of the poor:* Jesus in our midst."[12] There is once again the identity between the suffering poor and the same suffering Jesus Christ, and other texts repeat the theme. "Today, the same Christ is in people who are unwanted, unemployed, uncared for, hungry, naked, and homeless."[13] In these poor and distressed persons, Jesus continues to live his own passion. "When we are caring for the sick and the needy, we are touching the body of the suffering Christ, and this touch makes us heroic; it helps us overcome the repugnance and the natural reaction that is in all of us."[14] Once again we find the realism of a self-emptying life devoted to serving others in need.

Precisely because of this daily contact with poverty and pain, Mother Teresa's spirituality does not refuse suffering. She even finds in it a gift of

10. Mother Teresa, *Essential Writings,* p. 103.
11. Mother Teresa, *Essential Writings,* p. 104.
12. Mother Teresa, *Essential Writings,* p. 106.
13. Mother Teresa, *A Gift for God,* p. 28.
14. Mother Teresa, *Essential Writings,* p. 43.

God, something with a mysterious redemptive power.[15] Of course, we are not talking about a sort of masochism that exalts suffering in itself, as she herself spells out: "Suffering is nothing by itself, but suffering that shares in Christ's passion is a marvelous gift, a beautiful donation, a proof of love. I have to be ready to give all that may be necessary to do good to others. This requires me to be ready to *give until it hurts*" (111). The key is not suffering but love: "A living love hurts. Jesus, to prove his love for us, died on the Cross. The mother, to give birth to her child, has to suffer. If you really love one another properly, there must be sacrifice."[16] Suffering, therefore, has no meaning in itself, but only as an expression of love, of donation, of commitment. It is no wonder, then, that Mother Teresa's experience of sorrow goes hand in hand with an invincible joy: "The passion of Christ always ends with the joy of Resurrection."

This link with the paschal mystery reveals new dimensions of Mother Teresa's service and work, and once again it relates to its Eucharistic root. Thus, the universality of love and the gratuitous character of salvation appear in a more obvious way. "Our criterion for assistance is not one's belief, but one's need. *All are the body of Christ;* all are Christ under the appearance of those in need of assistance and love, and they have a right to receive it."[17] Notice the twofold aspect of service and identification: Jesus Christ gives himself up for all human beings, and he identifies himself with them in his own body. This is particularly true in the case of the poor of the earth.

The Eucharistic root of Teresa of Calcutta's life introduces a new and vital element: prayer. We have already seen how the dimension of personal encounter and intimate friendship with the Lord is always present in a prayerful life: "After the sisters have finished their day — carrying out their service of love in the company of Jesus, and through Jesus — we have an hour of prayer and eucharistic adoration. Throughout the day we have been in contact with Jesus through his image of sorrow in the poor and the lepers. When the day ends, we come in contact with him again in the tabernacle by means of prayer."[18] At the same time, a more profound level appears, one that we could call "mystical" and that opens up to personal

---

15. On this topic, see some additional texts in *A Gift for God*, pp. 20-23.

16. Mother Teresa, *A Gift for God*, p. 13.

17. Mother Teresa, *Essential Writings*, p. 44.

18. Mother Teresa, *Essential Writings*, p. 54.

transformation through a radical unification in Christ. In this regard, we find some very telling texts: "Prayer is nothing but being in the family, being one with the Father in the Son to the Holy Spirit. . . . We have given it that name, but actually prayer is nothing but that *oneness with Christ*."[19] Mother Teresa can even, with no sign of pride, make such a powerful assertion as "Jesus and I are one,"[20] convinced as she is that spiritual life consists in union with Jesus Christ. After all we have seen, it is no wonder that Teresa's radical transformation roots itself in the Eucharist: "By nourishing ourselves on his body and blood, we shall become one body with Jesus and through Jesus, thanks to his great love."[21]

Therefore, it is not difficult to understand that "the more we receive in our silent prayer, the more we can give in our active life."[22] Our own bodies, broken by and through love, united to the broken bodies of the poor, become one in the broken body of Christ. Eucharistic life, understood as an incarnation of the received gift and the offered service, requires spaces and times of silence, precisely to make that free gift incarnate. Mother Teresa relates a significant story: "Once I was asked by someone what I consider most important in the training of the sisters. I answered: Silence. Interior and exterior silence. Silence is essential in a religious house. The silence of humility, of charity, the silence of the eyes, of the ears, of the tongue. There is no life of prayer without silence."[23] The reason lies in the fact that "silence leads to charity, and charity to humility."[24] In silence we find new energy and true unity. For this reason, Mother Teresa reminds us that "the fruit of silence is faith. The fruit of faith is prayer. The fruit of prayer is love. The fruit of love is service. And the fruit of service is silence."[25]

This section has thus taken us from self-giving to silence, from service to prayer, from the broken body of Christ to the silent body of the same Christ. In a word, this section has introduced us to the mystery. Let us now move on to consider how Charles de Foucauld lived, in a different context, this same mystery.

19. Mother Teresa, *Essential Writings*, p. 54.
20. Mother Teresa, *Essential Writings*, p. 55.
21. Mother Teresa, *Essential Writings*, p. 121.
22. Mother Teresa, *Essential Writings*, p. 52.
23. Mother Teresa, *Essential Writings*, p. 65.
24. Mother Teresa, *Essential Writings*, p. 59.
25. Mother Teresa, *Essential Writings*, p. 64.

Silent Body: Charles de Foucauld

On Friday, December 1, 1916, Brother Charles de Foucauld was murdered. "Three weeks after his death, his tiny monstrance, still containing the Host, was found in the sand. Like the Host, like Christ, poor and hidden, it had sunk into the ground of man. It was buried there, like a grain of wheat, to ripen and become, with Jesus Christ, the daily bread of men, his brothers."[26] His biography ends with these words, just as his life ended — in the radical silence of full identification with the Lord Jesus.

This section presents another approach to the integral mystery of the body of Christ, by following the footsteps of Charles de Foucauld. This man lived in radical fashion his vocation "to preach the Gospel from the housetops, not by word, but by your life."[27] This man was dominated by a deep desire, which he formulated thus in a letter to a Trappist friend, on September 30, 1897: "All we are trying to do is to be one with Jesus, to reproduce his life in our own, to proclaim his teaching from the rooftops in our thoughts, words, and actions, to let him rule and live in us. He comes to us so frequently, through the Holy Eucharist!"[28]

Charles de Foucauld was born in France in 1858 into an aristocratic and military family. At the age of eighteen, he joined the army, where he earned a well-deserved reputation for being a high-living carouser. In 1882 he decided to leave his military career, and he dedicated himself instead to a life of adventurous exploration of Algeria, Tunisia, and Morocco. Religious conversion struck him suddenly and sharply in 1886. He himself clearly recognized that "as soon as I believed there was a God, I understood that I could do nothing else than live for Him." However, he actually had to search for years to find a concrete way to live out his vocation. He felt a strong call to share the life of poverty and humility of Jesus of Nazareth, and in January 1890, that led him to Our Lady of the Snows Trappist monastery in France. Despite the austere life and the snowy winter there, Brother Charles felt called to ever greater radicality. Six months later he moved to a much poorer monastery, that of Akbes in Syria. He stayed there several years, but he continued to feel called to still greater radicality in his

26. Jean-François Six, *Witness in the Desert: The Life of Charles de Foucauld* (New York: Macmillan, 1965), p. 274.

27. Charles de Foucauld, *Essential Writings,* selected with an introduction by Robert Ellsberg (Maryknoll, N.Y.: Orbis, 1999), p. 67.

28. Foucauld, *Essential Writings,* p. 117.

identification with Jesus, the worker of Nazareth. His experience of the habitual life and the security of a Trappist monastery did not allow him to be completely faithful to this call. The year 1897 was an important one in his life: Brother Charles was released from his religious vows and settled in Nazareth, living as a hermit and serving as a messenger for the St. Clare nuns. He lived there four years, during which time he grew closer to the Lord and continually sought to do his will. The nuns and his confessor helped him to clear the way toward priestly ordination, which took place in France in June 1901, after several months of preparation in his former monastery, Our Lady of the Snows. In September Charles de Foucauld traveled to Algeria and settled in Beni-Abbes, where he set up a chapel with the idea of founding a fraternity of monks. His mission was to continue in the Sahara the hidden life of Jesus of Nazareth; his aim was not to preach but to live in solitude and poverty and do the humble work of Jesus. Taking a step further, Brother Charles moved out into the desert and took up residence in Tamanrasset in 1907. That is the place where he was killed in December 1916.

This brief sketch of Charles's life may indicate why we spoke of the silent body when we first referred to him. His whole life was marked by kenotic descent, by radical identification with Jesus of Nazareth, by complete divestment of self, by radical commitment to poverty and humility, by apparent failure, by fecund silence. Within this general framework, I wish to point out two highly significant moments in the life of Charles de Foucauld, one in 1901 and another in 1907. These moments especially stand out from the particular perspective of my study, that is, my attempt to formulate a radical Eucharistic theology.

The first day is June 9, 1901, the day of his ordination as priest in Viviers. Brother Charles had at first resisted being ordained for ministry because he felt a clear call to silence, service, humility, and absolute poverty, and he feared that priesthood would give him a life of excessive dignity, privilege, and power. "My life continues to be the same, silent and still more deeply buried," he wrote in February 1900. One can understand his inner struggle, and one can also understand why he finally obeyed his confessor, Father Huvelin. What is not so easily understood is what happened as a result of his ordination: his fears dissipated, his concern about privileges dispersed into the air, and his confidence that God would continue directing the course of history increased dramatically.

"It was a radical rupture comparable to that which had taken place at his conversion."[29] It was a brusque change from his recent past and his earlier ideas. Until that moment the dream of Charles had been to lead a life of poverty and silence as a hermit in Palestine. After his priestly ordination he received a strong call to go forth in service to the most abandoned brothers and sisters. His own words express for us the Eucharistic depth of this vocation: "The divine feast of which I am the minister must be offered not to the brethren and their relations and the rich neighbors, but to the lamest and blindest of men, the most abandoned souls, those without priests."[30] What might have been a source of privilege became for Brother Charles a way of greater dispossession and radicality in his commitment. For this reason, as J.-F. Six rightly notes, after his priestly ordination Charles de Foucauld experienced a love for God that was united with love for the people farthest from God.

Just a few weeks later, on June 23, he wrote an old friend, who wanted to help him in his new mission, and he explained to him the heart of his project: evangelization based on the presence of the Blessed Sacrament and the celebration of the Eucharist, on the practice of hospitality, and on "a charity that is fraternal and universal, sharing the last crust of bread with every single pauper, every guest, every stranger who comes, and receiving every human being as a beloved brother."[31] Notice should be taken once again of the identification between the body of Christ in the Eucharistic bread and the body of Christ in the life of the poor. It is no accident that what is to be shared with the poor is precisely "the last crust of bread." Another very important detail that might go unnoticed is the practice of receiving each person "as a beloved brother." For years, especially during the time when he was with the St. Clare nuns in Nazareth, Charles de Foucauld regularly referred to the Lord Jesus as "the Beloved." This is just one more proof of his radical identification with the one and only body of Christ. We can imagine, then, the profound joy with which he celebrated the Eucharist for the first time, as he did in Benni-Abbes on October 29, 1901.

In light of this, the reader may also comprehend the dramatic nature of the second moment I highlight. As Six states, "December of 1907 and January of 1908 are for brother Charles a time of extreme nakedness.

---

29. Six, *Witness in the Desert*, p. 73.
30. Foucauld, *Essential Writings*, p. 76.
31. Six, *Witness in the Desert*, p. 76.

Brother Charles is in a dark night, even more painful than the one he experienced in 1897. It is God's great purification. It is the final donation that God asks of him."[32] He was in Tamanrasset, a place where he had gone with the desire to enter ever farther into the desert, in order to make the gospel present there. His living situation was very difficult, involving extreme hunger, two years of total drought in the Hoggar region and French exploitation of the Tuareg tribespeople. Besides, Brother Charles's sickness obliged him to maintain complete repose in radical solitude, and his sensation of spiritual failure overwhelmed him as he drew close to fifty years of age.

As if this were little, Charles de Foucauld was not able to celebrate the Eucharist. Even though he had been ordained a priest precisely to take the Eucharistic body of the Lord to the peoples of the desert, he was deprived of that grace. He was already anticipating the possible difficulties when he decided to go to Tamanrasset, for he pondered: "Is it better to stay in the Hoggar, unable to celebrate Holy Mass, or is it better not to stay?" (July 1907). Out of love for the poor he decided to go to the Hoggar region, even though he knew that he would be able to celebrate the Eucharist only sporadically (recall the liturgical norm at the time, which prohibited the celebration of the Eucharist without at least one companion). Various of his writings during those months reveal the pain that this situation of "Eucharistic fasting" caused him. The prospect of Christmas sharpened this pain further. On December 25, 1907, he wrote: "I find it hard to spend Christmas without Mass." "Until the last minute I had hoped that someone might come, but no one did, neither a Christian traveler nor a soldier, nor the permission to celebrate Mass alone."[33] He continued: "Tonight, without mass, for the first time in twenty-one years. May the Beloved's will be done!"

His situation was already awesomely radical, but Brother Charles insisted on submerging himself even further into his kenotic process of configuration with the Lord. On January 15, 1908, he explained his way of evangelizing: "The means which He used in the crib, in Nazareth and on the cross are: poverty, abjection, humiliation, abandonment, persecution, suffering, cross. These are our arms. . . . Our acts are no longer ours, human

---

32. Jean-François Six, *Carlos de Foucauld: Itinerario espiritual* (Barcelona: Herder, 1962), p. 276.

33. Six, *Witness in the Desert*, p. 161.

and miserable, but his, divinely efficacious."[34] During the month of January Brother Charles recovered little by little, and on January 31 arrived the message that for months he had been longing for: permission to celebrate the Eucharist without a server. "He wrote in his diary for January 31st: '*Deo Gratias*! How good you are, O Lord! Tomorrow I shall be able to celebrate Mass. Christmas! Christmas! Thank you, Lord!'"[35] To understand this explosion of joy and its connection with the Nativity, even a month after the liturgical date, we should recall that he himself had written in 1905: "Each Mass is like Christmas, and charity is more important than poverty." We can affirm, then, without fear of being mistaken, that his purification during Christmas 1907 had given Charles de Foucauld an even more powerful Eucharistic strength, for it had grafted him even more tightly into the body of Christ. From that point on he dedicated himself even more definitively to radical self-donation in loving service to the poor.

I end this section with a reference to Brother Charles's Christology. It is evident that his spirituality and many of its expressions are the fruit of his cultural ambience and context, but their strength is such that they are difficult to dismiss. In our own times, when there is so much talk of ascending and descending Christologies, the spiritual experience of Charles de Foucauld offers a healthy synthesis, one made authentic by the coherence of his life of commitment. Brother Charles always considered Jesus to be absolute Lord (descending Christology), even and especially in his hidden life in Nazareth (ascending Christology). We might say that Foucauld's Christology is descending in a twofold sense, because it links the descent of his divinity to the concrete descent of his historical life: the Lord Jesus never stopped descending, lowering himself, serving, becoming incarnate in radical kenosis. Charles heard a striking phrase at the very origin of his conversion ("You deliberately took the last place and no one wanted to take it from you"),[36] and it stayed with him to the end of his days. For that reason he wrote, during his time in Nazareth:

> My Lord, I do not know how it is possible for certain souls to see Your poverty and still remain willingly rich, to see themselves so much more exalted than their Beloved Master and not want to resemble You in everything as much as they can, especially in Your humility. I should like

34. Six, *Carlos de Foucauld*, p. 278.
35. Six, *Witness in the Desert*, p. 166.
36. Foucauld, *Essential Writings*, p. 30.

to think that they love You and yet I feel that their love lacks something. In any case I cannot conceive of love without a need — a great need — of sharing all the pains, difficulties, and hardships.[37]

It is precisely the radical following of this poor, humble Lord that leads Charles de Foucauld to a life of absolute commitment and service among the poorest and most abandoned people. The Beloved leads him to love greatly all people, especially the poor Tuaregs of Hoggar. The descent and the dispossession of the Lord lead him to strip himself completely in order to serve everybody. His union to the Eucharistic body of Christ opens him to even deeper dimensions of his love for the body of Christ in the poor. The kenotic descent of his life makes him into a "universal brother." Only from below, in the loving descent of committed service, is the universal Christ truly to be found. The following section will allow us to move farther along that path.

Cosmic Body: Pierre Teilhard de Chardin

In 1916, the same year that Charles de Foucauld was killed, the French Jesuit Pierre Teilhard de Chardin wrote his first theological essay, entitled *The Cosmic Life*. Writing in North Africa while he was serving as a stretcher-bearer during the First World War, the author affirms that "each encounter that caresses me, pricks me, bothers me, offends me or wounds me is a contact with the multiform but always adorable hand of God. Each element that is a part of me overflows with God. In abandoning myself to the arms of the visible, palpable Universe, I can commune with the purifying Invisible and incorporate myself into the immaculate Spirit."[38] And Teilhard turns this experience into prayer: "I love you, Jesus, for the Multitude that throbs within you and that is heard, along with all other beings, to whisper, pray and weep when we press up close to you. . . . To live the cosmic life is to live with an overriding consciousness of being an atom of the body of the mystical and cosmic Christ" (p. 61).

In contrast to the other two authors considered earlier in this chapter,

37. Foucauld, *Essential Writings*, p. 63.

38. Pierre Teilhard de Chardin, SJ, *Escritos esenciales*, introducción y edición a cargo de Ursula King (Santander: Sal Terrae, 2001), p. 57. For greater clarity I will always quote from this edition, putting the page references in parentheses within the text.

Teilhard is an intellectual. For this reason, rather than concentrate on his life, I offer a simple sampling of his thought, which without doubt represents one of the most profound and original syntheses of the twentieth century. Since there already exist excellent presentations, both analytic and synthetic, of Teilhard's work,[39] I merely review here, following a chronological order, the seven principal books in which he refers to his experience and explanation of the body of Christ.

During the First World War period, Teilhard wrote some short texts that are quite important, both for the incipient revelation they give of his great creative vision and for the vital context in which they were written, that of a young priest (ordained in 1911) in the middle of war. In 1916 Teilhard related a vision of the transfigured face of Christ; after tracing the shades of cross/resurrection in the visage, he concludes, "I seem to have glimpsed it again in the look of a dying soldier" (p. 122).[40] Two years later, in an essay entitled *The Priest*, he wrote: "The tiny, inert Host has become before my eyes something as vast as the World, as devouring as the bonfire. It dominates me absolutely. It seeks to enclose me once again. An inexhaustible and universal Communion is the culmination of the universal consecration" (p. 196). He continues with the plea: "May the fleeting and circumscribed contact with the sacramental species lead me to a universal, perpetual communion with Christ, with his all-active will, with his unlimited mystical Body!" (p. 198).

With this we now enter into the content and the focus of one of Teilhard's best-known spiritual works, *The Mass on the World*, written out of his experience on the Feast of the Transfiguration, August 6, 1923, when he was in the desert steppes of China and without possibility of celebrating the Eucharist. "Since once again, Lord, . . . I have no bread, no wine, no altar, I will lift myself above the symbols to the pure majesty of the Real, and I, who am your priest, will offer you, on the altar of the entire earth, the labor and pain of the world" (p. 91). Once the offering is made, Teilhard in-

---

39. Besides the collection of texts cited in the previous note, see also Henri de Lubac, SJ, *La oración de Teilhard de Chardin* (Barcelona: Estela, 1966), pp. 47-78, and Christopher F. Mooney, "La encarnación y la eucaristía. El cuerpo de Cristo como centro físico de la humanidad y del mundo material," in *Teilhard de Chardin y el misterio de Cristo* (Salamanca: Sígueme, 1967), pp. 89-136.

40. The three narratives of 1916, called "The Picture," "The Monstrance," and "The Ciborium," can be found in Pierre Teilhard de Chardin, SJ, *Himno del universo* (Madrid: Trotta, 1996), pp. 43-54.

vokes the power of God ("Blazing Spirit, fundamental and personal Fire") over cosmic matter, he recognizes its transforming presence and, prostrated, he enters into intimate communion with the total Christ. Before the double mystery of the universal consecration and communion, he concludes with this magnificent and powerful prayer: "In your body, with all that it encompasses, that is, in this World made by your power and my faith into the magnificent living crucible in which all disappears in order to be reborn, . . . I hand myself over to live and die in your service, Jesus" (p. 127). With amazing force, with radical honesty and with noonday clarity, Teilhard unites together the cosmic aspect and the personal aspect of Christ, by combining his own material and mystical dimensions in a vigorous Eucharistic realism.

The Divine Milieu, written in 1926-27, deepens and expands this vision in a work whose spiritual intensity can hardly be matched. Drawing on the Christian tradition of *deiformation,* Teilhard envisions the divinization of both activities and passivities, whether these have to do with growth or with diminution; that is, he recognizes that the process of divinization encompasses all of reality. The divine omnipresence is converted into the network of organizing forces of the total Christ, since the divinization is in truth Christification. "Acceding to the Divine Milieu is, in effect, finding the One Thing Necessary" (p. 83). Loving service is precisely that which manifests and actualizes the divinizing power, because charity brings about, in the course of history and through human relations, the annexation of all reality to Christ, the incorporation of all into his body. With good reason Teilhard can pray: "In a true sense, the arms and the Heart that you open are nothing less than all the forces of the World together. . . . The Eucharist must invade my life. My life must become, thanks to the sacrament, a contact without limit and without end. . . . In every sense you have so filled the Universe, Jesus, that now, happily, it is impossible for us to escape from You" (pp. 133-34). Immersed in the Divine Milieu, thanks to the unifying force of charity, we are gradually transformed into the same cosmic body of Christ: we become Christified, and all reality becomes divinized.

We thus arrive at *The Human Phenomenon* (1938-40), possibly the work of Teilhard that best displays his philosophic genius, capable of uniting the physical, the biological, the anthropological, the social, and the spiritual from a perspective that is at once scientific and Christian. Teilhard offers a profound and original reading of creative evolution and postulates the "law of complexity-consciousness," which deploys itself progressively, giving meaning to the cosmos. The emergence of the Noosphere points toward a personalizing Universe, where the hyper-personal goes beyond the collective, that is to say, where community fully integrates the personal and the universal. Without falling into superficial harmonies, Teilhard indicates that this universal dynamic converges in the Omega Point, which cannot be anything else than the total Christ. "The Universe, culminating in a synthesis of centers, in perfect conformity with the laws of Union, God, the Center of centers — this is the final vision in which Christian dogma culminates. . . . And I am thinking here of Christian love" (pp. 186-87). In other words, what unifies reality is communion, a communion that we receive from God in Christ, a communion that already became present in the incarnation (the Omega Point is not outside the Universe, but is its very center), a communion that we receive in the Eucharist, a communion that we exercise in a life transformed by love. Once again we meet up with the unfathomable mystery of the body of Christ, with the indivisibility of its dimensions, and with the transformative force of its dynamism, into which we are all incorporated.

We now examine a text written in 1950, called *The Heart of Matter,* which may be considered a spiritual autobiography of Teilhard de Chardin. There he explains how he has "experienced, in contact with the Earth, the Diaphanous nature of the Divine in the heart of the ardent Universe — the Divine radiating from the depths of flaming Matter" (p. 37). As we have already seen several times in earlier chapters, the true Christian vision has never divided up the material, the human, the spiritual, the social, and the ecclesial. The concept and the reality of the body of Christ has served for centuries to unite all those dimensions of reality. In Teilhard this traditional vision acquires new tones thanks to the advance of science, concretely as regards evolution; the vision also acquires new energy thanks to the depth of his faith experience. In Jesus Christ he discovers the "immersion of the Divine in the Carnal" (p. 116), and more concretely, he finds in the Heart of Jesus "a Fire that is capable of penetrating everything and that little by little extends to all parts" (p. 117). It is hardly surprising that the thinker falls prostrate once again, asking in prayer "that your universal Presence arise, through both Translucence and Flame. O Christ ever greater!" (p. 129). The *Deus semper maior* of mystical tradition or the Augustinian *Christus totus* finds here an innovative formulation that stresses evolutionary dynamism and material concretion. The body of Christ keeps advancing, acting, Christifying, and incorporating all of reality into its heart. It becomes present to us, to be sure, but it also thrusts us toward the eschatological fullness.

We finish our review of Teilhard with another autobiographical text, written in the year of his death, 1955. The essay is entitled *The Christic* and affirms that, since the world is not a static Cosmos but is evolving, Christ the King must be conceived as having a dynamic lordship, one that deploys its transforming strength in order to take possession of all reality. None of Teilhard's great words — Christogenesis, Divine Milieu, Christification, Omega Point — is a mere concept: "Right here, before the amazed gaze of the believer, is the Eucharistic mystery itself, which extends itself toward the infinite in a truly universal 'transubstantiation,' in which the words of Consecration are no longer pronounced just over the sacrificial bread and wine, but rather over the totality of the joys and pains that are engendered by the Convergence of the World in its movement forward. And there also, as a consequence, the possibilities of universal Communion become real" (pp. 131-32). At this point we are hardly surprised by this lucid and powerful Eucharistic connection in the Teilhardian vision. We always speak of the constitution of the body of Christ and of its dynamics of communion, but now we do so by including levels that are often forgotten and by awakening genuine energies of transformation. Living enrooted in Jesus Christ has radical consequences that reach from the subatomic particles up to the most complex social structure. The cosmic Christ is the universal Lord of all that, by the revolutionary force of his love and communion.

Transfigured Body: Archbishop Oscar Romero

The fourth approach to the body of Christ that we make in this chapter takes us to El Salvador, a small Central American country that at the end of the twentieth century became known throughout the world for the structural injustice that dominated the country, for the brutality of the repression there, and for the steadfast testimony of evangelical faithfulness that the church offered. Out of this context emerged an exceptional pastor, the archbishop of San Salvador, Oscar Romero, who knew, as did few others, how to be at the side of his people and how to incarnate God's option for the poor in a decisive way. Examining his spiritual experience and his pastoral labor will lead us to discover the centrality for him of the mystery of

Christ's body, found in the fragility of the bread and the fragility of the oppressed faithful, in the glory of the Lord and in the strength of the church.

Romero became archbishop of San Salvador in February 1977. The following months were marked by great social and political upheaval, by the church's dedication to serving the people as an agent of reconciliation, and also by the criticism and growing persecution that followed on the church's option for the poor. Given such a setting, the archbishop decided to write his second pastoral letter in August 1977, in order to help discern the difficult situation. In the letter he first presents the changes that have taken place in the last years and then explains the reason for the changes. The changes have occurred, he states, precisely because the church is the "Body of Christ in history" and therefore must communicate the message and prolong the mission of the Lord, in accord with the constantly changing history. Romero writes: "The Church is that flesh in which Christ makes present down the ages his own life and his personal mission. . . . They [the changes in the church] are needed if the church is to be faithful to its divine mission of being the Body of Christ in history. The Church can be church only so long as it goes on being the body of Christ."[41] Concretely, he says, this means announcing God's reign especially to the poor, denouncing sin without forgetting its structural dimension, and calling all to conversion. He does this not only in abstract terms, but affirming "the pressing obligation to encourage and promote the concrete mechanisms that best seem to help towards the partial realization of that Kingdom." Only by fulfilling its mission in this way, insists the archbishop, will the church realize its own mystery of being the body of Christ in history. He then goes on to review the accusations, attacks, and persecutions of recent months and concludes that "nobody should be surprised that the Church is persecuted precisely when it is faithful to its mission." Paradoxically, this difficult situation shows that "service of the gospel and the persecution of the church have brought forth, as a precious fruit, a unity in the archdiocese to a degree hitherto unknown." The pastoral letter therefore concludes on a note of hope and reaffirms the conviction that "all we who are baptized form the Church which makes Christ incarnate in history." In summary, then, this valuable document states that the church is the body of

41. Archbishop Oscar Romero, "The Church, the Body of Christ in History," in *Voice of the Voiceless: The Four Pastoral Letters and Other Statements*, introductory essays by Jon Sobrino and Ignacio Martín-Baró (Maryknoll, N.Y.: Orbis, 1985), pp. 63-84; here, p. 70.

Christ, which prolongs his mission by taking up the cause of the kingdom and which does so in growing unity, despite the persecution.

This pastoral letter was published on August 6, 1977, the liturgical Feast of the Transfiguration of the Lord and titular feast of the archdiocese of San Salvador.[42] The date is not inadvertent; rather, it has great theological significance, as Romero himself recognized when he published on that same liturgical date the rest of his pastoral letters. Let us examine why and how this date is so important. In El Salvador the most immediate, daily experience is the suffering of a people that is impoverished, oppressed, repressed, massacred — we might even say with Ignacio Ellacuría, a crucified people. The vision and experience of faith make the claim, however, that this is not the whole truth, because that same people has already been touched by the divine grace that will thrust them toward resurrection. How might we define this Salvadoran people that is the body of Christ? It is not really a crucified body, but neither is it a resurrected body. We can properly call it a transfigured body. The Synoptic Gospels narrate the episode of the transfiguration of the Lord when he is on his way to Jerusalem, immediately after the first announcement of the Passion (see, for example, Luke 9:22-36). The liturgy has maintained this connection by including this Gospel of the transfiguration in the liturgy of the second Sunday of Lent, that is, in the process of preparing for Easter. In similar fashion, Archbishop Romero succeeded in grasping the meaning of the transfiguration only by walking toward the cross alongside his people, the body of Christ. As Margie Pfeil has keenly observed, "the luminous hope of Jesus' transfigured body shines forth precisely in the crucified body of Christ in history."[43] Here are to be found the profundity and the force of this mystery of liberating communion.

In what follows I illustrate, with some texts of Romero's homilies, the doctrinal synthesis of his second pastoral letter and the theological truth of the transfiguration of the broken body of Christ. For example, on December 3, 1978, the first Sunday of Advent, he states: "Christ is now in history. Christ is in the womb of the people."[44] Therefore, continues the arch-

42. Recall the importance of the Feast of the Transfiguration in the life of Teilhard de Chardin, concretely in his work *The Mass on the World*.

43. Margie Pfeil, "*Gloria Dei, Vivens Pauper:* A Theology of Transfiguration," *Sign of Peace* 4, no. 2 (2005): 6-9; here, p. 9.

44. *The Church Is All of You: Thoughts of Archbishop Oscar Romero,* compiled and translated by James R. Brockman, SJ (Minneapolis: Winston, 1984), p. 39. As I have done in other sections of this chapter, I cite this text in parentheses when referring to the homilies.

bishop, "a Church that knows how to feel as its own all that is human, a Church that wants to embody the pain, the hope, the anguish of all who suffer and rejoice — that Church will be Christ beloved and awaited, Christ present. And that depends on us" (p. 114). It becomes clear that the incarnational dynamic is the same as the dynamic of in-corporation, as this takes place in the church itself as the body of Christ. "Advent should alert us to discovering the face of Christ in each brother we greet, in each friend we welcome, in each beggar who asks us for bread, in each worker who exercises his union rights, in each peasant who seeks work in the coffee plantations. No one would be capable of robbing them, deceiving them, denying them his rights. There is Christ, and all that is done to them, Christ will take it as done to himself. This is what Advent is: Christ living among us" (p. 41).

In his homily of December 17, exactly two weeks later, he recalls that the Holy Spirit "made the body in the womb of Mary and keeps making the Church here in history" (p. 119). From this point on, Archbishop Romero replaces the word *body* with the word *flesh,* with all the connotations that such a change implies: "The flesh is the concrete situation of humans, of sinful humans, of humans in anguish over their situation, of humans who are a homeland with a history that seems to have detoured into a dead-end street. The flesh is all of us who live incarnated. The flesh! That fragile flesh, that flesh that begins and ends, that grows sick and dies, that sins, that becomes distressed and delighted, according to its obedience to God. The Word became that, became flesh. . . . God became human and has taken on this concrete flesh of crimes, of violence, of suffering. Flesh is all that, a mixture of justice and assault, of innocence and sin. All this has been taken on by Christ in order to redeem us from sin and obtain for us God's life, so that we might be converted and participate in the divine life" (pp. 119-22). In other words, even though the fragility and ambiguity of the flesh remind us that we are not yet the glorious body of the Lord, the strength of his incarnation assures us that we are still called to be that.

For Archbishop Romero, situated in the Christian tradition, "there is no dichotomy between the image of God and the human being. Anyone who has tortured humans, anyone who has offended or assaulted humans, has also offended God's image, and the Church feels that that cross, that martyrdom, is also hers" (p. 42). No doubt, the Salvadoran church has been a church of martyrs; it has been such in virtue of the large doses of persecution and suffering that it has undergone, and for having experienced this situation out of fidelity and witness to the gospel. Several times the radio station of the archdiocese was attacked with bombs, with the intention of silencing its prophetic voice. In this regard, Archbishop Romero said on January 27, 1980: "God's best microphone is Christ, and Christ's best microphone is the church, and the Church is all of you. Let each one of you, in your own job, in your own vocation — nun, married person, bishop, priest, high-school or university student, workman, laborer, market woman — each one in your own place live the faith intensely and feel that in your surroundings you are a true microphone of God our Lord" (p. 105). The church is "God's microphone" precisely because it is the body of Christ in history, a history in which the powerful attempt to silence God.

Finally, I dedicate a few lines to recalling that the force of Archbishop Romero's word did not derive simply from its incisiveness or its wisdom, but came precisely from its being an incarnated word, a word made body. By this I mean that the very life of Archbishop Romero, along with that of the Salvadoran people, reproduced the paschal way of the Lord Jesus. It was, therefore, the true body of Christ. Let us recall just four significant moments of the last stage of Romero's life. On March 16, 1980, he reaffirmed the inviolable value of human life and stated that the attacks on the poor truly touched "the very heart of God," because those poor are the same body of Christ. Exactly one week later, on March 23, in what would be his last Sunday homily, Archbishop Romero raised his voice to denounce the armed forces "in the name of God and of this suffering people": "I ask you, I beg you, I order you in the name of God, stop the repression!" That was just too much for his enemies, and on the next day, March 24, 1980, Archbishop Oscar Romero was murdered while he was celebrating the Eucharist in the Chapel of the Divine Providence Hospital, exactly at the moment of preparing the table to receive the body of Christ. There is perhaps no more graphic, powerful, explanatory emblem than that of seeing a bishop martyred for defending his people, the body of Christ in history, while he is offering the Eucharistic bread, the Body of Christ on the altar.

Archbishop Romero was buried in the cathedral on March 30, and his funeral was an immense manifestation of the people's solidarity, affection, and communion. The repressive forces, nonetheless, broke into the celebration, killed an undetermined number of people, and wounded several hundred more. The body of Christ, united to its head and guided by its bishop, keeps moving toward Easter, really and mystically.

Conclusion

Thus do we reach the end of this chapter's survey of four different persons who have offered us as many unique ways of viewing the mystery of the body of Christ. We have heard from a missionary religious, a nearly hermitic priest, a Jesuit scientist, and a martyred archbishop. We have traveled to India, Algeria, France, El Salvador, that is, to the four corners of the world: Asia, Africa, Europe, America. We have submerged ourselves in the one and only body of Christ: broken body, silent body, cosmic body, transfigured body. And we have discovered, once again, the profound unity that that body of Christ produces when we allow ourselves to be grafted into it. We have heard from four radical witnesses that speak to us of the need to root ourselves in Jesus Christ; we have received four invitations to display in our own lives the radicality of the body of Christ. The following chapter offers some suggestions for how we can advance in that direction.

8. A Radical Counter-Politics

This final chapter has vital importance for the coherence and proper understanding of this book. Admittedly, the central category that I have used, the body of Christ, provokes serious suspicions in many thinkers. As Michel Foucault has pointed out, the category "body" has often been used to justify and legitimize the established order,[1] since it always favors the powerful classes and sometimes gives rise to practices that offend the dignity of the human person.[2] For many readers the category possibly sounds like a very conservative socio-political church doctrine. Nonetheless, in the course of this book I have been defending the thesis that the body of Christ grounds a "radical theo-politics," one that cannot be consigned to devoutly hollow words, but must take on flesh in concrete, visible, and operative proposals. This chapter, therefore, may be viewed as the touchstone of the whole system I propose. Can the body of Christ really provide the basis for articulating an alternative to the dominant system? That is what I must show in this chapter.

---

1. The essential work is Michel Foucault, *Discipline and Punish: The Birth of the Person*, trans. Alan Sheridan (New York: Vintage, 1979).

2. To take just one example, St. Thomas Aquinas states that it is licit to kill sinners, just as "if it were necessary for the health of the whole human body to amputate some member; for example, if the member were gangrenous and could infect the other members, such an amputation would be laudable and beneficial" (*Summa Theologiae* II-II, q. 64, a. 2).

Methodological Considerations

The General Analytical Framework

In this chapter I employ a schema that has been gaining currency in the last few decades as a framework for social analysis. It involves a threefold division of reality that has been used by neo-conservative authors like Daniel Bell and Michael Novak, as well as by Neo-Marxists like Jürgen Habermas. Pope John Paul II himself adopts this schema in his 1991 encyclical *Centesimus Annus*. Referring to chapters 4 and 5 of this encyclical, a recognized specialist points out that "the study of both chapters together allows us to discover the analytical model that the encyclical employs, which appears to us to be one of its important contributions, namely, the distinguishing of three levels: economic, political and (ethico-)cultural."[3] The encyclical speaks of economics in the fourth chapter (*CA* 30-43), while the fifth chapter is dedicated to politics (*CA* 44-49) and culture (*CA* 50-52). Using this schema, the pope explains the collapse of the Soviet system and offers insights for a devastating critique of globalized capitalism.

Obviously, there are different ways of ordering and interrelating these three spheres, and one's analysis will clearly be affected by the ordering pattern he or she decides on. The most conservative authors, for example, are known to have used the schema to legitimize capitalism, arguing that a return to moral values (the cultural system) allows for maintenance and reinforcement of the other two systems (economic capitalism and political democracy). This line of argument is in clear disagreement with what the pope is actually saying. More enlightening and more coherent with Christian doctrine in this regard is the proposal of Habermas, who, in critical dialogue with the main currents of modern sociology, distinguishes between the "world of life" and "systems." The central concept of the world of life *(Lebenswelt)* is taken from Edmund Husserl; it is understood as the shared horizon, the depository of "self-evidences" or unquestioned convictions, the transcendental space common to the different people who participate in it. This world of life unfolds in three spheres (objective, social, and subjective), which correspond to the three dimensions of communicative action and to the three aforementioned subsystems (economic, politico-administrative, and socio-cultural).

It is generally agreed that the good functioning of any society requires

---

3. Ildefonso Camacho, SJ, *Creyentes en la vida pública* (Madrid: San Pablo, 1995), p. 153. The author develops this model of analysis on pp. 155-56.

that the world of life take priority over the system, that communicative action take priority over strategic action, that emancipative interests take priority over practical interests, and that the person take priority over the structure. What happens in practice, however, is that the rationalization of the world of life brings about an increase in systemic complexity; the complexity overdevelops to the point that the systemic imperatives, now uncontrolled, exceed the world of life's ability to absorb them, so that the world of life ends up being manipulated by them.[4] In such a case, we witness an uncoupling of the world of life and the social subsystems, with the result that the world of life becomes "technified" and instrumentally colonized. In other words, the roles are reversed: the system takes priority over the world of life. What is even more serious, as in the case of capitalism, is the domination of the economic subsystem over the political, which leads to rampant commercialization.

What needs to be emphasized is that for a society to function properly and in coherence with the Christian vision, the systemic mechanisms must be subordinated to the world of life (or, if you wish, to the civilization of love or the Christian worldview). Such proper functioning does not come about, as some neoconservative authors state, simply by doing some superficial retouching in the realm of cultural values. In reality, such cultural remodeling leaves the social structure basically intact and decidedly favors the powerful. In contrast, giving primacy to the world of life allows ethics to be given a preponderant role, without ceding either to moralism or to a sterile affirmation of abstract values. When we state that the world of life must take priority over the political, economic, and cultural subsystems, we are striving to restore daily life as a space for shared practices (an ethos that shares mores, customs), we are placing the person and his or her socio-communitarian relations in the center of social life, and we are underscoring the role of the church as an alternative social space, precisely as the body of Christ present in history.

For this reason, what I have expressed up to this point must be linked closely with the principles of the church's social doctrine. While it is true that these principles have not always had the same formulation and that they are made to relate to one another in a variety of ways, I offer here a proposal that is completely faithful to the pontifical magisterium and also coherent with the analytical framework I am using.[5] I posit, first, the con-

---

4. See Jürgen Habermas, *The Theory of Communicative Action,* vol. 2, *Lifeworld and System. A Critique of Functionalist Reason,* trans. Thomas McCarthy (Cambridge: Polity, 1989).

5. See Pontifical Council for "Justice and Peace," *Compendium of Social Doctrine of the*

ception of the human person as the image of the living God, which leads to the principle of the primacy of the life and the dignity of every person. This principle constitutes what in philosophical terms we have called the *Lebenswelt,* the world of life, the Christian worldview. It will form the basis of the other principles, which in turn will orient the comprehension of the diverse social systems. Accordingly, the principle of subsidiarity, which seeks the most suitable and effective plane for responding to society's challenges, according to each case, applies to the political system. The economic system, for its part, is oriented by the principle of the universal destiny of goods, the horizon that orients all the economic initiatives aimed at bringing about a world of justice and solidarity. Finally, the cultural system finds its orientation in the principle of participation, of both individuals and organized groups, at all levels of social life. In sum, the following schema summarizes the position that is argued in these pages:

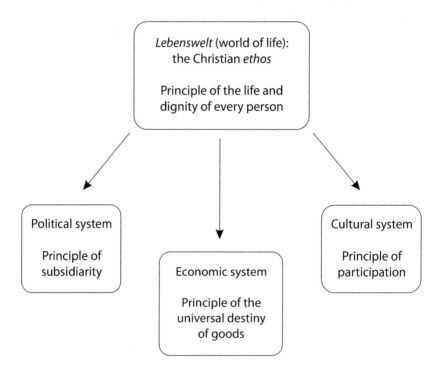

_____

Church (Città del Vaticano: Libreria Editrice Vaticana, 2004), chapter IV, numbers 160-208. Accessible at www.vatican.va.

The Interrelation between the Two Levels of Discourse

The second topic I need to clarify is how my proposal links the theological level together with the socio-political level. Although we already touched on this matter in the second chapter of the first part of this book, we would do well to recall some of the conclusions arrived at there and to make them a bit more concrete. My position clearly distances itself from every kind of fundamentalism and so avoids identifying the body of Christ with any specific historical formula (or even with the Catholic Church!). At the same time, I do not want to be accused of naiveté and so I avoid uttering ethereal generalities that have no relation at all with concrete historical mediations, as partial as they may be. What is more, the selection of these mediations is clearly important in a double sense. From an ecclesial and theological viewpoint, we must make plainly manifest the Christian alternative and do so in complete coherence with what we believe. From a social and political viewpoint, the asphyxiating disruption being caused by globalized capitalism points insistently toward the need for a potent, vigorous alternative. Such is the challenge I have before me, and I must therefore specify quite clearly how the two levels relate to one another.

To that end I am going to draw on the distinction that Michel de Certeau makes between strategy and tactic.[6] This author argues that strategy is the calculation, utilization, and manipulation of relations of power that become possible for a given social subject (for example, an enterprise, an army, a nation, or a scientific institution). For their part, tactics are defined as the discrete, isolated actions that take advantage of opportunities as they arise. Thus understood, then, strategy is an instrument of the powerful, while tactics constitute the art of the weak. This position is liberating in a way, because it offers tools for public action and social transformation to all kinds of people, no matter how fragile they seem to be, they are in fact, or they believe themselves to be. Of course, this focus smacks of the postmodern; it goes well with fragmentation and is suspicious of meta-narratives. In terms of the general image that guides this book, tactics interconnect with the "rhizomes" and are suspicious of all that sounds like "root" or strategy. It is small wonder that a large part of contemporary alternative radical thought feels comfortable with this distinction and settles on tactical means, without greater pretensions.

6. Michel de Certeau, SJ, *L'invention du quotidien*, vol. I, *Arts de faire* (Paris: Gallimard, 1990), pp. 50-68.

My disagreement with the distinction begins precisely at this point, because my position is that, along with tactics, a strategy is necessary. I hold that the rhizomes are vigorous only when they are anchored in a root. The radical Christian position I defend in these pages does not depend solely on the historical opportunities that might or might not arise; it grounds itself fundamentally in the gift of Jesus Christ, victor over all the thrones and powers, the one who opens up for us the horizon of the kingdom with its total liberation. We know what we want, we already have a strategy, and precisely on the basis of that we adopt particular tactical alliances, not only with Christian communities, but also with all the forces that are opposed to the predatory system that dominates us. Such forces might include worker-managed socialist projects, anarchist groups that opt for direct participation, cultural minorities that struggle creatively to maintain their identity, nonviolent groups that practice civil disobedience, cooperative organizations, or anti-globalization movements that believe another world is possible.

In chapter 2 of the first part of this book I stated that the Christian vision is founded on the primacy of the *analogia fidei*, but insisted that this analogy does not exclude, but actually requires the *analogia entis*, in a relation of subordination. What I formulated then in theological terms I now transfer to the political realm: it is necessary to cultivate a Christian strategy, but this strategy needs tactical alliances that give it substance, that make it concrete and visible. Having a clear strategy or laudable values is of no use if we are incapable of molding them into human community with a certain tactical realism. Neither is it of much use to throw ourselves into concrete projects (always limited and partial) if we forget the core passion that moves us. The primacy always belongs to the strategy, but the strategy, in accord with the basic principle of Christian incarnation, always requires tactical alliances. The root produces rhizomes, just as the vine produces branches.

In this sense, my proposal coincides with the posture of conservative Christians in that we affirm our specific identity. It coincides also with that of progressive Christians in its political commitment on behalf of the impoverished. I would like to urge the former to refrain from isolating themselves in their identity ghetto, and I urge the latter to avoid diluting themselves and letting themselves be swept away by currents that are culturally dominant and politically correct. Both sides need to go beyond the false conservative/progressive dichotomy, without falling into the error of a centrist theology that leads to naïve idealism, mediocre praxis, and, implicitly, a defense of the status quo and the interests of the powerful. Indeed, mine is a radical theology. It does not water down the Christian position or renounce anything positive in that position. I affirm both extremes at the same time. I invite the one side to take seriously the church, the body of Christ, our most authentic root. I invite the other side to opt with radicality for the poor and to struggle for justice. My proposal may perhaps sound excessively radical to those who (consciously or unconsciously) maintain alliances with the powerful, and excessively Catholic to those whose affection for the church has been seriously eroded. However, we will be faithful to the tradition we have inherited and to the challenges of our world only if we live firmly rooted in Jesus Christ, giving fleshly substance to a radical alternative to the dominant world system.

The Body Is Fragile: Active Nonviolence

The Catholic principle of the inviolable dignity of human life (every human life) leads directly to defining the Christian worldview precisely as active nonviolence. In the first part of this book I already defended this connection between a consistent ethic of life and active nonviolence, but I continue to insist on the point for two basic reasons. First, fidelity to the gospel of Jesus Christ, which announces the good news of peace and total liberation, requires such linkage. "Christ is our peace" (Eph. 2:14), and it would be an error to limit the gospel of nonviolence to a secondary, subordinate chapter of social morality, for it expresses the very heart of the revelation of God in Jesus Christ. Second, the need for this interconnection between a human life ethic and active nonviolence arises as a response to the historical situation we find ourselves living in, a world pervaded with structural violence.

Notes on Evangelical Nonviolence

The Gospel passages that support active nonviolence are so numerous that trying to present them, consider them, or simply mention them would be an unmanageable task. Moreover, excellent studies are available that develop the biblical foundations of nonviolence.[7] It is well recognized that many of the most important nonviolent leaders of the twentieth century emphasized the powerful inspiration that they derived from the Gospels for their lives and their action. This is true not only of those who were explicitly Christian and church-related (Martin Luther King Jr., Lanza del Vasto, Jean and Hildegarde Goss-Mayr, Adolfo Pérez-Esquivel, César Chávez, to mention only a few), but also of many others who were non-Christian (Gandhi) or alienated from the church community (Tolstoy). Gandhi, for example, always referred to Jesus of Nazareth, and concretely to the Sermon on the Mount, whenever he explained the profound bases of his nonviolent project.

The command "Thou shalt not kill!" of the biblical revelation on Sinai (Exod. 20:13) finds a strongly radicalized resonance in the mouth of Jesus (Matt. 5:21-26). Love for one's enemies to the point of giving one's life for them may be considered, furthermore, a condensed summary of the life of Jesus, the full revelation of the living and true God, and the synthesis of active nonviolence. In chapter 3 of the first part I explained how the Christian vision surpasses the lex talionis and invites people to resist evil by the force of goodness (Matt. 5:38-42). A great many more passages could be cited to the same end; indeed, a whole Christology of nonviolence could be elaborated.[8] We are going to focus, however, on just one central moment in the life of Jesus that is essential for giving a solid foundation to evangelical nonviolence.

The episode of the expulsion of the merchants from the Temple is usually adduced as a proof that the praxis of Jesus was not always peaceful and that, consequently, defending active nonviolence in all situations is an exaggeration. The criticism is a serious one, and if it proved true, it would substantially change our argument. Moreover, the importance of the event is shown in its having been recorded in all four Gospels (Matt. 21:12-17; Mark 11:11, 15-17; Luke 19:45-46; John 2:14-16). Indeed, it is considered to

---

7. François Vaillant, OP, *La no violencia en el evangelio* (Santander: Sal Terrae, 1993); Walter Wink, *Jesus and Nonviolence: A Third Way* (Minneapolis: Fortress, 2003); Juan Driver, *Una teología bíblica de la paz* (Guatemala: Semilla, 2003); André Trocmé, *Jesus and the Nonviolent Revolution* (Maryknoll, N.Y.: Orbis, 2004 [orig. French ed., 1961]); Jean and Hildegarde Goss-Mayr, *Evangelio y lucha por la paz* (Salamanca: Sígueme, 1990), pp. 25-41.

8. See James Alison, *Knowing Jesus*, 2nd ed. (London: SPCK, 1998), translated into Spanish with the subtitle "Cristología de la no-violencia," and John H. Yoder, *The Politics of Jesus. Behold the Man. Our Victorious Lamb*, 2nd ed. (Grand Rapids: Eerdmans, 1994).

have led directly to the death of Jesus. For all these reasons I have decided to examine this scene closely. I wish to state clearly, even if some readers are surprised, that this episode does not describe the exceptional use of violence by Jesus; to the contrary, the event is a true model of direct nonviolent action, whose aim is non-cooperation with evil. Let us look at the scene in detail, fixing our attention on certain contextual elements and on the narration itself.[9]

In the Synoptic Gospels the expulsion of the merchants occurs immediately after Jesus' entry into Jerusalem (Matt. 21:1-11), which is portrayed not only as a gesture of humility, but also as a veritable dramatization, with clear symbolic intent, of Jesus' nonviolent alternative. Verse 7 is key for interpreting the event, since "the donkey and the colt" on which Jesus is riding refer directly to a prophecy of Zechariah, which announces that the king "will cut off the chariot from Ephraim, and the horse from Jerusalem; and the battle bow will be cut off; and he will speak peace to the nations" (Zech. 9:10). Accordingly, Jesus' entry into Jerusalem is a symbolic action constituting a nonviolent, countercultural parody of the dominant imperial political power. The Gospel of Mark provides another important contextual element: his text (Mark 11:11) states explicitly that Jesus and his companions went to the Temple, observed everything, and then left for Bethany. The following day the expulsion of the merchants took place. What does this indicate? No doubt it means that the expulsion was not a violent and uncontrolled explosion, fruit of sudden indignation; rather, it was a foreseen, planned, organized nonviolent action.

If we examine the action in itself, what actually happens? First, the whip is mentioned only in John's version. Even though that whip figures large in most people's imagining of the scene, it is completely absent in the three Synoptic Gospels. Most exegetes agree that the whip was used to drive out all the animals, not the sellers (John 2:15). The whip that Jesus used to lead the animals out of the Temple, then, was the same kind that shepherds and cowherds used to guide their livestock. Precisely for that reason, the text relates that Jesus goes on to speak to the sellers, who are still inside the Temple (John 2:16). That is to say, no violence is committed

---

9. My reading of this passage is in part inspired by Vaillant, *La no violencia en el evangelio,* pp. 45-59, and by Richard A. Horsley and Neil Asher Silberman, *The Message and the Kingdom: How Jesus and Paul Ignited a Revolution and Transformed the Ancient World* (Minneapolis: Augsburg Fortress, 2002).

against any person; the expulsion of the animals consists in a strong symbolic action that opposes an unjust system; it is an action that refuses to cooperate with evil, that takes the initiative, that purifies the Temple and restores to God the initiative of universal salvation. Jesus is convinced that God must not be manipulated or commercialized, and certainly not at the expense of the poor. This perverse, commercialized sacrificial system had to be opposed, and the initiative taken against it was a nonviolent action that was direct, symbolic, and well planned — so much so that this same action unleashed the events that led to the arrest, trial, torture, and execution of Jesus, who was accused precisely of destroying the Temple (Matt. 26:61). Through his death Jesus manifests clearly the radicality of his nonviolent faithfulness: he hands himself over out of love and pardoning his mortal enemies.[10]

Notes on Twentieth-Century Theological Reflection

The Second Vatican Council invites Christians to "examine war with a completely new mentality" (*Gaudium et Spes*, 80). The Council texts display a certain tension between the traditional affirmation of legitimate defense, within the framework of the just war doctrine, and the recognition of conscientious objection and active nonviolence. The subsequent doctrinal development has maintained these two poles, though with a most interesting evolution that is not very well known.

The pronouncements of several episcopal conferences during the 1980s did much to help clarify this point. Most especially, the pastoral letter *The Challenge of Peace*, published by the U.S. bishops in 1983, advanced markedly in the formulation of the twofold Catholic tradition concerning nonviolence and just war.[11] In paragraph 120 the letter points out that "the

---

10. See James W. Douglass, *The Non-Violent Cross: A Theology of Revolution and Peace* (New York: Macmillan, 1968). The most brilliant and enduring pages of this book are those that refer precisely to the role of the cross in forging the nonviolent life of Christians. For example: "The logic of non-violence is the logic of the crucifixion and leads the man of nonviolence into the heart of the suffering Christ" (p. 71). "By the crucifixion violence and injustice have everywhere become crucial, cross centered" (p. 72). "The cross is revolutionary not simply because it raises men to other life but because it transforms them into the fullness of that life on this earth" (p. 76).

11. See Joseba Segura Etxezarraga, *La guerra imposible. La ética cristiana entre la 'guerra*

new moment in which we find ourselves considers the just-war doctrine and non-violence as different, but interdependent methods for evaluating war." The document recalls that both doctrines "are founded on the Catholic theological tradition" and argues that "the two perspectives support and complement one another mutually, preventing one from deforming the other" (no. 121). This double approach had perhaps never before been formulated with such clarity, and it received strong and definitive backing from John Paul II, even if few people seem willing to recognize this.

While the episcopal documents of the 1980s were framed within the context of the cold war, the arms race, and nuclear determent, the fall of the Berlin wall in 1989 and the subsequent collapse of the Soviet bloc produced a new geopolitical framework. In this new context, the ordinary magisterium of Pope John Paul II constantly reassessed the Catholic posture with respect to modern war and the challenge of peace. With persevering coherence and in opposition to the main current of voices in the international political arena, John Paul II was tireless in raising his voice against war. His protests were especially clear in his resounding condemnation of the military aggressions of the United States and other countries against Iraq in the wars of 1991 and 2003. To mention only a couple of examples, on the eve of the allied attacks in January 1991, he warned that war is an "adventure without returns," and in 2003 he defined the occupation of Iraq as "a defeat for humanity."[12]

The persistence of John Paul II in this regard was so unmistakable that it might well be affirmed that it produced a very significant shift in the ordinary pontifical magisterium. Concretely, the discussion has usually centered on judging whether this or that war is a just war, by applying the classic criteria. The result of such analysis has led the magisterium, time and time again, simply to deny that any modern wars can be considered just wars. The arguments articulated by John Paul II in his ordinary magisterium seem to lead clearly toward that conclusion. My own theological reflection, however, seeks to clarify this situation and give further coherence to the official doctrine, perhaps even going a bit further.

---

justa' y la 'no-violencia' (Bilbao: Desclée de Brouwer, 1991), pp. 126-99; Paul Thibaud, "Les évêques américains entre la guerre juste et le pacifisme," *Esprit* 7 (1983): 91-99; David Holllenbach, SJ, "*The Challenge of Peace* in the Context of Recent Church Teachings," in *Catholics and Nuclear War*, ed. Philip J. Murnion (New York: Crossroad, 1983), pp. 3-15.

12. See Drew Christiansen, SJ, "Un papa no violento en una época de terror," *Razón y fe* 1285 (November 2005): 175-82.

To sum up my argument and draw conclusions: we have seen that traditional Catholic doctrine on war and peace derives from two complementary approaches (just war and nonviolence), but we have observed also that the ordinary magisterium of John Paul II in practice eliminates the possibility of a just war. We are therefore in a new situation, one in which church thought and action are strongly inclined toward active nonviolence. No other alternative really exists for the Catholic Church. This situation is fundamental and has extremely important consequences; it is the basis of the argumentation that runs through this whole book. This situation might well be compared to the evolution of Catholic doctrine concerning the death penalty, a doctrine that has been abandoned in practice, even if not completely in theory (see *Catechism of the Catholic Church,* no. 2267; *Evangelium Vitae,* 56). Something similar may be happening with the just war doctrine: it might be preserved as a theoretical possibility, but, in practice and given the historical circumstances, it is completely discounted. I repeat once more my basic conclusion: the only practical alternative possible for the Catholic Church is the practice of active nonviolence.[13]

From Word to Action

If such theological reflection leads us to take active nonviolence as the central integrating theme of a Christian ethics of peace and war, then we must be ready to draw out the obvious consequences. Active nonviolence requires serious ecclesial responsibility and much commitment from everybody. Nice words and rigorous theological formulations are not enough — we must take action. As we have said, strategy must be made concrete in tactical proposals. That is why we speak of active nonviolence or nonviolent action. In order for my proposal to be understood correctly, however, two prior clarifications are required.

First, a distinction should be made between action and activism. Nonviolence is above all a style of life, an integral vision of reality, a way of relating to the world. Gandhi insisted on this point constantly, and in Europe his Catholic disciple Lanza del Vasto has stressed it with great vigor, espe-

13. The Catholic Peace Fellowship (CPF) has put forth the line argument with rigor. See www.catholicpeacefellowship.org.

cially through the L'Arche communities.[14] Not only is it necessary to avoid a rush into frenetic activity, but, even more important, efforts must be made to overcome the public-private dichotomy through action that is truly human.

The second clarification concerns the very concept of nonviolence. We have been using this neologism systematically to indicate that we are not referring simply to the absence of violence, but to something much more integral, positive, and active. Despite what some people might think, non-violence is the opposite of passivity or resignation. The original term for nonviolence *(satyagraha)* literally means "force of truth";[15] many writers on nonviolence highlight this aspect of force in the concept. Accordingly, I prefer to speak of the *virtue* of nonviolence,[16] for two reasons. First, because virtue is a force that always needs to take on flesh and blood, to become concrete; we might say that the body of Christ is precisely the way that the virtuous force of nonviolence takes on corporal form. Second, my use of the concept of virtue allows us to avoid speaking of values, a confusing term that often is used in a biased sense, in order either to avoid descending to concrete particulars or to try to legitimize the dominant system with vague allusions to certain cultural values.

Consequently, as Christians we are called to incarnate the force of nonviolence in a visible social body. Our attention is thus fixed on the supreme responsibility of the church and on the immense potential it has as an alternative to the violence that dominates and bloodies the world. The thesis of this book is that our living rooted in Jesus Christ has radical implications for the life of the world. The body of Christ is called to give visible form to God's nonviolent alternative, to constitute itself as a true nonviolent body. If we were to take this seriously, many things would change. I mention just one example, alluded to earlier, namely, the significant consequences for society that would result from having all Christians who receive the sacrament of confirmation (in Spain alone there are 150,000 ev-

14. See, among other works, Joseph Jean Lanza del Vasto, *La fuerza de los no-violentos* (Bilbao: Mensajero, 1994); *Umbral de la vida interior,* 5th ed. (Salamanca: Sígueme, 1989); and *El arca tenía por vela una viña,* 2nd ed. (Salamanca: Sígueme, 1988).

15. For example, force of justice (Lanza del Vasto), force of love (Martin Luther King Jr.), force of liberation (Jean Goss), courage of nonviolence (Jean-Marie Muller), violence of the peaceful (Roger de Taizé), violence of love (Monseñor Romero).

16. "Non-violence is the moral and political virtue, the virtue that governs human action, that is, the first cardinal virtue": Vaillant, *La no violencia en el evangelio,* p. 155.

ery year) pass previously through a rigorous process of formation in the spirituality and the techniques of active nonviolence.[17]

Should this be thought completely utopian and unrealistic, then the arguments I have adduced thus far should be recalled. Of the two possible options in response to violence (nonviolence and just war), one has been dismissed in practice by the pontifical magisterium. There remains only the other option, nonviolence. The only remaining step is for us really to believe in nonviolence, and to dedicate ourselves to practicing it using the same efforts and resources (money, lands, soldiers, chaplains, researchers, etc.) that for centuries we have dedicated to preparing for war. Do we or do we not live rooted in Jesus Christ? "As far as the Church is concerned, the social message of the Gospel must not be considered a theory, but above all else a basis and a motivation for action," says John Paul II in the encyclical *Centesimus Annus* (no. 57).

We cannot rest satisfied with fine words, well-intentioned exhortations, or abstract principles. We must be what we are: the body of Christ. To do so, we need to move from the strategic to the tactical level, combining the ethical focus of nonviolence, which we have used until now, with a more pragmatic focus.[18] Only thus can we truly give substance to the virtue of nonviolence in our church community, as a sign and an instrument of God's liberation. Perhaps we cannot expect that any country will decide to abandon its armies and its military defense, but might we not hope that the church would help establish the nonviolent army that Gandhi dreamed of and that his disciple Vinoba attempted to create?[19] Or, even better,

---

17. If only 10 percent of those to be confirmed were to pass through this process, we would have 15,000 new nonviolent activists every year. Would it be too utopian to think of an objective of 1 percent? For educational suggestions, see Mercedes Mas, *Educar en la noviolencia* (Madrid: PPC, 2000). A very suggestive initiative, that is not centered directly on active nonviolence but has led to a rethinking of the alternative civil service, may be found in Joaquín García Roca and Guillermo Mondaza Canal, *Jóvenes, universidad y compromiso. Una experiencia de inserción comunitaria* (Madrid: Narcea, 2002).

18. Concerning this distinction between ethical and pragmatic nonviolence, see Pere Ortega and Alejandro Pozo, *Noviolencia y transformación social* (Barcelona: Icaria, 2005), pp. 47-49. I agree with these authors as regards the inadequacy of pragmatic nonviolence, but I hold that both aspects of nonviolence can and should be combined.

19. The *Shanti Sena*, or Gandhian nonviolent army, has inspired other initiatives that are still functioning, such as the International Peace Brigades, the Christian Action Teams for Peace, and the Non-violent Peace Forces. The French nonviolent current has especially developed, with rigor and creativity, alternative systems of national defense. Their proposal, though,

might not the church become itself such a nonviolent force, since that is precisely what it means to be an alternative social body? That is what is involved in keeping faith with the gospel of Jesus Christ, our peace. The great moral theologian Bernhard Häring stated it clearly twenty years ago: "By our faith in the redeemer of the world we are called, as Christians, to form the vanguard of the non-violent army of peace."[20]

The tactical proposals are numerous and could hardly be described in these pages, but I will simply refer to the well-known classification of Gene Sharp, who some decades back surveyed almost two hundred different types of nonviolent action and systematized them into three groups: actions of protest and persuasion, actions of non-cooperation (social, economic, and political) and actions of nonviolent intervention.[21] Depending on the action's legal or non-legal character and on its direct or symbolic character, we have four possibilities, illustrated below with an example of each:

Types of nonviolent action	Direct	Symbolic
Legal	Boycott	Vigil
Non-legal	Blocking a nuclear power plant	Occupation that does not impede construction

To close this section with a simple example, I would like to comment on conscientious objection in my home country, Spain. After the elimination of obligatory military service (the fruit of a prolonged, massive campaign, with more than a million conscientious objectors and more than

---

is still too dependent on territorial defense, the nation-state mentality, and the strategy of dissuasion. In our times it is necessary to insist on nonviolence as a tool of social transformation, although this also implies the vigorous formation of bodies of nonviolent action, an consideration that is not always taken into account. See also Anders Boserup and Andrew Mack, *War without Weapons: Non-violence in National Defense* (New York: Schocken, 1975); Colectivo Utopía Contagiosa, *Alternativas de Defensa Noviolenta* (Getafe: Bajo Cero, 2005); and the "nonviolent militia" proposed in Spain by Gonzalo Arias in 2005, www.milicianoviolenta.net

20. Bernhard Häring, *The Healing Power of Peace and Nonviolence* (New York: Paulist, 1986). Written in the German context of the 1980s, this book is a splendid introduction to nonviolence, insisting on its curative force.

21. Gene Sharp, *The Politics of Nonviolent Action,* part II, *The Methods of Nonviolent Action* (Boston: Porter Sargent, 1973), pp. 109-445. See also Colectivo Utopía Contagiosa, *Manual de Acción Directa Noviolenta* (Getafe: Bajo Cero, 2003).

fifty thousand resisters), it would seem that conscientious objection has lost its meaning. That is not the case, however, at least in the three spheres of action that we mentioned. First, selective conscientious objection is a direct consequence of the just war doctrine: it requires that every person, even one who is *not* nonviolent, decide in conscience whether a particular war fulfills or not the conditions necessary for it to be considered just. If it is determined to be unjust, then in conscience the person should refuse to participate in it. This position is crystal clear, and the U.S. bishops have insisted on its being recognized as legal in their country. Sadly and shockingly, such a position is practically unknown in Spain. How could the Spanish Catholic soldiers and chaplains turn a deaf ear when John Paul II insisted so strongly, in word and deed, on the immorality of the Gulf War? It was a clear case of the need for selective conscientious objection, but it was also an unfortunate example of how far the church is from being truly rooted in Jesus Christ. Two other examples on nonviolent resistance (refusal to pay taxes and objection to scientific research for military purposes) are still minority positions, but they ought to become a privileged field of action for Christian communities, if they truly wish to be the body of Christ present in history, assuming some of the radical consequences of being firmly rooted in the Lord Jesus.

Transition to the Following Sections

In speaking of active nonviolence within my analytic framework, I have singled out two elements. First, nonviolence constitutes the nucleus of the Christian worldview, the true ecclesial ethos, the *Lebenswelt* (or shared world of life), for the believing community. It might well be called the heart of the body of Christ. Second, nonviolence therefore involves an integral vision that encompasses all of reality — the everyday ways of relating, behaving, praying, working, producing, getting organized, sharing, and living — and approaches that reality from the perspective of love of enemies, option for the poor, and personal commitment. Active nonviolence is a spiritual force that should be deployed in all spheres of reality. For that reason I speak of revolutionary nonviolence or of nonviolence as a force for liberation and social transformation. Accordingly, in the following sections we look at the political, economic, and cultural implications of this nonviolent conception of life.

The Body, the Head, and the Feet: Politics

The question of violence is obviously related to the question of power. The state is generally considered to be the social body that holds a monopoly on the legitimate use of violence. It is understandable, therefore, that the nonviolent and anarchist traditions have been quite closely related in recent history (recall, for example, the figure of Leo Tolstoy). Furthermore, it is no accident that Jacques Ellul, one of the few Christian-anarchist thinkers, defines anarchy interchangeably as the nonviolent rejection of authority or as "the absolute rejection of violence."[22] In this section, therefore, we consider the implications of the body of Christ doctrine for the relations of the Christian communities with authority, power, the state, and politics.

Biblical Reflections

I do not pretend to elaborate here a complete theory on the biblical (or even New Testament) vision of political power and state organization. Such a task would be excessive considering the space we have, and besides it is hardly necessary. We should first recognize that, as Oscar Cullmann has pointed out, the New Testament does not contain a repudiation in principle of the state as such, but neither does it contain an unconditional admission of the state.[23] The reason for this attitude is found in the Christian conception of eschatology and historical time, in the "constitutive temporal tension" of Christianity: since we live between the "already" and the "not-yet" of God's kingdom, the state certainly exists, but only as something provisional, not definitive. Its value is therefore conditional and subordinate to the kingdom, the true homeland of Christians. With this initial framework, and having recourse to the splendid work of Walter Wink on the New Testament powers,[24] I will limit myself to three New Testament texts that seem essential for an accurate understanding of the matter at hand. I chose the texts precisely because they demonstrate the complexity of the matter and do not allow of a simplistic response.

22. Jacques Ellul, *Anarchy and Christianity* (Grand Rapids: Eerdmans, 1991), p. 11.

23. Oscar Cullmann, *Der Staat im Neuen Testament* (Tübingen: J. C. B. Mohr, 1961).

24. Walter Wink, *The Powers That Be: Theology for a New Millennium* (Broadway, N.Y.: Galilee, 1998). This book is a summary of his trilogy: *Naming the Powers, Unmasking the Powers, Engaging the Powers* (Philadelphia and Minneapolis: Fortress, 1984-92).

First of all, we have the well-known episode of the denarius, with the captious question of the Pharisees and Herodians about the payment of taxes. The reply of Jesus was: "Return to Caesar what belongs to Caesar, and to God what belongs to God" (Mark 12:13-17). This saying has often been used to justify a division of powers between state and church, and it has even been used as a basis for theories like that of the "two swords." According to this view, a certain sphere of state action is conceived to be outside God's dominion. This is precisely the posture of the Herodians, which Jesus refuses to accept. It should be noted that the verb used by Jesus does not mean simply "give," but "return, restore." We should therefore interpret Jesus' statement in the sense of restoring God's sovereignty, which by definition is an absolute sovereignty. "Restoring to God what is God's" means nothing less than returning to that primordial situation in which all reality is God's and God's alone: that is the essential meaning of the kingdom of God that has broken in with the arrival of Jesus. "What belongs to Caesar" (that is, the realm of state power) is now essentially superseded, although, in the time that remains before the definitive plenitude, it may still have some function to fulfill. Such a function, though, will tend to exceed its limits, and Christians should be ready to contain it within its limited, controlled condition.

The letter to the Romans offers another well-known text, one that often is cited to justify state power and defend Christian acceptance of it: "Let every soul be in subjection to the higher authorities, for there is no authority except from God, and those who exist are ordained by God. Therefore he who resists the authority, withstands the ordinance of God" (Rom. 13:1-2) The passage seems clear and has indeed been used many times to legitimize political power and to require total obedience to the established order. The most flagrant case in recent history was the use of this text to justify apartheid in South Africa. We should first take note that the passage at no point asserts that the state is "divine"; it simply affirms that the state is "ordained" by God, just as every reality forms part of the order willed or established by God. That is the order of this world: provisional and relative. Paul justifies his argument in view of the prevailing eschatological tension: "knowing the time" in which we live (Rom 13:11). That is to say, while the final times are still arriving, political power forms part of this order willed by God, and it has a defined field of action within this setting. Accordingly, I offer the following reading or interpretation of the verse, on the basis of my nonviolent perspective. Christians should maintain a critical distance with respect to this world's established order; such distance will lead them to active nonviolence, to non-cooperation with evil and with unjust power, and on occasions to civil disobedience. Such is their obligation as citizens of the kingdom. Of course, legitimately established authority may apply the laws and imprison nonviolent militants, and the militants will accept the consequences of their action because they know that they live in this world, in the order established and thus willed by God. The nonviolent Christian who practices civil disobedience knows and assumes that the constituted authorities will exercise repression. He or she accepts such a situation as something willed by God and as a way of welcoming the kingdom that is coming.[25]

This interpretation, which may possibly surprise the reader, gains greater clarity in the light of the book of Revelation, which is another essential reference point for understanding the posture of the New Testament with regards to political power. That book recognizes the imperial Beast for what it is: "It was given to him to make war with the saints, and to overcome them" (13:7); what is required therefore is "the endurance and the faith of the saints" (13:10). Jewish apocalyptic is, of course, a literary genre that was produced by those who were in clandestine resistance to the dominant forces, and for that reason it uses symbolic, coded language. In the particular case of Revelation, the author is referring directly to the persecution of the church by the Roman empire. Out of his Christological conviction that Christ has defeated all earthly powers, the author stresses two essential aspects of this historical moment, which are applicable to all believers until the end of time. First, he asserts the radical opposition and evident conflict between the Roman state and the Christian community (the Beast and the Lamb, Babylon and Jerusalem). Second, he calls Christians, not to armed resistance, but to unyielding perseverance, steadfastness, and active nonviolence. It is by no means happenstance that the Lord Jesus makes his appearance as the victor over history and over this world's powers precisely in the form of the slaughtered Lamb (5:6-14). Furthermore, the text makes clear that in the end those who "didn't worship the beast nor his image and didn't receive the mark on their forehead and on their hand, lived and reigned with Christ" (20:4) and that the final horizon is not Rome, but the new Jerusalem, "a new heaven and a new earth" (21:1). The political power of the state has

---

25. See Yoder, *The Politics of Jesus. Behold the Man. Our Victorious Lamb*, pp. 193-211.

been definitively redefined in the Christian worldview: "Behold, I am making all things new," says the Lord.

Theological Reflections

Following up on these New Testament conceptions, we consider in this section some of the church's reflection on the state and political authority. To do so, we concentrate on two crucial historical moments. First, I say a word about Saint Augustine, since it was precisely in the fourth century that a profound change took place in church-state relations, and Augustine was effectively the theologian who systematized the new situation. Second, we consider the doctrine proposed by the pontifical magisterium in the twentieth century, and concretely the principle of subsidiarity.

The critical duality between the state and the kingdom of God, or between political power and the Christian community, as we have seen it expressed in the New Testament, is found also at the center of Augustine's work *The City of God*. Although the work has frequently been interpreted along the lines of what is called "political Augustinianism," we would do well to recall that for Augustine the division between the two cities is not at all easy to discern in the concrete terrain of history. We cannot simply identify the church with the City of God and the empire with the City of Man. Furthermore, Augustine is often thought to view human beings as political by nature, so that the existence of the state is fully justified. Augustine's true conception, however, was that human beings are social by nature, but not political.[26] In other words, human beings are created by God to be open to interpersonal and social relations, but the use of political coercion (like slavery or private property) is the fruit of sin, not a part of human nature. This point is related to one of Augustine's key concepts, the *libido dominandi*, the lust for control, the desire for domination, or the perverse structure of political power.[27] This concept appears at the very beginning of the first book of *The City of God:* "although peoples are sub-

26. This is pointed out by Robert A. Markus, *Saeculum: History and Society in the Theology of St. Augustine* (Cambridge: Cambridge University Press, 1970), p. 95, and by R. W. Dyson, *The Pilgrim City: Social and Political Ideas in the Writings of St. Augustine of Hippo* (Woodbridge: Boydell, 2001), pp. 104-5.

27. See Miikka Ruokanen, *Theology of Social Life in Augustine's* De civitate Dei (Göttingen: Vandenhoeck & Ruprecht, 1993), pp. 96-101.

ject" to the earthly city, "it is itself ruled by its lust of rule."[28] In synthesis, then, the Augustinian vision of the state and political power is initially critical, negative (they are the fruit of sin), and suspicious (they tend to be motivated by the desire for domination). Such a posture is plainly coherent with the New Testament position.

We undertake now a consideration of the church's social doctrine concerning the state and political power. We leave aside for the moment the very important issue of participation, since I treat it in another section of this chapter. I first focus attention on the principle of subsidiarity, which was formulated by Pius XI in this way: "it is an injustice and at the same time a grave evil and disturbance of right order to assign to a greater and higher association what lesser and subordinate organizations can do. For every social activity ought of its very nature to furnish help to the members of the body social, and never destroy and absorb them" (*Quadragesimo Anno,* no. 79). In this same section the pope recognizes that the complexity of the world requires the intervention of large social organizations; he then indicates that "the State will more freely, powerfully, and effectively do all those things that belong to it alone because it alone can do them: directing, watching, urging, restraining, as occasion requires and necessity demands" (no. 80). This doctrine has been confirmed and reasserted by successive papal encyclicals, although it is not always interpreted correctly.

Frequently, for example, appeal is made to the principle of subsidiarity in order to attack the welfare state, promote privatization of the public sector, or advance economic policies of a neoliberal nature. Such is not the meaning of this church doctrine. The principle of subsidiarity states, first, that civil society and the intermediate social levels should be strengthened, so that they are able to produce a closely woven social fabric. Second, the principle argues that the higher levels of organization are necessary in order to respond to the realities and situations that affect large numbers of people. It is not a question of dismantling anything, but of acting at the most appropriate and effective level in each case. The principle also states that, while the state can and should play an essential role in public life, it does not have a salvific or definitive character. In other words, some mat-

---

28. Saint Augustine, *The City of God,* trans. Marcus Dodd (New York: The Modern Library, 1993), Book I, Preface. The original Latin reads thus: "cum dominari appetit, etsi populi serviant, ipsa ei dominandi libido dominantur."

ters, depending on their nature, should be resolved at the municipal, state, national, continental, or global level. Other matters can and should be resolved in the social, and not strictly political, sphere. What is considered a political matter or a public space (polis) is much broader and deeper than just "politics." This principle of subsidiarity may appear excessively simple or obvious, but it is little known or understood by either side of the political spectrum and is usually cited only to defend vested interests. The dominant discourse seems to comprehend only an individual/collective continuum, which sometimes leads to a very crass liberalism that often ends up supporting the powerful and at other times leads to a sterile, bureaucratic statism. Both options ignore the vital role of the community, civil society, independent organization, and intermediate initiatives. These latter are the major concern of the principle of subsidiarity. They form part of a political vision centered on the body of Christ. To them we now turn our attention, citing perhaps concrete instances that will surprise more than one reader.

Alternative Paths

To sum up what we have covered in this section up to now, I make two basic points. First, for the Christian vision, an affirmation such as "everything for the homeland" or pledging allegiance to one nation is plain and simple idolatry.[29] The only true homeland of the Christian is the reign of God. Everything else (including especially the state), even what is valued as necessary, is always relative, secondary, limited, and temporal. Second, the historical reality of the world in which we live requires instruments for organizing public life that we as believers cannot evade. As one specialist in social ethics points out, politics is the means for subordinating economics to ethics.[30] That is the realm of political power, even if the way it is usually exercised often appears to be far less than adequate.

In the rest of this section I offer a series of paths, some more theoreti-

29. See Michael J. Baxter, "God Is Not American: Or, Why Christians Should Not Pledge Allegiance to 'One Nation under God,'" in *God Is Not . . .* , ed. D. Brent Laytham (Grand Rapids: Brazos, 2004), pp. 55-75, as well as José Luis Sicre, SJ, *Los dioses olvidados. Poder y riqueza en los profetas preexílicos* (Madrid: Cristiandad, 1979).

30. Luis González-Carvajal, *Entre la utopía y la realidad. Curso de moral social* (Santander: Sal Terrae, 1999), p. 81.

cal and others more directly practical, which will show us ways to incarnate creatively the principle of subsidiarity and the Christian vision of political power. My listing of proposals does not pretend to constitute a compact and homogeneous system. Rather, it seeks to offer a spectrum of alternative approaches to our political reality — alternative because they presuppose "being born again" and because they involve "being born with others" *(alter-natus)*. That is to say, I offer a series of possible leads for viewing concretely the implications of the body of Christ in the political realm. From this perspective, what is important is not designing a global alternative in detail, but progressively incarnating alternative spaces. My hope is that Christian communities will set out to travel along some or many of these paths.

Recently, on the basis of the philosophy of law, and concretely migratory law, some authors have made a devastating critique of the logic of the nation-state; they invite us to take a renewed and less naïve look at nationalism. Fernando Oliván, for example, has convincingly pointed out that "nationalism, the nation itself, is nothing but the shadow of the principle of excluding others."[31] Such exclusion becomes especially evident in the modern nation-state, which arose, we should not forget, thanks to the political triumph of the bourgeoisie and the expansion of capitalism. Organizing public life according to the national mentality presupposes the triumph of what Oliván calls the vertical tension (or law of conflict) over the horizontal tension (or friendship principle); it also assumes a practical ceiling that makes it impossible to live out the fraternity proclaimed in the French revolution. I would like to stress at this point just two aspects: first, the political configuration of the nation-state is the fruit of a given historical situation; it is not the only alternative that has existed in human history; second, the universalistic dynamic provoked by the body of Christ simply cannot accept the limitation of a mentality as discriminatory as is nationalism. The Christian proposal, by definition oriented toward the principle of universal love, cannot remain captive to the biased narrowness

---

31. Fernando Oliván, *El extranjero y su sombra. Crítica del nacionalismo desde el derecho de extranjería* (Madrid: San Pablo, 1998), p. 17. Recall William Cavanaugh's theological critique of the myth of the nation-state, in his *Theopolitical Imagination: Discovering Liturgy as a Political Act in an Age of Global Consumerism* (London: T&T Clark, 2002), pp. 9-52. Seyla Benhabib, *The Rights of Others: Aliens, Residents and Citizens* (Cambridge and New York: Cambridge University Press, 2004), makes use of Immanuel Kant and Hannah Arendt to show the contradictions of the nation-state.

of the nation-state. The implications of this focus are more than evident, for example, with regard to North-South relations or migratory policy.

The solidarity movement that seeks alternatives to the lopsided globalization we are now experiencing concedes much importance to two interrelated concepts: *governance* and *empowerment*.[32] Many attempts to improve society "from above," that is, by gaining power and seeking social transformation through the political apparatus of the state, have proved to be disappointing, if not disastrous, experiences. As a result, new ideas and proposals are abroad concerning how to bring about authentic social change. The emphasis now is on bestowing power on the whole population, in the sense of generating an ambience in which the real possibilities and potentialities of the people can be deployed. The new proposals seek to change the world *without* taking power.[33] This perspective "from below" refuses to use the term *power* (in Spanish, *poder*) as a noun (we have "power") and considers it first of all to be a verb (that is, we "have power" — to act, help, love, serve, live in a different way). It emphasizes the potency of "power to (act)" in the face of the domination of "power over (others)"; that is, it prioritizes social *potentia* over antisocial *potestas*. In order for this new conception of power to become truly effective, the wide-ranging force of the market and of global capital must be brought under control by means of an equally global type of governance. As can be seen, these proposals find much resonance with and similarity to the gospel perspective and the principle of subsidiarity.

This focus may be considered a positive one, in that it makes a claim for participation and access to determined spaces of political power, even if these are profoundly redefined and transformed. We find other, more negative proposals, in the sense that they emphasize taking distance with respect to power and the state. In keeping with the active nonviolence that I defended in the previous section, it is necessary to validate here the role of *civil disobedience*[34] (or civic disobedience, as some authors prefer). For Christians it will always be a necessary reminder of the provisional character of the state, and on occasions it will become a moral obligation of conscience. Obviously, civil disobedience is a powerful arm for nonviolent

32. Kristin Dawkins, *Global Governance: The Battle over Planetary Power* (New York: Seven Stories, 2003).

33. See John Holloway, *Change the World without Taking Power*, 2nd ed. (Ann Arbor, Mich., and London: Pluto, 2005).

34. Francisco Fernández Buey, *Desobediencia civil* (Getafe: Bajo Cero, 2005).

struggle and should be used with prudence, wisdom, and firmness. It is also, however, a forgotten virtue that the Christian community should perhaps try to recover. Continually bombarded as we are by messages of the type, "Little child, you must be obedient," we have perhaps reached the point where we should actively promote creative education in favor of civil disobedience.

Certain innovative paradigms in the field of grassroots social action stress the importance of *community dynamicization* as a tool for social transformation.[35] Several trends flow together in this perspective: the decentralization of political power and the subsequent rediscovery of neighborhoods and districts, the coming-of-age of contemporary social work, the desires and needs of neighborhood participation, the suspicion of bureaucracy, and finally the need for effective response to the grievous injustices that still exist in our societies. On the one hand, such proposals are useful for reinforcing the community fabric and responding effectively to the social needs of the district; on the other hand, they expand participative democracy and continually generate new social alternatives. In this way both the excessive professionalization of social work and the sterility of purely political decentralization can be overcome. A promising proposal in this regard is the IAP/PAI of Tomás Rodríguez Villasante, which manages to progress from what might remain a simple social work technique (investigation-action-participation: IAP) to a dynamic proposal for radical democracy (programming-alternative-integral: PAI).[36]

Advancing beyond the old political mold, the nation-state mentality, and our purely formal representative democracy finds an echo in the ecclesial principles of participation and solidarity. One concept that allows us to progress in this direction is that of *mutual aid,* precisely because it reinforces the social fabric, centers responsibility on the very community that gets itself organized, and keeps power close to the base. What is quite interesting is that mutual aid has been used and practiced by two groups that appear to be at opposite ends of the socio-political spectrum: the anarchists and the Mennonites. Back in the nineteenth century Piotr Kropotkin was already arguing that mutual aid was an essential force for human

35. Marco Marchioni, *Comunidad, participación y desarrollo. Teoría y metodología de la intervención comunitaria,* 2nd ed. (Madrid: Popular, 2001); Marco Marchioni, ed., *Comunidad y cambio social. Teoría y praxis de la acción comunitaria* (Madrid: Popular, 2001).

36. Tomás R. Villasante, *Las democracias participativas. De la participación ciudadana a las alternativas de sociedad* (Madrid: Ediciones HOAC, 1995), pp. 183-297.

evolution, precisely to make such evolution truly humanizing and harmonizing.[37] At the same time, around 1850, a Christian pastor set up mutual aid banks that were self-managed by the community itself and offered loans without interest. Even today the Mennonite Church has an alternative social security fund, apart from the national system, that is called precisely "mutual aid."

No doubt there are many myths and much misinformation about the relation between anarchism and Christianity, and there are certainly areas of deep disagreement between the two. Points of coincidence can also be identified, however, as, for example, in their renunciation of violence (quite clear in some anarchists), in their emphasis on personal and community responsibility, or in their mistrust of the state as the realm of abstract and depersonalizing power. Indeed, since when has it been necessary to ask permission of the state for people to help one another and to organize that help? As Christian philosopher Carlos Díaz states, in a properly anarchist proposal: "the elimination of the state should be maintained and complemented with a defense of civil society for the sake of communal relations and a defense of the self-managing (collectivist) system for the sake of productive relations, both being understood within a federalist and internationalist conception."[38] The central concern, therefore, is not simply opposition to the state, but the strengthening of alternatives on the relational and the productive planes, denominated here civil society and self-management. Clear points of convergence can thus be found between anarchist and radical Christian proposals. Since we cannot develop this point further here,[39] I limit my discussion to recalling and reemphasizing the

---

37. See Peter A. Kropotkin, *Mutual Aid: A Factor of Evolution* (Montreal: Black Rose, 1989).

38. Carlos Díaz, *Releyendo el anarquismo* (Móstoles: Madre Tierra, 1992), p. 75.

39. Given the great mutual ignorance that exists between anarchists and Christians, I think it appropriate to offer a brief bibliographical review. An obligatory reference continues to be Leo Tolstoy, *The Kingdom of God Is within You*, trans. Constance Garnett (Mineola, N.Y.: Dover, 2006 [orig. Russian ed., 1894]). The influence of Jacques Ellul, *Anarchy and Christianity*, is explicit in Vernard Eller, *Christian Anarchy: Jesus' Primacy Over the Powers* (Grand Rapids: Eerdmans, 1987). A fundamental study is that of Henri de Lubac, SJ, *The Un-Marxian Socialist: A Study of Proudhon*, trans. R. E. Scantlebury (New York: Sheed & Ward, 1948). Less rigorous, but interesting, is Linda H. Damico, *The Anarchist Dimension of Liberation Theology* (New York: Peter Lang, 1987). Also good is Frederick G. Boehrer III, *Catholic Anarchism and the Catholic Worker Movement: Roman Catholic Authority and Identity in the United States* (Syracuse, N.Y.: Graduate School of Syracuse University, 2001). The Catholic

importance of mutual aid as an expression of the life of the body of Christ and as a way of social transformation.

Other alternative paths might also be mentioned, proposals that diverge from the political configuration of the dominant system, perhaps along the lines of what Roberto M. Unger calls "democratic experimentalism."[40] Here also it is most definitely a matter of engaging "the imagination of a love" that is political (*Novo Millennio Inneunte,* 50). Mention might also be made of radical democracy, self-management, and direct democracy; or of the experience of participative budgets[41] and so-called economic democracy,[42] two proposals that serve as a bridge to introduce us to the economic themes of the following section. In any case, what is important is not so much the words we use, nor is it having all the answers. What is fundamental, for the Christian community and for society as a whole, is refusing to acquiesce to the established order or to a merely formal democracy that limits participation to simply voting every four years. We need to be creatively innovative and to seek out those formulas for effective participation that respond most adequately to the local and global reality that has been our lot to experience. We are irrevocably called to make concrete the radical alternative of the body of Christ.

The Body Breathes: Economics

Along with politics goes economics. We need not stress its importance in daily life and for a Christian social vision that aspires to just relations

---

Worker is essential for studying the possibility of a Christian anarchism; in this sense it is important to know the proposals not only of Dorothy Day but also of Ammon Hennacy and Robert Luddlow; see Ammon Hennacy, *Autobiography of a Catholic Anarchist* (New York: Catholic Worker Books, 1954). In Spain, reference should be made to several books that Carlos Díaz has dedicated to this topic, in the wake of Emmanuel Mounier.

40. Roberto Mangabeira Unger, *Democracy Realized: The Progressive Alternative* (London: Verso, 2001). See also Ivan Petrella, *The Future of Liberation Theology: An Argument and Manifesto* (Aldershot, England, and Burlington, Vt.: Ashgate, 2004); this book attempts to reformulate liberation theology based on Unger's theoretical model, but the results remain unsatisfactory.

41. See Ernesto Ganuza and Carlos Álvarez, eds., *Democracia y presupuestos participativos* (Barcelona: Icaria, 2003).

42. See Mimmo Carrieri, *No hay democracia sin democracia económica* (Madrid: Ediciones HOAC, 1997).

based on the option for the poorest of the earth. The importance of economics is so evident that we can enter directly into the matter, reflecting on its biblical, theological, and practical implications.

Biblical Reflections

A classic definition of the economy is that of Lionel Robbins, who in 1932 considered it to be "the science that undertakes the study of the satisfaction of human needs by means of goods which, being scarce, have alternative uses among which a choice must be made." Although this definition has different components and is not accepted by all economists, our main interest at this moment is to stress one element in the definition that appears obvious but perhaps is not so, namely, that of considering scarce goods to be the starting point of economic praxis and reflection. As biblical scholar Walter Brueggemann points out, the Christian vision takes a different perspective, for it opposes the myth of scarcity with the liturgy of abundance.[43] Our brief considerations in this section will be limited to clarifying this point. To that end I will draw on a few biblical texts, especially from the New Testament.

Starting from the book of Genesis, the Bible makes plain its emphasis on the abundance of gifts that God places with reach of human hands, provided for the benefit of all people. The statement "God saw everything that he had made, and, behold, it was very good" (Gen. 1:31) brings to an end the priestly account of creation, which completely shuns the paradigm of scarcity that dominates modern economics. Constant preoccupation with the scarcity of limited goods assumes a lack of confidence in God the Creator, encourages a tendency to idolatrize money (a central theme of prophetic preaching), endorses private appropriation of those same goods, and tends to justify violence in defense of scarce resources. It is not a minor matter, then, or simply a theoretical consideration. Let us look at how Jesus of Nazareth treats the matter.

One of the central images in the Gospels is that of the banquet of the kingdom, which links up quite clearly with the central theme of this book, the body of Christ. The banquets of Jesus with the outcasts and the sinners

43. Walter Brueggemann, "The Liturgy of Abundance, the Myth of Scarcity: Consumerism and Religious Life," *Christian Century* (March 24, 1999).

are a sign of the irruption into history of the kingdom, of the arrival of the God's overflowing grace. Two well-known examples illustrate this point from different narrative perspectives: the episode of the Cana wedding (the six jugs "filled to the brim" would mean about six hundred liters of wine: John 2:7) and the story of Zacchaeus, who returns fourfold what he has wrongly exacted of others (Luke 19:8). The exaggerated abundance of God's generosity in Christ is also quite present in the different narratives of the multiplication of the loaves: "They all ate, and were filled. They took up twelve baskets full of broken pieces and also of the fish" (Mark 6:42-43). Or again: "They ate, and were filled. They took up seven baskets of broken pieces that were left over" (Mark 8:8). The impression is given that with Jesus a new "economy of grace" (an expression that is neither casual nor superficial) has been inaugurated, in which the abundance of God's gifts eclipses the perspective of scarcity. Recognizing that the kingdom of God is like a wedding feast has clear consequences in practical life; it is another dimension of what we have been considering as the implications of the body of Christ. It is perhaps for that reason that the first Christian community in Jerusalem linked the "breaking of the bread" (Acts 2:42) with an alternative model of economic relations, in which "not one of them claimed that anything of the things which he possessed was his own, but they had all things in common," so that "there was no needy person among them" (Acts 4:32, 34). To claim, as is often done, that this summary is an idealization of the life of the community means ignoring the efficacy of grace and the novelty of Jesus Christ that is irrupting into history. Although it may be true that there is some idealization in these texts, what is important is recognizing what this ideal is pointing toward and where it finds its grounding.

Of course, many people may consider this to be naïve idealism and cry out, "exceedingly astonished," like the apostles: "Then who can be saved?" (Mark 10:26). Perhaps only then will we be able to sense again the earnest look of Jesus as he tells us: "Humanly it is impossible, but not with God, for all things are possible with God" (Mark 10:27). And hopefully our answer will be like that of Peter: "we have left all and have followed you" (Mark 10:28). We should note that this extremely important dialogue takes place immediately following the episode of the rich young man, and as a reaction to same (Mark 10:17-23). Jesus twice enunciates his judgment: "How difficult it is for those who have riches to enter into the Kingdom of God!" (Mark 10:23; cf. 10:25). The issue here is deciding between radical confidence in God or conceiving life in terms of economic security. The alternative is between the God of life and Mammon, the god of money. The choice is between a vision that trusts in the abundance of God's gifts and an outlook that focuses on scarcity and leads us to anxious hoarding. Finally, two important details of this passage deserve to be noted. One is that its economic repercussion becomes evident in verse 26, for what is normally translated as "then who can be saved?" would seem to make more sense if it were read, "then who could make ends meet?" The question is concerned with how to survive in a context of poverty that perhaps borders on destitution. Living idealistically on the basis of these naïve proposals, who can really make ends meet? The answer is given by Jesus himself and is the second aspect that I wish to point out: "humanly it is impossible" (v. 27). It should be noted that he does not say "it is very difficult," but that "it is impossible." We are dealing with another logic, the logic of God, in the economy of overflowing gratuitousness, the logic of sharing, the economy of the gift. The challenge presented to us is clear: Do we accept the radical consequences of living rooted in Jesus Christ?

Theological Reflections

We should not be surprised that, in keeping with these biblical considerations, the social doctrine of the church has emphasized the *universal destiny of goods* as one of its fundamental principles. Since God created the whole world for the benefit of humankind, the first principle that should govern the socio-economic order is the common use of goods. Such a principle is concerned with a natural, not a contingent, right, one that is fundamental and has precedence over any human intervention, juridical order, or socio-political system.[44] The pronouncements of the pontifical magisterium in this regard are clear and insistent; they offer a general framework for considering the remaining questions of economic ethics. Let us look at some of them.

As a first and significant example, I will say a word about *private property,* possibly one of the worst understood aspects of the church's social doctrine. Since the time of Leo XIII, the church has defended *above all* the right of poor and working-class families to have (or keep) enough goods

---

44. "Justice and Peace," *Compendium of Social Doctrine of the Church,* no. 172.

to live decently — a basic expression of the universal destiny of goods. Those who would claim that the church's posture on private property is mainly a defense of the private ownership of the means of production by capitalists are simply distorting the doctrine. Paul VI states, for example, that "the right to private property is not absolute and unconditional" and warns that it is possible for there to be conflict between "private gain and basic community needs" (*Populorum Progressio*, no. 23). The reference to acquired rights and basic community requirements is quite intentional and has strong and evident consequences. In this regard, the same encyclical states that "if certain landed estates impede the general prosperity because they are extensive, unused or poorly used, or because they bring hardship to peoples or are detrimental to the interests of the country, the common good sometimes demands their expropriation" (no. 24). Be it noted that the pope defends expropriation not only as a legitimate possibility, but also at times as a necessity. Once again, the reason is that private property must be considered subordinate to the universal destiny of goods.

For his part, John Paul II is concerned not only with such possible expropriation, but also with ways of guaranteeing a *socialization of property* that really is such (*Laborem Exercens*, no. 14). As we have seen in our previous reflections regarding that state and politics, the principle of subsidiarity raises questions concerning the state ownership of productive properties, but for that very reason the pope insists that nationalization is not synonymous with socialization, which he defends. In his last social encyclical John Paul II states: "Ownership of the means of production, whether in industry or agriculture, is just and legitimate if it serves useful work. It becomes illegitimate, however, when it is not utilized or when it serves to impede the work of others, in an effort to gain a profit which is not the result of the overall expansion of work and the wealth of society, but rather is the result of curbing them or of illicit exploitation, speculation or the breaking of solidarity among working people. Ownership of this kind has no justification, and represents an abuse in the sight of God and man" (*Centesimus Annus*, no. 43). After reading such clear and constant texts throughout the papal pronouncements, we can only conclude that the distorted perception of the church's social doctrine as an extreme defense of the rights to capitalist private property can only be due to biased, ideological interpretations.

John Paul II, in his encyclical *Laborem Exercens*, offers a profound analysis of the conflict between capital and labor. He affirms the primacy of labor over capital, denies that the conflict is insuperable, and denounces the present "economistic," materialist situation, in which the worker is subjected and subordinated to the requirements of capital. He therefore reaffirms the central value of the human person in the Christian worldview and supports *"proposals* for *joint ownership of the means of work,* sharing by the workers in the management and/or profits of businesses, so-called shareholding by labor, etc." (no. 14). As we have already mentioned, John Paul II in this document defends the socialization of the means of production, though he does make clear that "we can speak of socialization only when the subject character of society is ensured, that is to say, when on the basis of his work each person is fully entitled to consider himself a part-owner of the great workbench at which he is working with every one else. A way toward that goal could be found by associating labor with the ownership of capital, as far as possible, and by producing a wide range of intermediate bodies with economic, social and cultural purposes; they would be bodies enjoying real autonomy with regard to the public powers, pursuing their specific aims in honest collaboration with each other and in subordination to the demands of the common good, and they would be living communities both in form and in substance, in the sense that the members of each body would be looked upon and treated as persons and encouraged to take an active part in the life of the body" (no. 14). Clearly, such proposals are quite provocative and should stimulate action in the Christian communities, which are Christ's body in history.

A few years later, in 1991, John Paul II published the encyclical *Centesimus Annus,* written in the new context arising from the collapse of the Soviet model. It therefore poses the question of whether we should consider capitalism as the triumphant system and as the only possibility for socio-economic progress. "The answer is obviously complex. If by 'capitalism' is meant an economic system which recognizes the fundamental and positive role of business, the market, private property and the resulting responsibility for the means of production, as well as free human creativity in the economic sector, then the answer is certainly in the affirmative, even though it would perhaps be more appropriate to speak of a 'business economy,' 'market economy' or simply 'free economy'. But if by 'capitalism' is meant a system in which freedom in the economic sector is not circumscribed within a strong juridical framework which places it at the service of human freedom in its totality, and which sees it as a particular aspect of that freedom, the core of which is ethical and religious, then the reply is certainly negative" (no. 42). The paragraph is nuanced and precisely for that reason contains a certain ambiguity. On the one hand it defends the role of the business enterprise and the market, and on the other it roundly opposes the exaltation of capitalism.

A number of years have gone by since that encyclical, and perhaps we would do well to reflect a bit, from the perspective of church doctrine, on the new situation of globalized capitalism in which we live. If we analyze all the topics mentioned up to now (the universal destiny of goods, private property to guarantee the minimum needs of poor families, the possibility of expropriations, co-management as a way to overcome capital's domination of labor), we will not be surprised by the affirmation of Catholic economist Pierre Deusy, who defines capitalism as "the true enemy" of the church and sees the church as the only force capable of offering a credible alternative to globalized capitalism.[45] For this reason, I propose using the term *socialism* as a notion that expresses my own proposal. Despite its being a confusing and even bothersome term, the fact that Soviet communism has disappeared opens up spaces for reconsidering these matters with more calm. By speaking of socialism, I seek to make use of a provocative stimulus that might prod us into action against the one and only dominant system, which is indeed capitalist. Following theologian John Milbank, I defend a Christian socialism[46] that may present us with more than one surprise, but that is a topic for the following section.

Ways to Incarnate the Alternatives

In this section I offer a list of proposals that might serve to help us take some steps in a direction different from that of the dominant capitalism. We should not lose sight of our perspective: within a radically unjust world of grievous inequalities, we seek to make operative the Christian vision of the universal destiny of goods. Our strategy consists in doing ev-

45. Pierre Deusy, ¿*Una economía alternativa? Iglesia y neoliberalismo* (Madrid: PPC, 2005), pp. 21-78.

46. We read, "Socialism is founded on Christianity," in John Milbank, *Theology and Social Theory: Beyond Secular Reason* (Oxford and Malden: Blackwell, 1990), p. 208. See also his essay, "Politics: Socialism by Grace," in *Being Reconciled: Ontology and Pardon* (London: Routledge, 1999), pp. 162-86.

erything possible to advance in that direction, in generating spaces of power to make such a vision become reality. My objective in this section, therefore, is not to formulate a perfectly coherent universal framework, but simply to open up tactical paths that might lead in the right direction. What is important is that Christian communities, even in the realm of economics, give concrete form to their being Christ's body and that they do so by incarnating Jesus' alternative in diverse possible initiatives, as each community feels called within its concrete context. I organize the proposals along three planes: those that explicitly emphasize the Christian matrix, those of a more theoretical nature and finally those more directly oriented to practice.

Since I mentioned in the first part of this book the *communion economy* promoted by the Focolari movement, there is no need to treat it further here. It consists of a project of economic solidarity organized according to a Christian confessional perspective; it has an entrepreneurial focus, is mainly involved with the service sector, and is oriented to the middle classes. While the project does not emphasize the idea of being an alternative to the dominant system, it does show clearly that there are many possibilities and fields of action open to the creativity of Christian communities.

Two other interesting projects that are guided by an explicitly Christian perspective are the distributism and the economy of grace. *Distributism* is a current of Christian economic thought that G. K. Chesterton and other British authors, inspired by "guild socialism" and the philosophy of communitarian personalism,[47] promoted in the first half of the twentieth century. They relied on the social doctrine of the church, but sought to offer a third way, alternative to both capitalism and Soviet communism. Their influence extended not only to Dorothy Day and the Catholic Worker movement, whose activity we already examined in the first part of this book, but also to the well-known book *Small Is Beautiful* by Ernst F. Schumacher, which was published just two years after the author's conversion to Catholicism.[48] Distributism still exerts a certain influence, more testimonial than practical, by promoting an economic system that is

47. For a good first approach, see www.secondspring.co.uk/economy and www .distributism.com.

48. Ernst F. Schumacher, *Small Is Beautiful: Economics as if People Mattered. Twenty-Five Years Later, with Commentaries* (Point Roberts, Wash.: Hartley & Marks, 1999).

sound, cultural, ethical, and anchored in a Christian anthropology of love as self-donation. Distributism defends a "society of owners," in which property belongs to as many persons and groups as possible. In contrast to the dichotomy of state control versus private ownership of the means of production, this movement proposes a diversity of formulas that effectively allow a wide distribution of the means of production, circulation, and exchange.

A sensation of utopian sterility hovers over the project of distributism, as well as a certain romanticism that longs for past times. Such impressions are precisely what U.S. theologian Kathryn Tanner seeks to avoid in her *economy of grace*,[49] which she situates within the framework of globalized capitalism. Her proposal is quite profound in the sense that, before posing the question of the concrete mode of organizing ownership, she explores from a theological perspective the question of what it means to possess something; likewise, before considering the mechanisms the market uses to distribute goods, she reflects on the dynamics and the meaning of gifts in different cultural contexts. Tanner adopts a realist posture in the sense of assuming the capitalist framework in which we find ourselves living, but at the same time her theological depth leads her to propose extremely suggestive alternatives. To that end she seeks out the spaces where theology and economics might converge, granting priority to Christian discourse itself. Concretely, she highlights four theological elements (universal inclusion, unconditional donation, noncompetitive ownership and use, and the conversion of private goods into public goods) that allow our imagination and our praxis to expand, but without ignoring the game rules of the market economy. Starting from these theological principles,[50] Tanner defends full employment, action plans against poverty, effective and nonexclusive globalization, the right of poor people to receive aid that is not conditioned on compensatory activities, the need to develop the full potential of excluded people, and the overcoming of the zero-sum mentality. And all of this takes place precisely where God's absolute gratuitousness intersects with the far less generous mechanisms of global capitalism.

Having presented these explicitly Christian examples, we now proceed to consider a number of contributions that arise directly from the field of

---

49. Kathryn Tanner, *The Economy of Grace* (Minneapolis: Augsburg Fortress, 2005).

50. These principles are developed in Kathryn Tanner, *Jesus, Humanity and the Trinity* (Minneapolis: Augsburg Fortress, 2003).

economic theory. In the previous section I used the term *socialism,* even though I admitted it might cause misunderstandings and appear to contradict the defense of the market economy found in *Centesimus Annus.* It is important to recognize that the term *market* is quite flexible: it is not always used precisely and can refer to different realities. For that reason, I first of all describe the proposal of David Schweickart for a type of *market socialism* that may also be called economic democracy.[51] His proposal is inspired by a combination of experiences: Yugoslavian self-managed socialism, the Mondragón cooperative movement in Spain, and Japanese capitalism. He proposes an economic model based on three basic characteristics: democratic self-management of the business by the workers, a restricted market for the distribution of consumer and capital goods, and social control of investment. With these elements, Schweickart claims that his model can compete with the dominant capitalist system, not only as regards justice and equality, but also as regards efficiency and growth potential. Besides, he presents several scenarios for the transition toward the new economic model he proposes. Evidently, we cannot try here to evaluate the diverse elements contained in Schweickart's proposal, which is already fairly well known in Christian circles, but the reader will appreciate the striking convergence that exists between his proposal and the viewpoint of the church's social doctrine.

The second proposal that we will consider is the *participative economy,* or *parecon,* defended by Michel Albert,[52] which consists in a type of socialism that is participative, decentralized, and marketless. Although the similarities to Schweickart are evident, the differences are also clear, to the point that Schweickart considers Albert's proposal to be "completely absurd" for being utopian and impossible to put into practice. Nonetheless, Albert not only defends his proposal on the theoretical level, but also labors and participates in a publishing enterprise that is guided by the same principles. The central question concerns not so much the values being defended (solidarity, diversity, equity, self-management, and efficiency), as noble as they are necessary, but above all the change of mental configuration that the proposal presupposes. Concretely, the two central principles stressed in the *parecon* model are the workers' councils that guide a process

51. David Schweickart, *Against Capitalism* (Boulder, Colo.: Westview, 1996).

52. Michael Albert, *Parecon: Life After Capitalism* (London and New York: Verso, 2003). See also www.zmag.org/parecon.

of participative, decentralized planning and the redefinition of the work-post as a "complex of tasks." The horizon presented is doubtless stimulating, humanizing, and communal; at the same time, the difficulties in extending the model to a universal level are considerable, even with strong support from advances in information technology. Despite such criticism, the model suggests many possibilities for putting into practice communal experiences of a participative economy that is decentralized by definition. Indeed, it provides a great stimulus and a wide field of action for the Christian community.

The third theoretical model that we consider comes from Latin America, concretely, from the organizing experience of impoverished communities there. We refer to the so-called *popular economy of solidarity,* spelled out by Chilean economist Luis Razeto.[53] Possibly one of this model's greatest virtues is that it takes as its starting-point the praxis of the communities and of the so-called informal sector or submerged economy (as an example of cohesive self-organizing), but does not remain there; rather, it carries these activities further, to the point of presenting an alternative vision with a focus on solidarity and labor. By so doing, Razeto manages to surpass the habitual focus that considers these experiences and projects as merely anecdotal, marginal, and provisional. He insists on the "C factor" (community, cooperation, sharing [*compartir*], companionship, quality [*calidad*], charisma, communion, and — why not? — Christ) as one more factor to be considered in the technical analysis of economic life, along with the other classical factors: labor power, financial capital, material means, technology, and management. He thus introduces into the very economic system of production and distribution a new rationality, one that is not limited to beneficence or ethical values. The experience of popular organizations shows that this "C factor" has generated an alternative way of people's relating together and of participating effectively in economic life.[54] Three elements

53. Among other works, see Luis Razeto Migliaro, *Economía popular de solidaridad. Identidad y proyecto en una visión integradora* (Santiago de Chile: Área Pastoral Social de la Conferencia Episcopal de Chile, 1986) and *De la economía popular a la economía de solidaridad en un proyecto de desarrollo alternativo* (Santiago de Chile: Programa de Economía del Trabajo-PET, 1993). See also www.economiasolidaria.net.

54. There is an evident connection with the "R factor" of the so-called relational economy promoted by the British Christian group Jubilee Center. See also Michael Schluter and David Lee, *The R Factor* (London: Hodder & Stoughton, 1993) and *The R Option: Building Relationships as a Better Way of Life* (London: The Relationship Foundation, 2003).

are especially worth conserving from Razeto's proposal: first, its direct link with the option for the poor; second, its situating itself right in the heart of the productive economic structure; and third, its provenance from the decades-long daily praxis of ordinary people.

We move now from models of theoretical economics to the third group of proposals that I wish to present, initiatives of a practical type, and we begin with a brief mention of *cooperativism*. The cooperative model is no doubt stimulating and has become concretized in great variety of projects over many years. Without mystifying the concept, we would claim that the cooperative model offers effective ways of overcoming the sensation of inevitability that is sometimes engendered by the rule of global capitalism. It is important to recognize that there is no one cooperative movement and that possibly there never could exist such a unified movement. Indeed, the term *cooperative* includes a variety of very diverse models. Drawing on the work of Alfonso C. Morales,[55] I would propose a four-fold typology of cooperativism in accord with the social visions that guide each type:

(1) "utopian" cooperativism responds to a religious or ideological world-view: for example, the Hutterite communities in Canada
(2) "political" cooperativism is often simply an instrument used by a determined regime: for example, the Soviet *koljos*
(3) "contextual" cooperativism is based on collective action and on local, endogenous development: for example, the cooperatives of Mondragón, especially in their first decades
(4) "entrepreneurial" cooperativism is moved by the dynamics of the market: for example, the Danish agricultural cooperative movement.

Obviously, the lines dividing the four types are not sharply drawn; rather, a dynamic perspective needs to be adopted in defining a cooperative, one that takes account of overlapping models, of the cooperative's own evolution, and of hybrid situations. In any case, my main concern at this moment is highlighting the impressive convergence that exists between cooperativism and the Christian worldview. Clearly, this movement pro-

---

55. Alfonso Carlos Morales Gutiérrez, "Una tipología sociológica del cooperativismo: aplicación a diversos casos a nivel internacional," *Revista de Fomento Social* 60 (2005): 561-88.

vides us with yet another exciting possibility for exercising the creativity of Christian community. Each concrete community context will make it necessary to discern the cooperative strategies that are best able to incarnate the Christian ethos and the tactical opportunities that are thereby opened up. In this way, the community will be able to advance toward a social vision and praxis that is finely tuned to the territory, the market, and the political situation in which it is immersed.

A second practical example is the proposal of a *basic citizen's income* (also called a guaranteed universal income), which should not be confused with the minimum income concept.[56] The basic income is a universal economic allowance that is granted to every citizen for the mere fact of being a citizen and that is sufficient to cover his or her vital needs. What is most radical and innovative in this proposal is that it aims to sever the connection between work and economic income; it does so in order to highlight the intrinsic dignity of every person and to assign more value to the many labors that are not remunerated, but that contribute greatly to improving the quality of life (neighborhood cohesion, family life, home care, local political work, volunteer work, spirituality, etc.). We should not be surprised, therefore, that the proponents of the basic income are in general agreement with those who reflect on the meaning of labor in our time and who advocate such policies as full employment, the reduction of the workweek, and other conditions that make work a truly humanizing experience.[57] Apart from the technical details that would make it operative, the proposal for a basic citizen's income implies a major change of mentality, one that would link economics up with more cultural or ideological factors. For that reason, its proponents insist on the need for society to take intermediate steps and to generate immediately viable alternatives that will not for the moment be universally assumed by the state or other political forces. Is not this movement for a universal income yet another case of a fertile field in which the Christian community can experimentally sow creative initiatives within its own sphere of activity? Might we not as church

---

56. One of the first works in Spain in this topic is that of Eduardo Rojo and Juan García Nieto, SJ, *Renta mínima y salario ciudadano. Lucha contra la pobreza y cambio social* (Barcelona: Cristianisme i Justícia, 1989). See also Daniel Raventós, ed., *La renta básica: por una ciudadanía más libre, más igualitaria y más fraterna,* 2nd ed. (Barcelona: Ariel, 2002). Interesting websites are www.basicincome.org, www.redrentabasica.org, and www.rentabasica.net.

57. Such is the case, for example, with Imanol Zubero, *El derecho a vivir con dignidad: del pleno empleo al empleo pleno* (Madrid: Ediciones HOAC, 2000).

free up resources in order to establish a model of gratuitous, unconditioned, universal assistance, which, even as it helps the people now excluded, serves to mold our own mentality and to spur us on politically?

The Body and the Members: Culture

Having considered in earlier sections the Christian worldview in terms of active nonviolence and its deployment in the political and economic spheres, I now treat some of the implications of that same world of life in the cultural sphere. On the one hand, *culture* refers to the complex of practices, relations, values, institutions, customs, and conceptions of reality that a given human group shares. In this sense it may be synonymous with the concept of worldview, and thus indeed we have used it in proposing a certain "Christian culture." On the other hand, *culture* may also be given a more restricted meaning, defining a specific subsystem of society, one that is differentiated from the political and economic subsystems. Understanding culture in this sense, especially in contemporary societies, we are confronted with the question of how to manage the cultural plurality of our societies.

In the following pages we explore how and to what extent the vital experience of the body of Christ can illuminate the situation of contemporary cultural pluralism. For reasons I will explain later, I deviate slightly from the schema of the earlier sections and divide the present exposition into four sections.

Biblical Reflections

A helpful way to frame the question of cultural plurality in a Christian perspective is to consider two well-known biblical narratives: the story of the tower of Babel (Gen. 11:1-9) as a symbol of misunderstanding and confusion and the story of Pentecost (Acts 2:1-13) as an image of understanding and communication.[58] Our own concrete reality, desires, and efforts seem to move back and forth between those two poles. Plurality is a specifically

58. I take this proposal from Gabino Uríbarri, SJ, "Multiculturalidad. Una perspectiva teológica," *Razón y fe* 1288 (February 2006): 131-42.

human phenomenon, something that has always existed in our history — indeed, cultural linguistic uniformity almost seems foreign to God's plan for humanity. Nonetheless, because of globalization the phenomenon of diversity has taken on new dimensions in our times. A simultaneous reading of these two biblical accounts allows us to discover one quite interesting feature. While the dynamic of Babel is vertical (the people are building a tower to reach up to God), the process of Pentecost is horizontal: communication flows among people who are at once equal-and-different ("we heard them all speak in our own language": Acts 2:11). Using the terminology of Deleuze and Guattari that has accompanied us throughout the book, I propose that the first episode reveals the dangers of the root, while the second text points toward the advantages of the rhizomes. We could well find other nuances, though, since there is in fact a vertical dimension in both stories, but a difference in direction. In Babel the movement is upward, going from humans to God, while at Pentecost the movement is downward, one that gratuitously grants humans that which they were seeking to seize on their own. This descending gift of God is precisely what allows us to overcome the dangers of an ascending, grasping verticality. In summary, then, I would stress three points: God considers human plurality as something precious, such plurality comes intimately conjoined with the profound unity of the human family, and all plurality is oriented toward mutual understanding as a fruit of the divine gift.

Some years ago the well-known biblical scholar Walter Brueggemann offered some helpful reflections on this topic: he argued that the manifold biblical image of God offers a good basis for understanding, evaluating, and appreciating cultural pluralism.[59] If we read the Bible without any kind of reductionism, we find in it a series of images of God that show not only different aspects and nuances, but even tensions and ambiguities. Brueggemann stresses that it is precisely this varied aspect of divine action that allows us to understand God's own plural character and the necessarily dynamic and complex nature of its integration. Although Brueggemann does not mention them nor can we develop them here, the Trinitarian resonances of this point are evident.[60] Given that human beings are

59. Walter Bruggemann, "'In the Image of God' . . . Pluralism," *Modern Theology* 11 (1995): 455-69.

60. See Daniel Izuzquiza, SJ, "La Trinidad nos incluye a todos. Repercusiones sociales de la fe en un Dios comunión," *Sal Terrae* 91 (2003): 215-29.

created in the image of God, we are called to reproduce God's Life in our own processes of personal and socio-cultural integration. We cannot attempt to avoid plurality and complexity simply because uniformity gives us a greater sense of security. Rather, God himself makes us this gift of human plurality as an overflowing invitation to life.

The third and final biblical aspect that we will consider in this section has a more ecclesiological character and is based on the brief but very valuable study of Raymond Brown on the diverse models of church that appear in the New Testament.[61] Concretely, he points out seven different situations of the first-century Christian communities, all of which deal with a basic problem: how to carry on after the disappearance of the community's apostolic leader. What is interesting is that each of these diverse communities, within its own context, develops its own original response, and the sum of these responses is what constitutes the ecclesiology of the New Testament, which is therefore intrinsically plural. Thus, (1) the Pauline tradition of the pastoral letters stresses the importance of ecclesial structure, while (2) the other Pauline tradition (in the letters to the Ephesians and the Colossians) highlights love of the church as the body of Christ, and (3) the writings of Luke, also in the Pauline tradition, place the emphasis on the unity between church and Spirit. For its part, (4) the Petrine tradition of the first letter of Peter bases itself on the conception of the church as the people of God, while (5) the Judeo-gentile community of Matthew insists that authority is no substitute for Jesus. Finally, the two Johannine traditions show the community (6) as formed of persons who are individually united to Jesus (the Fourth Gospel) or (7) as guided by the Spirit-Paraclete (the letters of John). According to Brown, none of these communities and none of these writings sought to offer a complete image of the church. The only New Testament ecclesiology possible is, by definition, symphonic and inherently plural. His final recommendation is therefore quite wise: "In a divided Christianity, instead of reading the Bible to prove ourselves right, we would do better to try to discover that which we have not yet heard."[62] Of course, such a disposition is not to be limited to the questions of church, but should characterize our way of being in the world and of relating to plurality and difference of all kinds. Let us explore this further.

61. Raymond E. Brown, *The Churches the Apostles Left Behind* (New York: Paulist, 1984).
62. Brown, *The Churches*, p. 148.

Theological Reflections

The social doctrine of the church conceives participation to consist in the complex of actions by which the citizen (individually or associated with others, directly or by means of the proper representatives) contributes to the cultural, economic, political, and social life of the civil community to which she or he belongs.[63] Since I already discussed participation in earlier pages, I wish at this point simply to concentrate on one central topic that is frequently passed over: the organized participation of diverse groups in public life, as a manifestation and enrichment of our plural "living together" ("co-living"; in Spanish, *convivencia*).

All too frequently the processes of modern rationalization have tended to limit participation to the sphere of the individual (one person, one vote) or to impose a type of group participation that suppresses differences. Such procedures of pragmatic rationalization offer the lure of efficiency (not always attained), but run the risk of impoverishing common life and of not responding to the plural reality of society. As we saw in the previous section, the biblical proposal has a more positive view of such plurality — to the point of considering it intrinsic to God's desire for the world and the church — and for that reason promotes public action that not only respects plural participation but also empowers it by means of organized groups. As Jean-Marie-Roger Tillard reminds us: "Difference is inherent to communion in the Church. It is an element of communion. The Church is neither abolition nor addition but communion of differences."[64] This ecclesiological principle of union-in-difference has obvious repercussions in public life, since it promotes a definite style of presence and participation. Concretely, it allows us to go beyond the models of cultural assimilation (what Tillard calls abolition) and of "imposed multiculturalism" (summing up differences) in order to engage ourselves in a truly intercultural project that is far more dynamic, creative, and complex.

Perhaps here it becomes more evident than ever that the specific contribution of the church to politics or social ethics is precisely its being itself. At the same time, this terrain of politics and society makes more necessary than ever the church's own institutional coherence, stretched as it is between the

---

63. "Justice and Peace," *Compendium of Social Doctrine of the Church,* no. 189.

64. Jean-Marie-Roger Tillard, *Flesh of the Church, Flesh of Christ: At the Source of the Ecclesiology of Communion* (Collegeville, Minn.: Liturgical, 2001), p. 9.

horizon of communion that constitutes its most authentic self and the practical, concrete realizations by which it carries on its day-to-day life. As Medard Kehl puts it, it is necessary to interrelate "the *content* of communion and the empirical *figure* of the Church in such a way that precisely *in* this perceptible figure and *through* it the communion of God's love in human history is expressed and transmitted in a soteriological sense. Thus the Church fulfills its most intrinsic vocation of being the 'sacrament' of God's communion when its empirical form corresponds to what it should manifest."[65] In order to attain this indispensable correspondence between the theological content of communion and its expression as an empirical figure, I now examine the reflections of political philosophy, which is a field that has paid much attention precisely to the search for such institutional forms in the public arena. I will therefore modify somewhat the pattern I have followed in earlier sections, in order to consider the contribution of some outstanding "secular" thinkers. I will later return to a more directly ecclesial analysis.

Contributions of Political Philosophy

Evidently, we cannot mention here all the debates that have taken place in the realm of contemporary political philosophy concerning the fact of cultural plurality, its effect on the cohesion of society, and the juridical-political models that try to respond to this new plural situation. I thus limit myself to treating some of the more important matters related to the topic with which we are principally concerned.

The author who offers the most adequate overall framework for treating these questions is Michael Walzer, with his proposal of *complex equality*. His principal argument is "that the principles of justice are themselves pluralistic in form; that different social goods ought to be distributed for different reasons, in accordance to different procedures, by different agents; and that all these differences derive from different understandings of the social good themselves — the inevitable product of historical and cultural particularism."[66] It is not a question, then, of abandoning justice

---

65. Medard Kehl, *La Iglesia. Eclesiología católica* (Salamanca: Sígueme, 1996), p. 120. Original edition: *Die Kirche. Eine katholische Ekklesiologie* (Würzburg: Echter, 1992).

66. Michael Walzer, *Spheres of Justice: A Defense of Pluralism and Equality* (New York: Basic, 1983), p. 6.

(as some have complained), but of becoming more aware of the complexity of life and the plurality of the very goods that need to be distributed with justice. In this way we are able to correct a unilaterally individualist-rationalist interpretation that tends to think of equality in simple and homogeneous terms.[67] The matter thus goes beyond the realm of politics and situates itself on the plane of political philosophy; that is, it is not just a question of governmental decisions, juridical-institutional forms, or allocation of resources, but has reference to our very conception of society and human nature. As Walzer himself has recently written, "we need a political theory, and a politics, as complex as our own lives are."[68] Using this general framework, we now examine four complementary perspectives, which refer to four different areas of our human life in common.

In treating the question of cultural plurality in contemporary societies, Charles Taylor has defended an approach to multiculturalism based on a *politics of recognition*.[69] Taylor maintains that the dominant type of liberal politics has focused on the principle of equality, emphasizing that every person is equal in dignity. The problem is that, in doing so, there is a danger of falling into uniformity: the distinctiveness of each person and each group is forgotten, and the ability to recognize and distinguish one's own identity and that of others is lost. Such uniform assimilation becomes blind to differences and therefore prevents the development of each person's and each group's identifying authenticity and peculiarity. As a result, public life becomes impoverished; for the sake of greater efficiency, a formal artificiality imposes itself and dries up the wellsprings of our common

67. Walzer considers, quite rightly, that the Kantian tradition represented these days by John Rawls or Jürgen Habermas tends toward a rationalist individualism that does not manage to respond to the complexity of human life and its diverse socio-cultural traditions. Those who accuse Walzer of conservative communitarianism would do well to read his own final synthesis: "The appropriate arrangements in our own society are those, I think, of a decentralized democratic socialism; a strong welfare state run, in part at least, by local and amateur officials; a constrained market; an open and demystified civil service; independent public schools; the sharing of hard work and free time; the protection of religious and familial life; a system of public honouring and dishonouring free of all considerations of rank or class; workers' control of companies and factories; a politics of parties, movements, meetings, and public debate" (Walzer, *Spheres of Justice*, p. 320).

68. Michael Walzer, *Politics and Passion: Toward a More Egalitarian Liberalism* (New Haven and London: Yale University Press, 2004), p. 140.

69. Charles Taylor, *Multiculturalism and the "Politics of Recognition": An Essay* (Princeton, N.J.: Princeton University Press, 1992).

world. In response to this, Taylor, drawing on his experience as an English-speaker in French Canada, proposes a politics of difference that recognizes and foments the particularity of each person and each group (whether it be a national minority, a religious tradition, an ethnic community, or a social grouping such as the working class or the feminist movement). He stresses the importance of recognizing, valuing, and strengthening the public expression of the diverse voices that enrich the common life of the complex societies in which we live.

In this same direction, the feminist reflection of recent decades is also quite interesting. In its first years feminism concentrated on seeking equality between men and women; it critiqued gender roles as simple social constructions and proposed their modification on the social, cultural, and juridical planes in order to gain a true, non-discriminatory equality. Since the 1970s a so-called feminism of difference has been developing, which differs from the earlier feminism of equality in that it seeks the creative rediscovery of a specifically feminine way of being. A move is made from the politics of identity (we are identical) to the politics of difference (we are different), as two different modulations of equality itself (we are equal).[70] Now it becomes a matter, not just of participating in public life, but of doing so "with a different voice" (to use the well-known expression of Carol Gilligan). Women have values, styles, rhythms, strategies, and ways of functioning that are different from those of the men who have dominated public life for centuries. Turkish-American philosopher Seyla Benhabib expressed it with clairvoyance when she proposed moving from the "generalized other" to the "*concrete other.*"[71] The former refers to an abstract and rational universalism à la Kant, whereas the perspective of the "concrete other" aims at recognizing the particularity of each and every actor — their sexed condition, their family history, their cultural values, their social position, their religious tradition, and so on. Since the supposedly neutral abstraction of the "generalized other" is carried out in practice from the dominant social perspective (male, white, bourgeois, Western), it is therefore quite necessary to adopt the perspective of the "concrete other"

70. See Jodi Dean, *Solidarity of Strangers: Feminism after Identity Politics* (Berkeley: University of California Press, 1996). See also Anselm Kyongsuk Min, *The Solidarity of Others in a Divided World: A Postmodern Theology after Postmodernism* (New York and London: T&T Clark, 2004), pp. 47-64.

71. Seyla Benhabib, "The Generalized and the Concrete Other: The Kohlberg-Gilligan Controversy and Feminist Theory," *Praxis International* 4, no. 5 (1986): 402-24.

in order to avoid direct and indirect discrimination and to enrich shared public life.

A certain confluence can be noted between these proposals and those that come from the Marxist tradition or that are more sensitive to *differences of social class*. French sociologist Alain Touraine, for example, warns of the possible risk of ignoring relations of domination: "In a world of intense cultural interchanges, there can be no democracy without recognition of the diversity among cultures and of the relations of domination that exist among them. Both elements are equally important: the diversity of cultures must be recognized, but so also must the existence of cultural domination."[72] Recognition of cultural diversity must also be understood as related to economic redistribution. In order not to fall into sort of multicultural idealism, we must acknowledge the reality of a stratified society and, concretely, the reality of the groups that are marginalized or excluded from the system. It would be naïve to suppose that a group of undocumented immigrants laboring in the underground economy will be able to participate with their own voice in public debate, no matter how many multicultural promotion campaigns are carried out by the interested agencies. As long as the socio-economic question is not treated in depth, the cultural element will not be able to deploy its full potential. At the same time, any proposal that confines itself to formally juridical or economic criteria is also doomed to failure. For the Christian, all such considerations are related to the option for the poor, and for that reason some authors have criticized culturalist communitarianism on the grounds that "from the perspective of marginalized people, diversity and resistance constitute our very tradition."[73] But here we enter into the delicate question of identity, which is the final topic that we consider in this section.

What do we mean by identity?[74] Is there perhaps such a thing as a

72. Alain Touraine, *¿Podremos vivir juntos? Iguales y diferentes* (Madrid: PPC, 1997), p. 269. Iris Marion Young, *Justice and the Politics of Difference* (Princeton, N.J.: Princeton University Press, 1990), has shown the need to transcend the distributive paradigm. See also the dialogues collected in Nancy Fraser and Axel Honneth, *Redistribution or Recognition? A Political-Philosophical Exchange* (London: Verso, 2003).

73. Gloria H. Albrecht, *The Character of Our Communities: Toward an Ethic of Liberation for the Church* (Nashville: Abingdon, 1995), p. 152. Cf. Mark Kline Taylor, *Remembering Esperanza: A Cultural-Political Theology for North American Praxis* (New York: Orbis, 1990).

74. For a general introduction, see Joan Carrera, SJ, *Identidades para el siglo XXI* (Barcelona: Cristianismo y Justicia, 2007).

closed identity, a culture with neatly defined borders, a tradition in which the group consensus is unquestioned? Again, the reality is more complex; such pure identities exist only in books or in the ideological imagination of certain biased persons. Writer Amin Maalouf has depicted such pure identities as "killer" identities,[75] and he would clearly seem to be right, even for those of us whose cultural identity is not nearly so amalgamated as his (Maalouf is Christian by birth, with a Protestant father and a Catholic mother; his education was Muslim and his birthplace Lebanon; his native language is Arabic and his naturalized citizenship French). Sociologist Manuel Castells, for his part, argues that the central question of our time is the tension between the local and the global, between the sphere of identity and the sphere of flows, between the individual and the systemic. In our world there is "a fundamental division between an abstract, universal instrumentalism and particularist identities with historical roots. Our societies are becoming ever more structured around a bipolar tension between the network and the self."[76] In this context, Castells distinguishes three types of identity: the legitimizing identity, which reproduces and sustains the dominant system; the resistance identity, which has a reactive character and arises among marginal groups; and the project identity, which aims at creating a collective social force through which individuals can grasp a fuller meaning of their experience. The first two types, for different reasons, tend to become closed identities and so only with difficulty become compatible with Christian identity, which, anchored in the project of the kingdom, is by definition catholic, universal and open.

The five diverse proposals that we have considered in this section (complex equality, the politics of recognition, feminism of difference and the perspective of the concrete other, redistribution in response to class inequalities, and open project-identity) lead us to postulate a renewed con-

75. See Amin Maalouf, *In the Name of Identity: Violence and the Need to Belong,* trans. Barbara Brey (New York: Arcade, 2001). For her part, Seyla Benhabib, *The Claims of Culture: Equality and Diversity in the Global Era* (Princeton, N.J.: Princeton University Press, 2002), has defended a narrative foundation of cultures, rejecting cultural essentialism and affirming their internal plurality, the changing dynamics, and their porous boundaries.

76. Manuel Castells, *La era de la información: economía, sociedad y cultura,* vol. 1, *La sociedad red* (Madrid: Alianza, 1997), p. 29. In fact, the first volume of this trilogy is entitled *The Network Society* and analyzes the flow spaces that carry us to global interconnection by way of technology and community, but in the second volume he recalls *The Power of Identity,* based on community, self, and interpersonal relations.

ception of politics and a reconfiguration of the state itself. Such a new political vision will develop within a perspective that is at once participatory, subsidiary, grassroots, and both respectful of and enabling of differences. The differences would include ethnic and cultural minorities such as the gypsies,[77] the diverse voices of feminism, or the public presence of religions. All of these, as such, should attain recognition and acceptance in the civic realm.

Church and Plurality

In the previous sections we saw, first, that biblical revelation offers us a framework for considering plurality as something desired by God and essential for the church's very being. Second, we recalled that the church's theological reflection and social doctrine invite us to conceive of participation in terms not only of individuals but also of groups, and that the Christian community is called to give concrete form to the world's plural reality in its life and organization. Third, our study of certain contributions of political philosophy has helped us recognize the need for a complex equality that respects socio-cultural differences and helps integrate our plural society. As a final step we can now take up again the still outstanding question of how the church, as rooted in Jesus Christ, can also offer its specific contribution to the challenge of contemporary plurality.

At the very start I note that there is a confluence of two types of reflection concerning this contribution of the church. Both sociology and political analysis provide evidence that at this moment in history social transformation requires a plural subject.[78] From theology we hear that in our days "the theological task is the prolific creation of a complex space" that

77. The nearly eight million European Gypsies make up 1 percent of the total population. Concerning the conception of the Gypsy people as a non-territorial nation and the complexity of the political aspects of that perspective, see Nidhi Trehan, "Identidad étnica y representación político-institucional de las comunidades romaníes en Europa," *Documentación Social* 137 (2005): 99-114.

78. Imanol Zubero, *Las nuevas condiciones de la solidaridad* (Bilbao: Desclée de Brouwer, 1994), pp. 125-61. In the same line may be found the proposal of Michael Hardt and Antonio Negri, *Multitude: War and Democracy in the Age of Empire* (New York: Penguin, 2004).

feeds plurality,[79] a plurality that helps us understand better that "the truth is symphonic" (Hans Urs von Balthasar).[80] Our concern, nonetheless. is not so much with principles as with how to live this ecclesial communion concretely and meaningfully in our days.

Our examination of political philosophy has allowed us to perceive new dimensions of the complexity of our world, as well as to appreciate the importance of seeking institutional formulas that are able to channel this situation of plurality in a positive way. Our aim should not be to reproduce mimetically within the church models that have been advanced in the secular sphere. Rather, we should seek to study the valuable aspects of such experiences and consider how they can contribute toward an ecclesial experience that is at once faithful and creative. For the church to be meaningfully present in the world today, it must practice both a creative fidelity and a faithful creativity that become incarnated in concrete structures, institutions, procedures, and practices.

When we speak of ecclesial pluralism we refer to at least four different levels: first, an ideologico-theological plurality, which has always existed in the church and which refers not only to differences of opinion, but also to different spiritual sensibilities and ways of incarnating the mystery of Jesus Christ; second, the painful denominational differences that, again, go beyond the simply dogmatic-theological since they have now crystallized in different ecclesial forms and sensibilities; third, the growing cultural plurality within the local church itself, which is more acute in some areas than in others, but is impelled incessantly by phenomena such as migration; and fourth, the obviously immense cultural differences in a global and pluricentric church that encompasses the most diverse geographic areas.

Now that we have reviewed the general situation and the various proposals for dealing with it, I would like to stress just two things. First, it is essential that the church develop concrete organizational forms that are able to make communion-in-plurality an incarnate reality. Proclaiming the communion of the body of Christ is of no use if it is not subsequently implemented in concrete formulas and day-to-day practices.[81] Second, the

79. D. Stephen Long, *Divine Economy: Theology and the Market* (London: Routledge, 2000), p. 261.

80. Hans Urs von Balthasar, *Truth Is Symphonic: Aspects of Christian Pluralism*, trans. Graham Harrison (San Francisco: Ignatius, 1987).

81. See Jesús Martínez Gordo, "El gobierno de la Iglesia: síntomas de un malestar," *Razón y fe* 1279 (May 2005): 411-30.

church has within itself all the resources necessary to respond to these challenges and so to shine before the world as a sign and instrument of communion. Some examples of such practices might include a more creative running of bishops' synod meetings, in communion with the pontifical primacy; a dynamic restructuring of the relations between local and universal church; a renewal of the figure of the patriarchates; an updating of the role of the state and regional episcopal conferences; greater participation in eccesial decisions of all Christians, on the basis of their common dignity as baptized persons; effective formulas for making decisions and transforming conflicts; and a structuring of the church as a true community of communities. All of these elements would allow the church, rooted as it is in Jesus Christ, to give palpable form to the radical social alternative that it is called on to offer to our society.

Conclusion

Having reached the end of this long chapter, it would be beneficial to offer a general overview of what we have covered, in order to link together the diverse elements and to shore up the conclusions we have drawn. At the start of the chapter, to avoid the danger of using the notion of body to legitimize the established order, I affirmed that the body of Christ is a *fragile body.* I went on to develop the Christian worldview in terms of active, revolutionary nonviolence. The image of the body of Jesus Christ tortured, maltreated, put on display as king and savior (*Ecce homo:* John 19:14) and crucified becomes real in our days in the body of Gandhi, so emaciated and yet so powerful, or in the anonymous body of that university student who confronted the tanks in Tiananmen plaza in 1989. Despite these outstanding individual figures, the fragile nonviolent body is never a body in isolation, but always a body in communion. Precisely there we discover the force of fragility, for, as Saint Paul declares, "when I am weak, then am I strong" (2 Cor. 12:10).

Thus poised, the fragile human body deploys all its force (its *virtus*) in the different spheres of reality. We first considered the political subsystem, discovering there an interesting relation between *the head and the body.* All political power seeks to be the head that dominates the social order, its ruling principle. Christian faith affirms, with complete conviction, that there is no other head than Christ. Over against the monarchies, oligarchies, hi-

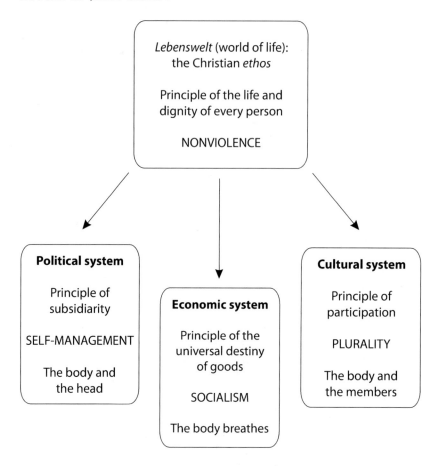

erarchies, autarchies, and whatever other kind of "archies" that demand our subordination, Christianity claims that the only *archē* (principle, power) is Christ the Lord. In this sense, I spoke of a Christ-archy that leads to a certain an-archy, rightly understood. The letter to the Colossians states that Christ "is the head of the body, . . . so that he might have primacy in all" (Col. 1:18). Thus is the link made between Christ's being head of the body and his primacy over all reality (including the political). Since talk of anarchism may result in a certain confusion, I proposed understanding this absolute primacy of Jesus Christ in terms of self-management, mutual aid, civil disobedience, community organization, governance, empowerment, and transcendence of the logic of the nation-state. That is to say, I sought to restructure the power relations between the body and the head, for these relations must also take the "feet" fully into account.

I proceeded to treat the problematic of the economic subsystem, using the principle of the universal destiny of goods, which is key for the church's social doctrine. Accordingly, I posited that *the body breathes.* This image of breathing highlights the fact that all the goods of society circulate and are distributed so as to reach effectively all the cells of the body. Clearly, breathing is not a mechanism external to the body's functioning (as the logic of capitalist market would seem to assume), but something absolutely intrinsic to the body itself. If it does not breathe, it dies. If oxygen does not reach every cell, the result is gangrene. Breathing occurs naturally and inconspicuously, because it is a key function for understanding how the body works. Thus the universal destiny of good should have the same qualities as breathing: fluid, natural, equitable, life-giving. In our world of global capitalism, though, we are far from such vivifying respiration, and we must therefore opt for formulas that I have called socialist but that are really nothing more than the breathing of the body, the equitable distribution of goods.

Finally, I treated the question of cultural plurality by appealing to the pontifical principle of participation, understood especially as the full participation of diverse cultural groups. Here my aim was to understand the relations between *the body and the members* and to harmonize their dynamics. Citing Saint Paul once again, we recognized that "it is true that the body is one . . . and its members form among all one single body" (1 Cor. 12:12). Furthermore, the principle of plurality interrelates closely with the principle of the option for the weakest, for "God combined the parts of the body . . . members are concerned equally one for another" (1 Cor. 12:25). The communion dynamics of the body of Christ offer an operative model for recognizing the value of plurality and otherness, for constructing unity-in-difference, and for avoiding a social imbalance that crushes minority groups or the most vulnerable people.

In the course of these pages we have indicated some of the practical implications of a theo-politics of the body of Christ. We have shown that living as a people firmly rooted in Jesus Christ is an adventure with radical consequences. We have insisted on the central role that the church plays in social transformation. What remains now is for us to live this all out.

Concluding Meditation

In the course of this book, I have repeatedly used two images to sketch out the main line of argument. The first image (roots and rhizomes) comes from the vegetable world and has allowed us to ground our proposal for a radical ecclesiology. The second image is that of the body and so comes from the animal world. This image has dominated the book's second half and has helped us make explicit the Eucharistic basis of the proposed ecclesiology.

The two images have accompanied me during the months of my researching and writing the book, not just in a figurative or imaginative sense, but also in a more real and tangible way. On the one hand, the image I use as wallpaper on my personal computer is a painting of Miquel Barceló called *Christ of the Roots;* this figure thus became a constant part of my spiritual contemplation and experience while I was giving shape to this book. On the other hand, the daily celebration of the Eucharist has allowed me to delve more deeply into new and varied dimensions of the unique reality that is the body of Christ. Some of these experiences have been recorded in another book, which in a way is complementary to this one.[1] In any case, these two images and these two experiences will serve as a connecting thread for this book's concluding considerations.

1. See Daniel Izuzquiza, SJ, *Con-spirar. Meditaciones en el Cuerpo de Cristo* (Santander: Sal Terrae, 2006).

Christ of the Roots

From the viewpoint of composition, Miquel Barceló's *Christ of the Roots* is completely dominated by the figure of the Crucified. In this sense, the image underlines the centrality of Jesus Christ in my life, in the proposal of this book, and in my conception of a radical ecclesiology. Jesus Christ is the Lord. The curious and almost festive powers of the crucified and crowned Christ indicate his true lordship over reality, in the midst of his poverty and humility. The picture in this way represents the universal dominion of Christ, the only true Lord of my life, of the church, of history, and of society. We Christians cannot simply take for granted such an amazing affirmation, one that forms the framework of my spiritual experience, my theological reflection, and my political proposal. Time and again we must return to the personal encounter with the Root that makes us live. Thus, living rooted in him, we solidify our faith in Christ's lordship over all reality, and we gain in liberty before all the powers that seek to dominate the world. The inevitable mystical experience of Christians, then, has an evident political dimension.

Besides the picture's composition, other notable features include the use of color, the materials, the texture, the size, and the disposition of the canvas. Everything speaks to us of an enrooted Christ. The predominance of the ochre tones serves not only to underscore the blackness of the silhouette of the Crucified, but also to accentuate the perspective from which we contemplate the reality. It is a view from below, in contact with the earth, close to the poor, essentially humble. The ochre earth is a reflection of the roads along which the Lord walked and along which he continues to makes his way. It is a reminder that the power of Christ emerges from and is grounded in the humble service that includes all humanity (humus-humility-humanity). It is no accident that Barceló painted the picture while in Mali, one of the poorest countries on earth; nor is it an accident that the canvas is thrown on the earth, immense and unframed, as if embracing all humankind, opting for the poor with all their diverse cultural traditions. All these aspects help us to capture a second vital element: the roots in the painting, going deeper into new dimensions of the Christ of the roots. Affirming the absolute lordship of Jesus Christ might possibly lead to theocratic readings or to individualist impositions, if we forget the permanent reminder of Jesus' own heart: closeness to the poor, radical service, humanizing humility, and universal siblinghood, as children of God.

A third captivating trait of this work of art has to do with pluralism. We see how a Majorcan artist paints in Mali a picture that is contemplated by a Madrid Jesuit in Boston. Three continents in a line. We observe a Christian who, precisely by being rooted in Jesus Christ and becoming ever more so, drinks also of agnostic and Islamic founts — three Abrahamic minorities in these times when secularization prevails. In this book I have emphasized much, indeed I have defended almost vehemently, the need to recover Christian identity as the root of ecclesial praxis. Since the risk of being misinterpreted is great, allow me to say once again that Christian identity is by definition open, plural, catholic. Something of this is plain also in the picture I am describing, and above all in the spiritual experience that the picture reflects and makes possible (or at least in my own case).

Finally, I wish to stress a fourth point, one that emerges from the mere fact of contemplating the picture. I am referring to the importance of art in itself, of expression that is not strictly rational, of the diverse modalities of language and communication. In different parts of the book I not only have defended a Christian identity shared and expressed in community practices, but have also reaffirmed the essential role of liturgy for a correct radical ecclesiology. On the one hand, the world of liturgy breaks with the logic of secular rationality and opens us up to mystery, to gratuity, to divine Life. On the other hand, liturgy introduces us into a sphere of shared meanings that reconfigure existence and show that the expression "another world is possible" is not only a well-intentioned slogan, but a reality that is already anticipated in the believing community itself. Liturgy, then, far from being a sentimental escape, plays an essential role in radical ecclesiology, insofar as it gives shape to the mystico-political character of the Christian community; it thus also embodies an alternative to the instrumental logic which, under the form of globalized capitalism, dominates our world.

Radical Practices in the Body of Christ

All through this book I have insisted on the need for us to live rooted in Jesus Christ, as the foundation for a radical ecclesiology. I have argued that Christian experience has evident and radical consequences in public life. Concretely, I have emphasized that the challenge we are invited to accept consists in "Eucharisticizing the world," that is, understanding and transforming all of reality on the basis of Eucharistic categories. In a way, then, this book on radical ecclesiology is also a proposal for a Eucharistic ecclesiology.

Naturally, the convictions that underlie this theological proposal are nourished by the daily celebration of the Eucharist as a space for radical encounter with the Lord and for radical transformation of the world. It is now a commonplace to affirm that the four actions of Mark 14:22 (taking, blessing, breaking, and giving) constitute a "basic form of liturgy" around which are structured the celebration of the Eucharist and Eucharist life as a whole. The Eucharistic liturgy begins with the presentation of the offerings (taking), continues with the consecration (blessing) and the breaking of the bread (breaking), and concludes with the communion (giving or sharing).

In what follows I offer a political reading of the Eucharist that is based on this four-part schema. I do not pretend to limit the Eucharist to this political dimension, for it of course includes other aspects that have to do with the personal and the community spheres. What I do argue is that every authentic encounter with the God of Jesus in the Eucharist (every mystical experience) has an unavoidable political dimension. Concretely, in the following paragraphs I suggest that we consider the four Eucharistic actions in contrast to their opposites. In this way the implicit nonviolent import of these same actions will become clear, the interconnection of the different themes treated in this book will be made more explicit, and their profoundly Eucharistic root will become more obvious.

The first action is that Jesus took the bread and the wine. *Taking* versus not taking. Taking means recognizing and valuing all the gifts, abilities, contributions, talents — of all persons, of all groups, of all society. The taking has to do with the active, creative aspect of nonviolence, which is always wary of passivity, ingenuousness, and absence of conflicts. The Eucharist requires that everybody be able to participate, and it therefore has radical consequences for the public sphere. A privileged witness of this aspect is Archbishop Romero, who was murdered for taking seriously his fidelity to the body of Christ, with all the requirements of people's participation and organization that that involved.

Jesus then blessed all these gifts. The second opposition is *blessing* versus grasping. When we bless, we recognize that what we have is a gift that we receive gratuitously and that we are invited to bestow it likewise. Instructive in this regard are the reflections of Saint Francis of Assisi concerning the relation between poverty and peace (or put negatively, between possessions and violence): when we grasp gifts for our particular use and convert them into private property, then violence becomes necessary to defend those possessions. Blessing the gifts is also opposed to cursing, and the fact that we speak of gifts in the plural makes us aware of the rich diversity of gifts that we are offered in humanity. From this perspective, the testimony of Teilhard de Chardin (with his hopeful hymns of blessing for material reality and his openness to the diverse cultural traditions unified in the cosmic Christ) allows us to identify new dimensions in this mystery.

The third verb in the series, *breaking*, refers not only to the material aspect. In Jesus and with Jesus we learn that breaking also means being broken: being broken for others. The capacity for sacrifice versus mere comfort is another of the basic elements of nonviolence. The great figures of contemporaneous nonviolence have given clear and concrete form to this capacity in their own lives. For that reason, fasting is an essential complement of the Eucharistic banquet and a central element in nonviolent praxis. Breaking bread with the hungry to the point of "being broken" oneself in service to the poor is one of the condensed formulas that best express the dynamic of a life with Eucharistic roots. And the witness of Mother Teresa of Calcutta is one that has superbly exemplified such service in our day and age.

Fourth, we have the fact that Jesus shares and gives the bread. Giving and *sharing* versus storing and amassing is a polarity that clarifies the dynamic of communion, common-union. The gifts we receive ("he took") are there to be given out among all. Without this, communion is a farce, sharing (*com*-partir) is an empty word, and *com*-panions turn out to be strangers. Accepting this, we will denounce the alienating aspects of the endless cycle of production and consumption that characterizes globalized capitalism, and we will genuinely live the alternative, with its Eucharistic roots. The universal destiny of goods, on which the ecclesial magisterium has so insisted, is still another of the radical implications of the Eucharist. Someone like Charles de Foucauld, who made himself a "universal brother" by sharing with the poor even his last morsel of bread, becomes an incarnate icon of this profound truth.

*   *   *

I end now. This book has sought to formulate a truth as simple as it is impressive: we Christians are called to live rooted in Jesus Christ, and this invitation has radical consequences for our world (not only for the church). If I have expressed this in a way that seems complex or cumbersome, it is simply because there are so many aspects involved, some more focused on grounding the proposal and others more oriented to explaining it. I have addressed questions that are epistemological, dogmatic, pastoral, mystical, liturgical, biblical, cultural, economic, political, ecclesial, educational, because all of reality is radically affected by the Lord Jesus Christ. All parts of reality spring from the same Root, and all are called to form part of a single body.

Index